Bouncing Outside

A Picaresque Romp Through
American Life

Steve Cassady

Steve Cassady

All rights reserved
Copyright 2010
Steve Cassady
Revised 2019

ISBN: 978-0-9881921-1-9
Literacy, Ink, Atwater, CALIFORNIA

Table of Contents

Prologue: The Dardanelles — 4

1. Into the Present: Chesapeake — 19
2. Back Roads: Altamont — 46
3. Alameda: The Raiders — 72
4. Lake Tahoe: Renrob, Part I — 116
5. Lake McSwain: Renrob, Part II — 157
6. Back Waters: The NFL Experience — 201
7. Highway 12: The Aviator — 249
8. The American: Around the World — 288
9. Out of the Past: California Remains — 324

Epilogue: Elkhorn Slough — 349

Steve Cassady

Prologue: The Dardanelles

With one stroke of the paddle I leave village politics and personalities...behind....
--Ralph Waldo Emerson
From "Nature"

State Route 99 once US 99, a big-time American thoroughfare—the principal highway artery from Blaine, Washington, at the Canadian border, to Calexico at the Mexican border. US 99 was decommissioned in 1964, subsumed by the modern freeway system, the "Greatest Public Works Project in History", the Federal-Aid Highway Act of 1956: a 41,000-mile cross-county system of restricted-access interstate roadways costing 114 billion dollars.

President Dwight D. Eisenhower endorsed the national freeway system, in part for reasons of civil defense. Ike favored uninterrupted traffic flow as much as the next guy. More than the next guy, ex-ETO General Eisenhower, Supreme Allied Commander of the D-Day invasion, favored four-lane routes across America for convoying military personnel and ordinance in the event of hostile attack.

As a result of the Federal-Aid Highway act of 1956, US 99 was reduced to SR 99, a 400-mile system of freeways, highways, two-lanes roads and business routes starting in the north Sacramento Valley near Red Bluff, ending at Grapevine, the southernmost tip of the San Joaquin Valley, where SR 99 merges into Interstate 5 just as I-5 rises through the Tehachapi Mountains and descends into Southern California. Though federally less significant, SR 99 still is integral to mass transit through the California's midsection.

Bouncing Outside

Clogged with automobile and semi-truck traffic 24 hours a day, seven days a week, SR 99 belches exhaust through Central Valley towns and cities parallel both to the Pacific Ocean and the Sierra Nevada. Mostly a north to south runway, SR 99 cuts through the San Joaquin Valley town of Merced as a freeway 70 miles below Stockton, the point at which the contours of the California coast line dog-leg to the southeast. Consequence: SR 99 re-compasses west to east as it passes through Merced.

SR 99 is steeped in California history. Dust Bowl sharecroppers from Oklahoma migrated to the Valley along US 99 during the Great Depression of the 1930s. They lumped with evacuees from Kansas, Missouri, Texas, and Arkansas under the pejorative tag, *Okie*. Disenfranchised Okies drove overheating jalopies along the Mother Road, US Route 66, another highway since decommissioned.

The Okies took Route 66 through Amarillo, Texas, Gallop, New Mexico, Winslow, Arizona, Needles, California, across the Mojave Desert to the junction of Highway 58 en route to the Promised Land— California's soil rich Great Central Valley.

The Okies stacked meager belongings into the beds of their ratty Model-T trucks. Overloaded crates topped out at 30 mph and barely crested the heartless elevations of the Tehachapi along the high desert. From the peak of the Tehachapi northeast of Bakersfield on highway 58, the Okies beheld the bounty below: a dun and green patchwork quilt of orchards and fields stretching west and north almost without horizon.

The Okies were stoked by promise that proved a cruel mirage. They dropped into the sizzling summer heat of the valley floor and found only intermittent work as cotton pickers and fruit tramps in the farmlands

Steve Cassady

along US 99. They found conditions spiritually worse than what they had left: poverty, unemployment, scab wages, discrimination, and exploitation. Some rose with the occasion, retooled, and assimilated into upper and middle- class security. Too many didn't.

    John Steinbeck wrote about the latter in *The Grapes of Wrath* and *In Dubious Battle*. Steinbeck was a liberal, sympathetic to migrant suffering. Steinbeck also was an ecologist since his studies of tide pools near Cannery Row with Doc Ricketts. Steinbeck captured the relocated Okies as destined to occupy the lowest strata of California's mighty agrarian economy. He had seen the marine species scrabbling through the backwash of outgoing tides and applied the lesson. He said all species, Okies included, evolve or stagnate. Steinbeck romanticized farm workers in their innate dignity, their family solidarity, their Job-like patience. He embodied them as "Joads". He despaired of the Joad's stagnant plight and scathed the cruelties of the socio-economic system that fostered it.

    Merced was named when dry-lipped Spanish explorers on horseback crossed the tall brown weeds of the valley and discovered a serpentine waterway between copses of willows and cottonwoods. The explorers looked upriver and down, saw some of it, and could imagine the rest. Short form: the river gives life. Long form: it is an eco-system, and Merced County is arid without it. The Merced River rushes whitewater fast from the snow-packed Sierra. It gorges through Yosemite, descends to the valley, and flattens into the San Joaquin which flows north to form the Delta at the confluence with the Sacramento.

    The explorers thought the river was a gift from God. 12 inches of annual rainfall produce scrub oaks and rattlesnakes. Sierra snow-packs thawing into an intricate river system yields cornucopia. The river system permits prolific hydration for pastures, shrubs, flowers, fruits, nuts, berries, grains, and vegetables.

Merced still clings to its bucolic roots. Merced still is heavy into agriculture—peach and almond orchards, cotton fields, dairy farms, and cattle ranches. 18 percent of Oklahoma's share-cropping population fled west seeking agricultural respite during the Dust Bowl, and Merced County took in its share. Mexican migrants followed a generation later, and their demographics are worse than their Dust Bowl forbearers.

Latinos comprise 36 percent of Merced County's population but have unemployment rates 75 percent higher than whites, with high school graduation rates lower than any other ethnic group. A generation later, Hmong farmers, collaborators during the war in Viet Nam, fled Southeast Asia communism after the fall of Saigon. American foreign policy resettled the Hmong and spaced them evenly across the country, in Arkansas, Minnesota, and California. The Hmongs networked their refugee groups. They broke ranks and tilted the balance: Minnesota and Arkansas cousins resettled disproportionately into Merced County.

All the migrants were ambitious for the same thing—a better life through crop work. The Hmong culture had no intrinsic written language, but the feds offered education benefits, so the refugees became college students. They bootstrapped the system and persevered. They worked their way into ventures other than stoop labor. Merced's demography is a mixed bag with stunted economic opportunity.

Agriculture money still drives the town, but agriculture as an industry distributes immense wealth in crippling disproportion. Ag profit creates deep pockets of plutocratic wealth. Depressed farm labor wages create pockets of poverty as pronounced as anyplace in Appalachia. John Steinbeck wrote about it in *The*

Steve Cassady

Grapes of Wrath: agricultural rich gaining wealth by breaking the backs of the working poor.

Merced is an undistinguished valley town with famous criminal connections. Steven Stayner was kidnapped at age seven from Betty Street in Merced in 1972 by a chicken hawk named Kenneth Parnell. Steven Stayner remained captive in a series of one-room dwellings for seven years. He eventually escaped but had no luck. He had trouble adjusting to normal life. He died at age 24 of head injuries from a motorcycle crash when an unlicensed Green Card driving a beater pickup T-boned him one rainy afternoon on Santa Fe Drive. Steven Stayner was not wearing a helmet—his had been stolen two days earlier.

The Chowchilla school bus kidnapping happened in 1976, 22 miles from Merced. Three indulgent youths from the San Francisco Peninsula, delusional from cocaine, brainstormed the idea from the first *Dirty Harry* movie. They carried out one of history's most inept crime, kidnapping, instead of one rich kid and holding him ransom, 26 poor ones. Their plan: extort $5 million from the state of California. The plan was preposterous. The variables all were loose ends, and the loose ends broke containment. The kids and their bus driver, Ed Ray, were ingenious and escaped. The perpetrators were convicted, LWOP, but in fact are paroling out after 40 years.

Steven Stayner's brother Carey turned serial killer. Carey Stayner beheaded female tourists in Yosemite in 1999. The FBI apprehended him in a nudist camp in Wilton, below Sacramento. Carey Stayner said his woman-killing fantasies began when he was seven. He said he was jealous over the attention Steven received as a kidnap victim years before. Carey Stayner awaits the needle in San Quentin's green room.

Bouncing Outside

The congressman representing Merced at the turn of the century, Gary Condit of Ceres, would have been a lock for reelection in 2002. But Gary Condit was drummed from office when his paramour Chandra Levy disappeared in 2001 and was found a year later decomposed in wooded park in Washington, D.C.

Gary Condit lied about his relationship to Shandra Levy. Gary Condit's wife sued the *National Enquirer* for defamation and settled out of court. Condit told Connie Chung on *60 Minutes* that he wasn't perfect man, and he didn't have a perfect marriage. He chanted his imperfect marriage mantra in lieu of direct answers. He sounded as stiff as the Manchurian Candidate.

Gary Condit appeared on *60 Minutes* in a futile attempt to rehabilitate his public image. Gary Condit's TV hair never mussed, but his facial features fidgeted through every question. He was wound tight as hell and came across as guilty of something rancid. Gary Condit lost it all. He had been politically insulated, a conservative blue dog democrat in a rural conservative congressional district. No more.

He lost to former aide, Dennis Cardoza, in the November, 2002, election, and left office in January, 2003, after 13 years. His adult children forwent gravy train jobs with then Governor Gray Davis, because Davis failed to support their father. They delivered bitter exit speeches. Gary Condit won a defamation judgment against celebrity muckraker Dominick Dunne, but it was small potatoes redemption. Gary Condit is a political cadaver.

Scott Peterson lived in Modesto, 38 miles north of Merced, straight up SR 99. Scott Peterson was convicted of murdering his pregnant wife and dumping her body into San Pablo Bay. Scott Peterson was a criminal dunce. His alibi placed him at the scene of the crime. Forced to cover a Christmas Eve parking stub

Steve Cassady

from the Berkeley Marina found by authorities, he claimed he had been fishing alone—two miles from where his wife and unborn son washed ashore three months later. He couldn't remember what kind of fish he was trying to catch. He couldn't answer basic questions about bait. San Pablo Bay fishermen testified Scott Peterson's boat and tackle were unsuited for stripers, his most likely prey. Scott Peterson sits in death row, San Quentin.

 Scott Peterson probably never mused over life imitating art—probably never read Theodore Dreiser's 1925 *An American Tragedy* or saw George Steven's 1951 screen version, *A Place in the Sun,* starring Montgomery Clift and Elizabeth Taylor. But his crime was a dead steal. The Montgomery Cliff character George Edwards (Clyde Griffiths in the novel) loves high-society Elizabeth Taylor but knocks up a factory girl played by Shelley Winters. Inconvenient. Edwards concocts a drowning scheme for unloading Winters. Raymond Burr is the relentless DA. George Edwards pays for his crime in the electric chair.

 Merced hosts a county fair every summer when the weather outside is hotter than the hinges of hell. The fair always has an agricultural theme. The fairgrounds sprawl across 11 acres five blocks south of the 99 freeway, which effectively segregates the town. Oversimplified, money lives north of the freeway, poverty south. On average, 75% of the homicides committed in Merced are committed south of the freeway. 69% of them are gang and/or drug related, including the first cop killing in Merced history, the shooting of gang suppression officer Stephan Gray.

 In his unmarked car one April night in 2004, Gray pulled over validated gang dude, Tao Rivera, riding in a car driven by a girlfriend. Rivera fled from the passenger's side on foot, Gray chasing. Rivera stopped, turned, and fired his Tech-9, fatally hitting Gray just above his bulletproof vest. Rivera's nicknames are "Bullet" and "Trigger". Gang-mark tattoos ring his neck. "Bullet" Rivera's 2007 trial was venue-switched to Colusa, a Sacramento valley farm town.

Bullet Rivera was a big hit with the redneck jury. My friend, C. Logan McKechnie defended him. Logan didn't bother to deny the charges or present his client in a favorable light. He knew it wouldn't have played to the hicks. He only argued the technicalities of premeditation. It's not Logan's fault. He is a death-penalty defense attorney. Sometimes he has a crappy job. The hicks convicted on all charges. Bullet Rivera joined Peterson and Stayner in Death Row.

The Fairgrounds sits on what used to be J Street. In the 1980s, it was renamed Martin Luther King Jr. Way, a dead giveaway. When my younger son was in the first grade, he said Martin Luther King Jr. was his favorite black man. He insisted his mother bake a cake on MLK Jr. Day and we all sing happy birthday, Martin. Martin Luther King Jr. was martyred with honor after Tennessee Cracker James Earl Ray and persons and causes yet unknown conspired to assassinate him in Memphis in April of 1968.

Martin Luther King Jr. has been honored with renamed streets all across America. MLK, Jr. streets never run through affluent sections of town, unless the town is Berkeley. In Berkeley, MLK replaced Grove Street, ironically the de facto color line for segregation in Berkley. Until liberal opposition overwhelmed the trend late in the 1960s, blacks were red-lined from owning property east of Grove.

The MLK Jr. Way entrance in Merced floods with fairgoers on Saturday night--the most impacted crowd of the week. Fairgoers find slow rides for the kids, fast rides for bigger kids and adults. They find overpriced food ranging from chow mein to funnel cakes, calamari to corn dogs. They find rodeo events, tractor pulls, and demolition derbies in the main arena, country music in the outdoor theater, rock music in the bandstand near the beer garden. They find beer.

They congregate to become everything pressed in and odious about 21st century weekend diversion. Security guards and sheriff's deputies patrol for the drunk and the disorderly, the numbers of which burgeon before the gates close at 12:30 am Sunday. County probation officers troll for bail skips and parole absconders more needy to attend the fair than they are smart enough to avoid recapture. Gang suppression units comb the crowds for weapons and drugs.

The Merced County fair is a fine event as fairs go. It wins awards every year. But it gets on my nerves by Saturday night. On Saturday night, the sheer mass of fair-goers makes it aversive. They concentrate and embody all that is bothersome outside the gates. Moods in high summer heat are aggravated by long lines to rides, beer, and bathrooms. Fools and drunks abound. Conversations coarsen with shrill profanity.

Violence is by and large contained by law enforcement presence, but stupidity is not. No one in attendance is too poor to own a cell phone or disciplined enough to stick said phone into pocket or purse. Fairgoers trudge elbow-to-elbow through the throngs, phones grafted to their earlobes. Cell networks jam. Clamor drowns out calls, most of which are impulse gabble to begin with. Young people and their selfie social media imperatives dominate. Every new generation finds its ways of offending its elders, and the millennial generation offends big time..

Before my children grew into adults, I attended the fair under some duress. My wife was a 4-H leader; our children raised, bred, showed, and sold sheep. Sheep are dumb as shit. I am domesticated, a supportive spouse and father. Sundays on fair week, I used to ramrod volunteer 4-H parents to set up the barn. Tuesdays and Wednesdays are show days. Saturday culminates with the auction.

My wife and children were preoccupied with fair week. They fed, cleaned, and groomed dumb-ass sheep. I appeared now and then to run bobo errands. They mucked pens. I hid. They toured exhibits. They socialized with leaders, parents, and 4-H kids. I drank beer at the Blue Devil Saloon. They like demolition derby. I maintain they've seen it all with the first collision—anyone with imagination can extrapolate the rest. I have zero interest in the fair, no role beyond barn set up on Sunday and spectator on Tuesday, Wednesday, and Saturday.

I chafe at being peripheral. I learned to break out for sanity between Thursday and Saturday, if only for a day. I took Emerson's advice. I cross-referred it with a principle from football. Emerson says, *Cities give not the human senses room enough.* He's dead-on correct. Overcrowded conditions, endemic in urban California for decades, have hit small towns such Merced, post-millennium. They scream for escape. Emerson talks about cities in his essay on Nature.

Post-millennium, seeking new perspective I studied Emerson's insight on capital-N Nature. It resonated elliptically: *Nature is loved by what is best in us...Man is fallen; nature is erect, and serves as a differential thermometer, detecting the presence or absence of the divine sentiment in man.* Emerson nails it: nature provokes deep but inarticulate awareness: *The whirling bubble on the surface of a brook admits us to the secret of the mechanics of the sky. Every shell on the beach is a key to it. A little water made to rotate in a cup explains the simpler shells.* Nature doesn't explain but modulates: *One look at the face of heaven and earth lays all petulance at rest soothes us to wiser convictions. To the intelligent, nature converts itself into vast promise, and will not be rashly explained. Her secret is untold.*

Football holds a supporting principle. If the hole between the tackles is filled, *bounce it to the outside.* John Madden adds: *keep the long axis of your body perpendicular to the goal line*—meaning always adjust body position for a quick cut toward the prize, the end zone. The country fair clogs the middle between the tackles. It always does. I bounced to the outside between show and sale days.

The first year, on a Friday, I hitched my kayak trailer to my Mustang and drove three hours along two-lane roads through the foothills into the gold country and up toward the high Sierra. I settled in for the night at a B & B on Highway 4, 22 miles above Arnold, 88 miles above Stockton. I woke before five on Saturday and put in at Spicer Meadows Reservoir. A quarter moon still hung bright and low in the blackened sky; stars still shone through the alpine treetops. I was in full paddle when the sun crested the horizon to the east and spread morning light into the blue water.

Lakeside terrain in the high Sierra tends to swelter from typical mid-summer climate. Southwest winds kick in about 10 a.m. Stifling heat peaks into the 100's by late afternoon. It mixes with the breezes and chops the lake into ripples. The hot winds reverse themselves about mid-day and gain intensity. They blow in from the northeast, churning lake water into whitecaps that don't play out until evening. Embark even an hour too late at Spicer, and the return trip means enervating heat, stiffening headwinds, choppy water sloshing over the bow, and cross currents requiring constant corrective

Bouncing Outside

strokes. Afternoon embarkation is all the way worse: a distracting 13-mile skirmish with wind and weather.

But at first light, the paddler senses everything a pristine alpine Sierra Nevada lake has to offer, every secret about itself and its origins—its silent immutable truths. The still air of dawn is pine-smell redolent; the water is as flat as a tabletop. The rising sun, harbinger of broiling midday temps and high-elevation winds, reassures with softening warmth.

Morning light twinkles off the placid blue water as resplendent as diamonds in an array as profuse as the lake is wide. The rock formations on the banks are endless variations on the theme of granite, some of them in their own small scale as profound as Stonehenge. The Dardanelles loom to the southeast, formed prehistorically by molten lava, rising to 9,500 feet, ranging 150 miles from Lake Tahoe to Sonora peak. At Spicer, first light pours through the saddle of the Dardanelles, shadowing alpine evergreens and red heather that cascade down granite inclines.

A kayak sits in the water not on it. Kayak paddlers participate in the flow of water; hence the flow of scenery as it passes the periphery. I participate with Spicer Meadows reservoir, pushing five miles an hour in a 17-foot kayak I built myself—a three-hour expedition of some 10,000 paddle strokes. The blades dip into the water right-left, right-left, until an alpha state forms and connects with insight unavailable in the temporal crush of 21st century odium.

Flash: it's all within striking distance, all around California—room enough for the senses. Back roads and water are integral. The abridged James A Michener version of northern California geophysics: three million years ago, the earth convulsed and roared; water separated from the soil and receded to become the Pacific Ocean; the mountains rose and formed the

Steve Cassady

Sierra Nevada; the snows melted, the rains came down, and the rivers found the paths of least resistance, carving canyon courses to the Pacific.

Civilization entered in its inevitably clumsy fashion and found its direction by sheer riparian imperative. Water sustains life and the lakes and rivers connect at points that men would be Promethean foolish to contradict. Roads followed rivers, towns followed settlements, and cities followed towns. The railroads came and, in its time, the internal combustion engine. And with it, all hell broke loose.

In the period following World War II, population and growth exploded into California. California post-World War II created the modern highway/freeway system to accommodate mass movement (and military contingency): trucks and cars congesting wide concrete lanes detouring towns rather than entering them—blazing four-lane macadam trails from the foot of the Grapevine to the Oregon border, Monterey to Yosemite, San Francisco to Reno.

Merced sits right in the middle. Merced is rapidly shedding its small-town identity—it is home to the 10th campus of the University of California—but it is growing more in numbers and problems than in any other way: gang problems, crime problems, poverty problems. Merced has Hicksville roots with pride over being a nice town belied by ugly statistics.

In 1970, Merced's census registered 22,670. In 2005, it was 73,610. It is calculates to 240,000 by 2025. Merced is growing in population but not productivity. 39 to 42 percent of its economy is welfare-based. Fresno 60 miles to the south is the nearest large urban presence, 500,000 population, but Fresno is an overgrown version of Merced. Fresno has springs of wealth inverse to pockets of poverty at a higher ratio than anyplace in America. California produces 75-90 percent of nation's supply of illegal methamphetamines, and rural Merced County contributes its share, with crystal meth's concomitant culture driving down social denominators.

In 2004, to cite one millennial year, Merced ranked 17th nationally in incidence of car theft: 1,688 thefts out of a population of 74,000—one theft for every 44 people in Merced. Car theft is as intrinsic to the Central Valley as fruit trees. Modesto ranked number one in 2004, Stockton, number 2, Sacramento number 5, and Fresno, number nine. Merced in the 21st century has some undeniably bad features. Merced quadruples the national average in homeless people. It ranks third in the nation in failure to feed its population. It doubles the state statistics in unemployment.

Merced is hastily overbuilt. The prospect of the University brought in housing speculators and with them hyenas offering sub-prime loan packages. Real estate inflated. Housing prices escalated. Merced was rated the most overvalued in the nation. The local economy could not contain the market forces. The bubble burst. Merced shot to the forefront in home foreclosures. Merced high schools average 2.4 fights a day. Air quality ranks with Los Angeles and Houston as some of the worst in the US.

Unpalatable truths scream for escape. Merced, once a small town in the central San Joaquin Valley, no longer is exempt. Merced is afflicted with crosscurrent realities. Merced is the town where I live, the spring source of much that follows. On the flip side, Merced specializes in escape routes. It trails to every back road and river getaway in California.

I took the roads to the rivers overloaded with fair-induced animus and returned serene. Back road river trips can do that. They can magnify the picture big and attach its images panoramically to the soul. They can

Steve Cassady

minimize temporal disgust until temporal disgust detaches into transcendent calm. I knew it that first year sitting in the Blue Devil beer saloon at the fair on Saturday night after returning from the sunrise paddle at Spicer Meadows along the Dardanelles. I watched the dreary cavalcade of fairgoers without a squirm of existential dread. Back roads and rivers: Nature's own Prozac: I was on to something. Emerson said, *Nature is loved by what is best in us.*

    The outside bounce brings it out, the best in us, I mean—our transcendent spirit.

Bouncing Outside

1. Into the Present--Chesapeake

*...I've known rivers...my soul has
grown deep with the rivers...*
                                --Langston Hughes
                        From "The Negro Speaks of Rivers"

New millennium, post 9-11: my time for despair. Work was flat-lining and metaphoric. The chain of command obsessed on picking the fly shit from the pepper flakes; bureaucrats expedited hence corrupted core values; PC suborned truth; disconnects everywhere. California, land of dreams, end of the rainbow, was bulldozing its promise and razing the common good.

Farmland had shrunk, population exploded. High-tech moved in. Real estate turned insane. Shady windfalls underwrote the tax base. Politics became babble. Texas energy tycoons grew rich off Californians sweltering in mid-summer brownouts. High-tech teetered; dot.com toppled.

The state recessed. Voters protested at the polls. Voters recalled political hack Gray Davis as governor in 2003 and replaced him with cartoon swagger, Arnold Schwarzenegger. By 2005, the cartoon figure couldn't pass a single measure in his special election reform initiative. Things sucked and got worse. Property values bubbled and burst. Fuel costs inflated. Crime rose...

Every which way, I judged books by their covers. I saw the populace as hostile Mongol hordes. In line at Circle K, I saw welfare recipients spending their public dole on lottery tickets. I read it as the numbers racket turned licit via government sanction. I heard uncensored hip-hop music, overt, angry, and vulgar, blasting out of cars in parking lots or idled at intersections. I saw wannabe badasses sagging pants below their butts making zoot-suiters look like Cary Grant.

I saw tattoos, once the province of male losers, turning bi-gender and epidemic. Tattoos don't adorn—they disfigure. Tattoos: rationalized as artistic expression of profound sentiment. Human skin: bad medium for artistic expression. Some skin ink has meaning. Most is as deep as a dog lifting his leg on a hydrant. Human skin turns every color of tattoo ink into spinach-shit green.

Tattoos were breaking out beyond skinheads, drunken sailors, college guys on a border town lark, convicts killing time with needles made from cassette recorder reels. I saw pretty women made ugly with tacky tattoos, shrill colored hair dye, and pierced body parts. Classic new millennium creatures: sagging their dirty denims, gang tats on their necks, vulgar hip-hop banging out their car windows. Added vision: girls' lips pierced by fish hooks, tongues studded with trailer hitches, tats across their backs scripted with the names of boyfriends currently in jail. Both genders were loud, profane, and graceless. Ezra Pound said, *The nation that loses its grip on its syntax loses its grip on itself.* The nation had lost its grip.

I coped with lifetime creeds. Don't settle. Think beyond the mood. Issues are not of themselves. Issues never disappear, but they can transmogrify and blend smooth. Hamlet: *nothing is so but what thinking makes it so.* Think past it.

Think. Twist the kaleidoscope until blending colors enlarge and de-size irritant issues. Birdseye the big picture. Fly above the gathering clouds.

Bouncing Outside

Outrun the storm. Ishmael in *Moby Dick* called it a *damp, dreary November in my soul,"* and went to sea. Huckleberry Finn pined for the freedom of a raft and *lit out for the territory ahead of the rest.* I needed to rediscover my territory ahead.

I hair-pinned to the roots of my intellectual awakening. I had graduated from UCLA in the mid-60s with a worthless degree in economics. Beyond chapter headings and catch phrases, *Supply and Demand, Diminishing Returns, Guns or Butter, Invisible Hand,* I had absorbed little about economics. I had spent my college days in LA watching Sandy Koufax and Don Drysdale pitch for the Dodgers; Elgin Baylor and Jerry West, for the Lakers. I had seen Walt Hazzard and Gail Goodrich lead Bruins basketball to its first NCAA titles. I went to the beach, first-run movies, film noir movies, and the Hollywood Bowl. I slept through classes and studied seldom. I have a BA from UCLA—I don't know how.

I had seen the black-and-white movie *A Thousand Clowns* with Jason Robards Jr. Robards junior played a misfit New Yorker named Murray Burns. Murray Burns had zero impulse control. I was struck by his iconoclasm set in grainy black and white urban surroundings. My econ degree was paper only. I had only odd-job qualifications. I had worked crops alongside Braceros in the produce fields of Salinas. I had tended bar at age 20 in a beer-and-pizza joint in West LA called McGee's. I had worked in a Chevron gas station in Beverly Hills. I had driven a school bus for private schools in Bel Air and Brentwood. I had a resume filled with go-nowhere skills. Prospects: grim.

I thought urban geography. Murray Burns was New York, but I was west coast. San Francisco sounded good. Macy's SF recruited UCLA for executive trainees. G. Luther Wiebel, Macy's VP for personnel, knew my uncle Ralph from the UCLA School of Business. Uncle Ralph had a tony title—He was the director of business and economic research. Macy's wasn't fussy—they couldn't afford to be. Macy's paid 500 a month starting salary—they weren't competing for Wharton MBAs. They offered a junior exec job; I moved north. Ellipsis: I stunk at retailing. I hated wearing a suit. I couldn't feature scrambling for promotion to a position more abhorrent than what I already held. I stuck it out for two years—wouldn't quit without securing the next step

My finest moment at Macy's: I was department manager in the stationary and notions department—where the store sold useless shit. A young black lady—can't recall her name—worked part-time, 20 hours in four five-hour shifts. The black lady was from Bogalusa; her grandfather had died; the funeral was three days hence. She stopped at personnel on the fifth floor before her shift began. She asked for time to attend the funeral.

She could afford only Trailways. She asked for two-weeks. A Louisiana black with a deceased grandfather—a bond running deeper than personnel could fathom. Personnel said she hadn't sufficient seniority to warrant more than her stipulated three days off. The mindless usual: *if we did it for you we'd have to do it for everybody*—like everybody had a dead Bayou grandfather. She was in tears. I said maybe I can help. This was Friday. She wasn't scheduled for Saturday; the store was closed on Sunday. I checked with the union steward.

I rewrote the schedule. The department ladies loved me; they co-conspired. They rearranged their

Bouncing Outside

own off days. I gave the black lady Monday, Tuesday, and Wednesday off the next week. I said, have someone call in sick for you on Thursday, Friday, and Saturday. Union rules: no doctor's excuse through three days of calling in sick. I said, I'll give you Monday, Tuesday, and Wednesday off the following week. I bought her 12 days. She hugged me still crying and hustled for the terminal after shift. Personnel had no heart. They grilled the caller, and the caller caved. Personnel terminated the lady via telegram. I told the union steward. The steward forwarded the matter. Union brass stuck it up Personnel's ass.

The lady was reinstated. Upstairs they marked me as insubordinate. My supervisor noted it during evaluations. He said I was more concerned with the employees liking me than being part of the management team. I stifled laughter. I said, no, I was concerned with them working for me.

I had interviews with top-floor executives. I met with E. Marian Trembley, manager of the San Francisco store. E. Marian was US Navy ret., WW II vintage. She looked like Julia Child only a foot shorter. I opened humble. I copped to less than stellar employee. E. Marian bore in. She wanted her pound of flesh. She was gouging me for disinterest in her profession and eager to dominate. I went from humble to obstreperous.

She said she couldn't recommend me for assignment anywhere in her store. She said her group managers were tight-knit—they'd eat me alive. I said I'll stipulate desultory performance. As for managers eating me alive—bring it. The meeting ended badly. I met with G. Luther Wiebel himself. G. Luther was sincere. He wondered why it wasn't working. I said, I get it, retailing, I really

Steve Cassady

do. It just doesn't mean anything to me. I copped to difficulty taking orders from so-called superiors greasing their own climbs up the ladder.

He assigned me for six months with the wine buyer, a Spaniard named Mario Peral, without cost to the fine wine and liquor department. Peral loved it. He had a free bobo. I took trips to the Paul Avenue warehouse out by Candlestick Park to check on booze shipments. I fantasized being a bootlegger. I wouldn't carry a briefcase. Eager junior execs carried brief cases and looked to me like dorks. I stashed all paperwork in my pockets. I learned enough about wine to order in a restaurant or buy for home. Senor Peral didn't expect much since he wasn't paying for it.

I gave him as much as I could. I had free time between warehouse trips. I always had a book. Senor Peral and I got along. He had a legitimate sense of humor. He called up a wine snob one day, bored, and asked the pairing of wine with baked beans. He didn't discourage my wit; most at the executive level did. I thought eventually I'd have to account for the Macy's phase on a job app. I asked Peral for a reference. He told me to write it, and he'd sign it. I scrolled it on Macy's letterhead. He laughed when he read it. He flourished his signature. The reference letter was shameless; it glowed with superlatives.

I waited for a next-step epiphany. I was a voracious reader. I could read before I entered kindergarten. I read PTA notes the teachers pinned to our shirts in the first grade. At Macy's, I snuck into the stock room at every opportunity to read. The epiphany hit when I read *Babbitt* and *Catcher in the Rye* the same week. Macy's didn't have a chance. I registered confluent truth from both:

conformity is spiritual death, but rebellion needs orchestration and purpose unless the goal is misfit lunacy. I wanted remuneration for reading. I wanted no part of business America, big or small.

I reckoned I needed a graduate degree in literature. I wanted to teach English in college. Obstacle: I had taken only the bare minimum of English classes in college. My GPA was passable only. I checked out San Francisco State. My uncle Ed taught American Literature at San Francisco State. Uncle Ed was cool—he had a loud booming laugh. He was quick, funny, and irreverent. He had cut a path to follow. I couldn't deal direct; my transcript didn't qualify me—average grades; no upper division English units.

I asked around. I sought the department with the lowest entry standards and found it: secondary education. I fed in my uninspiring econ degree and was admitted. I quit Macy's and found a job parking cars. I registered only for lit classes at SF State. I never went near the school of education.

1968, my first semester in grad school: America was on fire. Riots in the cities and political assassinations, the orders of the day—Martin Luther King, Jr. in April, Bobby Kennedy in June. They were killed by cranks: an ex-con Tennessee cracker, James Earl Ray, shooting MLK; an Arab extremist, Sirhan Sirhan, taking out RFK.

Add them to Lee Harvey Oswald: three lone-gunman marks for the gullible. Figure the odds of three leaders with the same enemies clipped by disparate losers. Figure the gunmen instead as cranks propped as murderous dupes. Figure instead a conspiracy of demon interests exercising its evil franchise with assassins' bullets.

Steve Cassady

Students in campuses across the land were striking for inarticulate goals. My father taught German and English at Hartnell Junior College in Salinas. A third-world student challenged the relevance of his policies. My father was sharp-tongued and funny as hell. He couldn't be Mau-Maued. The student was neither amused nor flattered by my father's snide rebuttals.

He threatened to log a complaint. My father stood and said, *Let's go.* The student said, *Where?* My father said, *to the administration building—I'll show you where you can report me.* The student balked. My father asked, *if you don't really want to report me, what do you want?* The student said, *Power.* My father was incredulous. He said, *Power—What would you do with it if you had it?* The student sulked and left.

My first year post-graduate, San Francisco State was on strike—intermittently all fall and five weeks into the spring. Liberal awakening rode the wake. Professors reassessed their relevance. Students revolted, making no more sense than the guy who tried to grab power from my father. Angry students and teachers with counterculture agendas. Power to the people.

I had a spring semester class in 19th century Brit Lit. It convened when the strike was settled. The first day, the professor announced a guest speaker: the leader of the SF State chapter of the SDS brought to discuss the radical impact of the recent campus events. The SDS dude was lame literally and figuratively. He limped in with a panting Airedale. The Airedale drooled while his left-wing master filled the room with deluded political platitudes. He said if we weren't part of the solution we were part of the problem.

His polemic was simple-minded. I wouldn't cop to being either. I rose to leave. He stopped his spiel. He asked me if I minded telling him where I was going. I said, I don't mind. I'm going home and take a nap. He was incredulous. Didn't I want to hear about the relevant issues? The cause? I said we'd been on strike for a semester and five weeks. If I didn't grip the issues by now, I was far too stupid for graduate school.

The incident left a mark. The professor was love-struck by rebellious thought. She was feeling it too late in life. She said we would read side-stream books and we wouldn't take tests or write papers. She wouldn't take roll. We would only have meaningful discussions on the reading. We would gather in a circle and love books. At the end we would determine our own grades.

I caught the good part—the side stream reading list. Not hers, mine. Why not—I already had an A for the class, because I was going to grade myself. The discussions were pointless—attendance was intermittent—and few read the assigned stuff. Avoiding homework without penalty—she had a serious misread of student psyche.

I spent time in the library. I read things that actually interested me. For the first time ever in school, I was emboldened to learn. Education was not solely the domain of teachers with tight-assed intellectual agendas and mind-numbing reading lists. Books, if they were any good, were better than confinement within academic rigidity.

I read Mickey Spillane and found him a crude American original. I read Dos Passos and linked him to WWI. I read about WW I and linked it to the Bolsheviks. I read about the Russian Revolution. I read H.L. Menken and howled.

Menken wrote about the Scopes Monkey Trial in backwoods Tennessee at which Clarence Darrow defended the *infidel Scopes*. I read about Clarence Darrow. I read about Louis Nizer and the atom bomb spies, Ethel and Julius Rosenberg. I read the collected works of Damon Runyon.

    I started with class syllabi and branched out. Robert Penn Warren said the study of William Faulkner was *the single most challenging undertaking for a student of American Literature.* Faulkner is abstruse. I took it on. I read everything Faulkner wrote—multiple times. I felt like an honorary citizen of Yoknapawtha County. I read Mark Twain, Frank Norris, Theodore Dreiser, John Dos Passos, Ernest Hemingway, F. Scott Fitzgerald, Jack London, John Steinbeck, Jack Kerouac, Raymond Chandler, Dashiell Hammett, James M. Cain. I assimilated literature into culture. I scoured America through American writers.

    Common themes came clear: the individual in pursuit of himself, alienation, nature, violence, the journey. It all resonated with Huckleberry Finn on the raft *lighting out for the territory ahead of the rest*. I read Emerson. Emerson wrote essays that came across as sermons that inspired. I intuited Emerson more than read him.

    His message boiled down: a central unity exists beyond human events. Right thinking and proper action transcend conventional thinking and conventional action. The individual has to push past temporal distraction toward right thinking and proper action whereupon he connects to the *Oversoul,* the central unity of existence.

    All things make sense upon connection with the *Oversoul.* The search was everything. The search *is* the destination. The need to penetrate the temporal is ongoing and incessant. One of Emerson's guys, Thomas Carlyle, called it *Sartor Resartis*—the tailor retailored. The challenge resurfaced 35 years later: head forward and back. Reconnect: rediscover meaning and value.

I flashed forward. Post-millennium—my spirit had skewed. I fought mono-polar depression. I was transcendence disconnected.

Somehow back roads and water coalesced. I had no articulate long-stride aims, but I hit on a gestalt fed by Emerson's ellipses on nature, the prospect of new experience, aerobic exercise; affinity and proximity to water, all at minimal expense. I went top-of-the-line cross connecting the categories of least expensive and most portable.

At an REI store in Concord, I bought a Stearns inflatable, a 9-foot, 6-inch neoprene kayak. I could air up the inflatable from the cigarette lighter in my car in two minutes. I could deflate it as fast and fold it up and store it in the trunk. It was very handy. I paddled canoes on family vacations as a ten-year old on the Russian River. Paddling skills were muscle memory implanted—they came back easy. I wasn't interested in generation-X death-defying white water acrobatics, just spirit-releasing flat-water exertion in rivers and lakes.

I knew of a guy in Hawaii who starts each morning paddling a kayak 45 minutes along a lagoon near his house. All advocacies for exercise start with the formula of 20-minute aerobic exertion at least three times a week. My seminal thought: double it—in the water three times a week for 40 to 45 minutes. I found a calm stretch of the Merced River above Snelling, easily accessed, below Lake McSwain, where I could chain my bike to a fence at the takeout point, put in a mile or so upstream, paddle down to the bike, ride to the car, and drive back down to pick up boat.

I did it twice. It was a logistically annoying and time-consuming workout. Lake Yosemite was a nearby alternative—five minutes' drive from Merced College, 20 from my house. Lake Yosemite is civic asset of an irrigation reservoir, the front yard of the new UC campus. Two-and-a-half miles long by a mile and a quarter wide, 450 acres: shady trees, green lawn down to the banks, banks, picnic grounds, boat rentals, a sailboat Marina and yacht club. But, Lake Yosemite has drawbacks. It is way too accessible for a community bereft of outlets.

The same people I was hoping to avoid spend summer days on Lake Yosemite. The drawbacks showed up one-by-one and stayed. Too many people, some of them sober. Too many powerboats or jet skis, not all with sober pilots. Bad statistic: jet skiers comprise 10 of boat owners nationwide and account for 55 per cent of waterway accidents. Jet skis: quintessential temporal activity.

North winds blow daily and unabated across Lake Yosemite from the rolling brown grass of treeless pasturelands. Winds froth Lake Yosemite into whitecaps. The lake is crowded at put in and takeout. The free side is overrun by sit-on-the bank fishermen, alone and with whole families and dogs. Bathers, boaters, sailors, and jet skiers proliferate on the pay-to-get-in side. I paddled Lake Yosemite that first summer. I engaged in low-impact aerobic exercise, 45-minute excursions that didn't deepen my soul. They wouldn't have stirred Langston Hughes to dip his pen into a well of ink.

A Chinese-Canadian doctor named Wong lived in the neighborhood that year. Wong had a wife and six kids. He was blessed with an MD's income and cursed by the instincts of an impulse buyer. He had a garage full of stuff, much of still in a box, including a Costco version of my Stearns inflatable that his wife as much as gave me without bothering to consult Wong himself.

I took it one autumn Sunday, so my friend Mike Gallagher and I could pursue an unexamined suggestion from Gallagher's back fence neighbor: paddle the San Joaquin from the Lander Bridge on highway 165 near our houses to wetlands at Great Valley Grasslands Park, where the river crosses highway140. The back-fence neighbor didn't say how long the trip would take.

Highway 140 to the east from Merced ends in Yosemite. To the west, it ends in Gustine 33 miles away. I live a mile north of the Gustine highway, 13 miles from its intersection with 165, which runs perpendicular to 140, east-west from Turlock through Los Banos, toward the vast nothing of California's Interstate 5. About a mile-and-a-half west of its intersection with 140, route 65 crosses the San Joaquin, forming one leg of a right triangle.

The other leg is formed from the four-mile distance along 140 toward Gustine at the Great Grasslands State Park takeout. The river forms the hypotenuse. Via Pythagorean Theorem, I put the river course at six miles. The inflatables topped out at three miles an hour in normal conditions. I figured less than two hours of paddling with a friendly downstream current--a good stretch from the normal 45-minute exertion.

The river exhibited as much disdain for Euclid's laws as I did while flunking 11th grade Geometry. The trip took three hours, 45 minutes of continuous paddling, and, excepting the first ten minutes and the last, it foretold in breathtaking—literally and

Steve Cassady

figuratively—fashion what the rivers had to say. The first ten minutes of the trip and the last ten minutes comprise the outer limits for riffraff straying from their cars. Riffraff detritus soils the ten-minute zone. Riffraff fishermen pop beer cans, drain them, drop them to the ground. Riffraff mothers drop dirty diapers where they change them. Riffraff swimmers litter cigarette butts, plastic bags, Styrofoam cups, soda cans, food cans, and paper wrappings of anything that can be packed in easily from the access point.

    Riffraffs' saving grace: no ambition—they don't head in too deep. A half-mile or so downstream, the river is refuse-free. The San Joaquin crosses the west side of the Valley through protected public wetlands. The San Joaquin in this stretch isn't scenic like a black water river through granite Sierra cliffs is scenic. The San Joaquin is a vast wildlife preserve. Civilization doesn't intrude and maybe never has.

    It is shallow brown water bounded by flat grassy terrain, a habitat for abundant waterfowl. It is rimmed with trees of multiple types. Luther Burbank could ID the types of trees; John Jay Audubon, the species of birds. That first trip, I could only view them with ignorant wonder. Trees deformed by decades of wind and weather had grown intricate and large and become rookeries, bird villages. Tall trees, short trees, wide trees—they house blue birds, brown birds, birds with long necks and short necks, birds with darker pin feathers and different colored cowls.

    They house birds that perch on branches and birds that skitter along the water. I found out later that I was looking at white oak, osage, willows, and cottonwoods. I was looking at mallards, gadwall, mergansers, red tail hawks and kite. I was paddling waters filled with crappie, bluegill, perch, and catfish. I was paddling along an immutable flow of nature within a timeless terrain accompanied by a chorus of bird sounds. The river flows the way it always has. Paddlers 150 years ago coursed the same waters and saw the same plant life, land contours and wildlife. The temporal doesn't extend this far downstream.

Long-run paddles release endorphins. The mind travels into spaces the mind goes when it goes off by itself—into Emerson's transcendent zones where I could spend deep draughts of time. Driving takes me there, paddling more so. Paddlers think free thoughts and tell spontaneous stories. Paddling generates uninhibited discourse. The mind conjures a story and wonders, *Where did that come from?*

Gallagher told one. He spent grammar school years in Shively, California, a map dot below Fortuna on Highway 101 on California's northern coast. Shively had one store owned by a bachelor storekeeper. The storekeeper was a town fixture with unspeakable urges. The storekeeper molested Gallagher's older brother Pat.

In the early 1960's molestation by a respectable storekeeper couldn't happen. Gallagher's brother's shame went suppressed and untreated. It came out in junior high, after the family had moved to Livingston, 15 miles northeast of Merced. Gallagher's brother had distinctive penmanship. He penned a mash note to the flirtatious wife of the owner of a downtown store. Gallagher didn't know what the note said. It must have been a doozy.

Gallagher's brother was arrested, found guilty, and remanded to Atascadero. In Atascadero, one of Gallagher's brother's fellow inmates was Edmund Emil Kemper, III. Edmund E. Kemper was wanted by neither of his divorced parents. He had spent the summer of 1964 with his paternal grandparents in North Fork above Fresno.

Steve Cassady

Edmund Kemper was 15. His grandfather had bought him a .22 rifle the Christmas before and taught him to shoot. Edmund Kemper was 6-4 at age 15; he would grow to be a monster 6 foot 9. Edmund Kemper's mother, Clarnell, was a big woman herself, plus six feet tall. She was a ball-buster. Kemper's dad had married in the image of his mother and then some. He withered under Clarnell's fierce domination and split for greener grass. Edmond had issues with impulse control. His grandmother berated him like his mother did. One day she was bent over a typewriter table—she wrote children's adventure stories—and Edmond shot her with his .22.

Edmund Kemper was sensitive to his grandfather's feelings. When he heard the old man's pickup driving in, he shot him too. He claimed he didn't want his grandfather to be sad over the sight of his dead wife. Edmund Kemper's mother, Clarnell, was in Montana. He called her. She said call the police and wait. He obeyed. The courts considered him a juvenile nut case and sent him to Atascadero.

Gallagher remembers visiting his brother Pat at Atascadero on Sundays and eating at the same table with Edmund Kemper and Clarnell. He remembers Clarnell as a huge ungainly woman with a big head and penguin legs. Edmund Kemper possessed a near genius IQ. At Atascadero, he was assigned to the prison shrink. He learned to interpret psychiatric assessments. He applied his knowledge during his own psych evals. He was diagnosed as cured by his 21st birthday. His crimes were juvenile; his records were sealed.

For no articulate purpose, I once had researched the serial killers of Santa Cruz in the early 1970s. I picked up the story. Edmund Kemper was released to Santa Cruz and against psychiatric advice moved in with Clarnell. Clarnell worked for UC Santa Cruz.

Bouncing Outside

As his roommate, she could verbally abuse him at close quarters. Kemper fell passive and deflected. He picked up female hitchhikers from UC Santa Cruz. He strangled them and penetrated them post mortem. Kemper was a ghoul though obedient. His lawyers in Fresno petitioned to have his juvenile records sealed. The judge granted the motion in a hearing in Fresno in September of 1972. In the parking lot, in the trunk of Edmond's 1969 Ford Galaxie: the head of 15-year old dance student, Aikoo Koo.

Paranoia crept in—homicide and necrophilia tend to incite paranoia. Edmond Kemper thought he needed a gun. He applied to buy a .44 magnum pistol. In California, gun purchases are cooled off two weeks while the sheriff vets the applicants. A retired FBI agent from Merced, Tom Walsh, told me this part.

Walsh said, the sheriff saw Kemper's file was sealed, the notation only revealing double murder in Madera County. He didn't know whether a sealed juvenile record could block a gun purchase. The sheriff told a deputy, Mickey Aluffi, to contact Edmund and confiscate the gun until a judge could rule.

The deputy spooked him. Edmund thought they were on him for killing coeds. He thought he could buy time by killing Clarnell—the shrinks said she was his subconscious target all along: the dead coeds were a dress rehearsal for the murder of his mother. Shrinks sometimes cite the obvious.

Edmund revealed his issues through matricide. He killed Clarnell and a friend of hers he had invited for dinner. He ripped out Clarnell's tongue and larynx and stuffed them down a running garbage disposal. The tongue and larynx popped back up, like the Coen brothers had scripted the action. Edmund drove away in his mother's friend's Chevrolet. Four days later, he called the Santa Cruz police from a pay phone in

Steve Cassady

Pueblo, Colorado and confessed to all his killings. Edmund Kemper, a giant with a genius IQ planned a moron's getaway.

By paddles' end that first long journey, my upper body felt strained but nowhere near overwhelmed. I knew three things taking out at Great Grasslands State Park: 45-minute excursions were not sufficient; a three-mile per hour inflatable boat, no matter its convenience, was not fast enough; and: Northern California water was endless with possibility.

I shopped for boats. I gravitated toward Sacramento. Sacramento is the state capital made interesting by the rivers. Gold was discovered on the American River above Sacramento in 1848 at Coloma. The American flows through town to meet the Sacramento River at Discovery Park. I found a kayak store near the American at Hazel Avenue up Highway 50, just below the town of Folsom. I bought a roto-molded 12-foot Necky Santa Cruze.

The Santa Cruze was faster than the inflatable by a mile and hour. It was stable. It was indestructible. I put in on the American above the kayak store at Willow Creek. The sign on the entry road to Willow Creek said *Free Area*. The price increased its appeal. The parking lot bordered the creek which fed into Lake Natomas, which actually is a dammed-up length of the American River. Willow creek has ample parking, good bathrooms, and a boat ramp. I paddled upstream toward Folsom Prison, where Edmund Kemper is incarcerated for life. Things tend to connect.

The American flows in that stretch under three picturesque Iron bridges. Bike paths and jogging trails line both shores. Parks and beaches are everywhere. The river narrows and grows faster. Granite formations on the banks dramatize the view. The water is dark and clean. The upstream current builds. It resists paddling within view of the high stone towers of Folsom Prison. Near the prison, a cable strings across the top of the gorge with signs hanging down. The signs are prison mandates—they prohibit further passage.

The prohibition is moot for kayaks. The current forces a turnaround and fast ride downstream toward the *Free Area* parking lot. The prison run had taken two hours in an inflatable. It took 90 minutes in the Santa Cruze. I frequented Willow Creek. I liked the easy put in and take out. I liked the run through urban life, under the bridges, through a gorge, to a famous prison. I liked the price. I paddled it six times before I actually read the sign. It didn't say, *Free Area.* It said, *Fee Area,* with small print instructions for feeding four dollars into an iron ranger.

The Santa Cruze is among the most reliable and versatile boats on the market. I paddled Willow Creek, Lake McSwain, the Delta, and the Oakland Estuary. I still went boat shopping. I wasn't settling for reliable and versatile. I wanted something fast and singular that cut closer to the bone of the experience. I went looking in kayak stores. I surfed the internet.

I kept returning to a website out of Annapolis, Maryland, Chesapeake Light Craft. CLC sold kits for home construction—kits for making plywood-fiberglass-epoxy composite kayaks. I obsessed on Annapolis. My wife's sister's husband works for Southwest Airlines. My wife's sister palmed a couple of standby passes. They were anytime destination anywhere. I set out spur-of-the-moment. I had not flown since before 9-11. I figured air travel would be depressed to the point cross country trips in small jets wouldn't be crowded. I figured way off.

In the aftermath of the World Trade Center bombings numbers of flight were curtailed. Every flight still aloft was booked six across on every row and was as claustrophobic as a rush hour subway under the streets of Tokyo. I figured a flight from Oakland to Baltimore with a stop in Utah on a Thursday in July for half-full. I figured security would be a bottleneck, but forecast everything else as sparse. All wrong.

Everything about air travel post 9-11 is a bottleneck. I wedged into the last standby seat, in the middle of the row by the starboard wing. On touchdown from a bumpy two-hour flight to Salt Lake, a scratchy PA voice instructed *standby passenger Cassady* to *deplane and report to the boarding gate.* I speculated as to why. I couldn't come up with positive possibilities.

The gate lady in Salt Lake said I had been bumped, but the plane wasn't technically full. She gave me a choice. A very large gentleman was occupying his seat and a portion of the one next to him. She said they could redirect me to Phoenix, where I could pick up a 7:30 p.m. flight to St. Louis, stay overnight, and take a mid-morning plane to BWI, arriving about noon.

Or, she said, I could scrunch into the seat overlapped by Fatty Arbuckle. I fly tense in good conditions. The USA Today weather page had Baltimore dark green—socked in with high winds and thunderstorms. I thought of being trapped by otherguy corpulence four hours while thrashing through an eastern seaboard summer storm.

I said Phoenix. Bad choice as it turned out. Info from Salt Lake was faulty. The St. Louis flight in Phoenix was overbooked. Disgruntled travelers stood in a long line rocking with bad moods. Some had been waiting since morning. The gate lady at Sky Harbor fished out a coupon for a discounted room at a nice hotel in Tempe. She said return at 5:30 in the morning and hope for a seat on a 7:30 flight direct to Baltimore.

In the morning the attendant took my standby ticket with body language that accused me of stupidity for even asking. Not one seat available. I conceded. I said take me back to Oakland. I ate an early lunch in San Francisco at *Swan Oyster Depot* on Polk, which serves the best Crab Louis on earth. I was across the Bay Bridge and home by early afternoon.

    I had burned half my standby ticket learning about air travel post 9-11. I built a new plan. I wanted to reach Baltimore ASAP, Annapolis, actually, see the factory first-hand and test drive a Kayak. Returning could take as long as it wanted and go wherever it goes. I booked an America West flight to New York leaving Oakland the next Tuesday night, with one stop in Phoenix, for $209. America West was the carrier that recently had fired some pilots for drunk flying. I didn't remember until after I endured the flight, sleepless across America. We scorched the tarmac at Kennedy sober and on schedule at 5:20 a.m. eastern.

    I followed the arrows toward baggage. The first person I saw was a bald guy in his 60s with white-hair fringes on the side. He was wearing dark brown polyester slacks and a short sleeve plaid shirt. He looked like the sadistic Nazi dentist in *The Marathon Man*. The dentist's named in the movie is Christian Szell, played by Laurence Olivier. Szell makes movie history extracting information by drilling into Dustin Hoffman's molar nerve endings without pain deadeners. Szell asked me where I was going—I said Penn Station. He said he'll take me for $45 plus tolls. I paid 25 bucks for a cab ride from mid-town to Kennedy 20 years earlier. 45 seemed about right.

    I lounged in the back seat of Szell's Lincoln town car through Queens into Manhattan. I sat at a counter in Pennsylvania Station underneath Madison Square Garden, eating a cheese Danish, drinking coffee out of a paper cup and reading hyperbolic takes from the *New York Post*. Reading the Post, eating a cheese Danish, and drinking coffee was New Yorkiest thing I could think to do while waiting for a train in Manhattan.

Amtrak's high speed Acela departed at eight a.m. and was scheduled to reach Baltimore at 9:30. At 8:30, somewhere between Camden New Jersey and Philadelphia, the fast train slowed, snorted, lurched to a stop. The trainmen were reluctant to say why. 30 minutes into a 90-minute delay, one conductor let it slip that a pedestrian had thrown himself into the path of the locomotive. He was dead on the tracks. I had traveled trains all across America in the early 1980s. I knew how long it takes time to clear the rails. I had plenty of time to scour the schedule. I read up and down. The Acela went fast but didn't stop in Annapolis.

Before I left I had called Harry Blauvelt. Harry was once the sports editor of the Merced Sun-Star. He had worked in Honolulu for the Star-Bulletin. Now he was the golf writer for *USA Today*. Harry said to detrain at BWI and call him. The plan was unreliable but all I had. Harry once phoned the former baseball coach at Merced College, Butch Hughes.

He called him at home in Merced and was told Butch Hughes was attending a party on the other side of town. Harry called him at the party. He told him he was in town at Amtrak and needed to be picked up. Butch Hughes was excited. He told everyone at the party who knew Harry that Harry was in town. He said he was going to pick him up and they all should meet at Butch's house. Harry was home at the time, in Chester, Maryland. He tipped off to bed after sending Butch Hughes on a fool's errand. He rat-fucked Butch Hughes because, drunk and bored, the idea amused him. Harry Blauvelt might by my best friend, but dealing with him I want options.

BWI is proximate to nothing. The Amtrak station is a rectangular building across a street from a multistoried parking garage, all amenities omitted. It caters to commuters who arrive late and are in a hurry to leave. A crow could take wing and fly 25 miles northwest from BWI Amtrak to Annapolis. I am not a crow. I called Harry Blauvelt at work, home, and on his cell. He answered none of them. I might as well have de-trained in McCook, Nebraska. I saw a bus stop across the street that offered free airport shuttles to BWI and took a chance.

Pre-Uber: I bussed to the airport—farther away from Annapolis—took the escalator toward baggage, and walked the long concourse, looking at wall signs. I saw the word Annapolis, with an arrow pointing the door toward a curbside pickup shelter.

A Dodge van drove up, and the driver asked my destination. I said Annapolis. He said 35 bucks. I said, *Let's go.* He flicked on his GPS, I had him call ahead for a hotel, and a little past noon, I was reclined in a commodious room looking at an out-of-scale city map for Prince George Street, which appeared within walking distance. Still without sleep, I didn't want to rest until I was completely situated. I reached the CLC building with my clothes sodden from a one-hour walk through the 100 per cent humidity.

A receptionist in the office was telling me the company ran demos on Chesapeake Bay. She said the next one was scheduled for eight days later. I said I had called John two weeks earlier, was here a week later than anticipated, and didn't plan on being in town more than 24 hours. John returned from lunch right then and said he remembered. He said he was in meetings all morning, but if I showed up at one the next afternoon—Wednesday—he'd put me on the water in a demo boat. I slogged back to the hotel, frittered around the rest of the day, and went to bed early, pretty much done with brisk strolls through high humidity. I rose at first light

Steve Cassady

and walked to a car rental agency that was just about as far in a different direction from the hotel as Chesapeake Light Craft.

I was back in the showroom by one. I tested several boats in an inlet, then took an LT 17 for a 40-minute tour of the back side of the Naval Academy though an armada of yachts and some very picturesque marina settings. A kayak doesn't sit on the water as much as it sits in it. About 3mm of mahogany, fiberglass, epoxy and varnish stands between a Chesapeake Light Craft and immersion. The Neoprene Stearns inflatable was little more than an inner tube floating on top of the water, but it was portable and convenient. The roto-molded plastic Necky Santa Cruze was virtually indestructible, stable, and versatile.

The CLC would not be portable, convenient, indestructible, or versatile. It would be a pain in the ass to build, involving patience, finesse, and construction skills that friends and relatives contended I didn't have and would bet I couldn't learn. The LT was fast, true, beautiful, and real. Each paddle stroke back to the inlet brought me closer to a very impractical decision. I made the transaction at the showroom, celebrated with a bottle of Rolling Rock and a plate of crab cakes at the Annapolis Crab Cake Factory.

Late that afternoon, I drove through pounding rain under leaden skies to BWI to activate my standby ticket home on Southwest. Airport security was the same long-ass tedium. I re-looped my belt, slipped on my shoes, and walked along the concourse to the Southwest gates, looking out the windows at thunderheads and lightning bolts. For the first time since the journey began, I rooted for no standby seats. I got the last one on the 5:30 to Oakland with a stop in Kansas City, though the plane was delayed while bad weather prevented any westbound takeoffs.

Bouncing Outside

Finally, they prodded us through the boarding chutes. I lucked into an aisle seat; a mother and small daughter were sitting in the same row and didn't want to separate. Southwest at its finest: Every seat taken, a long cross-country flight through threatening weather, the only sustenance a foil pouch of peanuts washed down with a plastic thimble of beverage.

The captain said through the intercom that takeoffs still weren't allowed to the west, so we were going to trick the computer by amending the flight plan and take off to the east. We would bend left up the Atlantic coast, turn left again around Buffalo and head west into Kansas City. The captain's intercom voice betrayed the fact she was a women. That shouldn't have bothered me, but I fly only upon illusion. I hypnotize myself into believing we're on the ground, not five-and-a-half miles above it, as the poet said, *loosed from its dreams of life*. I gull myself into believing the pilot is an *ubermensch*, not Russell Kellum or a woman.

Russell Kellum used to live behind me when I was growing up in Salinas. He was a good enough guy as I recall, and had a pretty sister named Alice. He ran cross-country in high school, and distance events in track. Once when I was flying in DC-8s charters with the Oakland Raiders, I climbed the jet way for a playoff trip to Pittsburgh. On top stair, dressed in a navigator's uniform, Russell Kellum greeted passengers.

I hadn't seen him for 5 years. Apparently, he had done well; he was flying for United. But Russell Kellum was just a guy, like I am just a guy. Just guys can't keep clumsy aircraft from falling out of the sky. As nice as it was to reunite on the jet way steps in Oakland in 1975, the sight of him finger-snapped me from my hypnosis on that flight to Pittsburgh, just as the sound of a woman pilot's voice brought me out on the flight to Kansas City in 2003.

Steve Cassady

That and the rolling turbulence accompanied by lightning streaks out the left side window. They might have been three states away, but huddled inside a Southwest 737, all seats occupied, they look like they're right above the wing tip. I remembered the John Wayne movie, *The High and the Mighty.* The bad shit began when a passenger looked out the window and saw an engine in flames. We were one lightning bolt from living out the movie. By the time we landed in Oakland at 11:20 local time, I was drained from terror. I had slept maybe eight hours since Monday morning and still had a two-hour drive home.

But at least I was on the ground again, and that reassurance carried me at high speeds from Oakland Airport to my own bed, where I settled in at 1:30 a.m., 66 hours after I had begun. I had been awake 22 hours that day. I was exhausted and welcomed sleep, but I had loved every minute of the trip, even the hideous hours aboard Southwest Airlines. I was on to a thing that made pure Emersonian sense. UPS wouldn't deliver the boat kit for a couple of weeks. It would take while to start construction.

I had to buy tools, including a million clamps. I had to find help for steps I couldn't fathom. I had to train myself to accomplish small tasks without aptitude or experience for completing them. I moved from one painstaking step to the next. I factored in competing preoccupations with work and the demands of family. I was bending the bow on a Saturday when my teenage son, Corey, had to be transported by ambulance with a 106-degree fever. It was the day of his first formal dance. I clamped the bow just ahead of fast-drying epoxy and rushed to the hospital.

My son said, *this sucks.* He meant paying rent for a tuxedo he would never wear. He missed the point but recovered without complications, and I hadn't trashed the project. Progress was slow; the boat wasn't ready for seven months. But it was beautiful when finished, and I was integral to its construction.

All that was left: formulating a scheme for how I would attack this thing.

Steve Cassady

2. Back Roads—Altamont

...I took the one less traveled by,
And that has made all the difference...

--Robert Frost
From "The Road Not Taken"

On October 17, 1973, the OPEC ministers in the Middle East ordered a five per cent per month reduction in crude oil imported to western nations supplying aid and weapons to Israel, then embroiled in nasty dispute with neighboring Egypt. The embargo ramified in America with electrical brownouts, rising fuel prices, long lines at the gas pumps, rationing of gas, gas stations going dry, something once thought as unlikely as A&W running out of root beer. Tense times.

President Richard Nixon faced a surly electorate. Nixon was beset by problems of his own. Vice-president, Spiro T. Agnew, was caught with a brown bag of graft from a Maryland contractor. Agnew resigned in disgrace. Nixon's politics could not contain the wars in Indo-China and the Middle East. Ghettos ignited. Protesters protested. Campuses flamed into riots. Nixon strained to outpace media jackals nipping at the ass of his Watergate scandals. His phlebitis throbbed. He knelt and prayed with Henry Kissinger in front of Lincoln's portrait at the White House.

My father watched him on the nightly news and believed Nixon had lost his marbles. I watched the same news and couldn't rebut. Nixon twitched on television. His upper lip beaded sweat. He did some strange and scary stuff.

He put the American forces in the Middle East on nuclear alert. Nixon looked batshit. Nixon augured fearful images right out of *Dr. Strangelove.* He concocted feeble responses to the energy mess. He didn't light the national Christmas tree. He mandated home heating tamped down to 68 degrees. He reposted speed limit on the nation's highways to 55 miles per hour. The 55, the *double nickel*—a Luddite maneuver. It saved no lives, and it affected me big.

I was flagged at 70 on I-5 in Oregon in the summer of 1984 somewhere between Salem and Eugene (the second ticket for 70 in a 55 that day—the first was in California, between Sacramento and Redding). The Oregon highway cop was friendlier than his California counterpart. He said Oregon considered the citation a conservation offense, not a moving violation. He reassured it wouldn't show up on my California traffic record. I thanked him. I burned the ticket that night in an ashtray at a sports bar near the Kingdome in downtown Seattle. I received a letter two months later stating that exceeding the 55 was not a moving violation. But…failure to pay the fine was a class-D felony with jail time implications. I remitted by immediate return mail.

In California, the *double nickel* was punitive. Eight months after he imposed it, Nixon abdicated. What the hell did he care what the rest of us would be stuck with for the next 22 years? He was pacing the sands of San Clemente mumbling to himself. I drove a 912 Porsche in that phase. 55 miles an hour wound the transmission too tight for third gear and lugged it in fourth. California highways are designed for Autobahn speeds. Cars with radial tires are engineered to cruise at 75. Nixon rolled us back to era of the prewar Plymouth Coupe—dirt roads, hand signals out the driver's side window.

Steve Cassady

Speeding tickets rolled in, all for 10 to 15 over the limit. My license was in Sacramento often. About that time, I saw a movie with Donald Sutherland, Jane Fonda, and Peter Boyle called *Steelyard Blues.* *Steelyard Blues* features a group of dropouts and misfits trying to refurbish a DC-3, mostly with stolen parts. The misfits wanted to fly away from a repressive and insensate establishment. Sitting on a warehouse rooftop at dawn watching him bite into a shoplifted apple, Jane Fonda says to Donald Sutherland:
"Veldini, when you're going to stop being a criminal and thinking its romantic"?
"I'm no criminal, Iris, I'm an outlaw."
"What's the difference"?
"I don't know".
I didn't know the difference either, but a difference exists. I read it in Emerson. I went outlaw on the 55 and sped with impunity, when Sacramento had my license, and when it didn't. I did it on the roads less traveled by, and that made all the difference.

I lived in Merced, a small valley town with no intriguing profile. I had made my peace with Merced. The job was great, the people were fine, and living was cheap compared to all the good places, which, by and large, were already taken. With a fast car, I was four hours from LA or Reno, two hours or less to the Oakland Coliseum, the toll plaza of the San Francisco Bay Bridge, Sacramento, or Yosemite.

I taught English at Merced College. I wrote freelance for the NFL working around the Oakland Raiders and San Francisco 49ers. I had connections in San Francisco and Los Angeles. My parents and sister lived in Salinas, my brother in Santa Cruz. My parents had a mountain house in Dutch Flat, halfway between Sacramento and Reno, midpoint between Auburn and Truckee. All those points are freeway connected, north-south by 99, 5, and 101; west to east by the 80's: 80, 280, 580, 680, and 880, but freeways are heavily patrolled. I went off the ramp to avoid the CHP. I drove to the same destinations as always. I found my way without difficulty along as many back roads as the map would yield.

To reach LA, I went downtown to J Street. I followed J to 152, ramped off to Dos Palos and sped onto highway 33 past the melon fields through dusty Firebaugh, Mendota, and Three Rocks. I crossed I-5, into Coalinga and out, past the intersection of 46, the James Dean highway, to Paso Robles. Highway 33 accommodated high speeds through tumbleweeds and oil rigs into Darby Acres, Maricopa and Taft, up the mountain and across a long sparse valley leading to mountains that crossed into Ojai. From Ojai, I jumped down into Ventura, for a short time on highway 101, before hitting the Pacific Coast Highway at Point Mugu and drove about 50 miles through Malibu and Pacific Palisades. I hit LA in Santa Monica and worked through town on boulevards.

To reach San Francisco, I took 140 toward Gustine, past the 165 intersection, to Keaton Road on the back side of Stevinson. I turned left on River Road along the Merced River. I went left on Kelly past the Hills Ferry Go-Cart track, right on River Road again, past the Fisherman's Bend trailer parks where the Merced River forks into the San Joaquin.

River Road curves and eventually becomes Marshall. I went right on Sycamore from Marshall to Las Palmas. Left on Las Palmas. Las Palmas, rimmed by tall Sega palms, runs into Patterson. I picked up highway 33 north in Patterson—the apricot capital of the world—and turned right past the town of Westley and community of Vernalis. Just past Vernalis, after the 132 overpass, I turned left on Koster.

Steve Cassady

I picked up 132 at the end of Koster, took 132 to I-5 and chose one of three two-lane alternatives to the freeway across Altamont Pass: Corral Hollow, which ends up near the Concannon Vineyards on the backside of Livermore, down from DeLaValle Reservoir; Patterson Pass, which runs over the hill through the wind farms, right into Livermore Labs, and my preference: Midway Road from Patterson Pass Road right past Altamont Raceway to Grant Line on the northeastern side of the pass. I turned left on Grant Line and followed it until it branches right to becomes Altamont Pass Road. Altamont Pass Road courses around the northern decline of the hills through the wind farms. It picks up the 580 freeway at Greenville Road in Livermore.

I fanned into a back-road Odyssey and saw by contrast virulent obtusity in the California freeway system. All points I travel are freeway linked. Freeways connect places directly; they accommodate masses wanting to reach destinations without detour or decision. Freeways clog from mass movement. Upon congestion, traffic slows; freeways almost inevitably defeat their own purpose. Freeways follow no natural path and seldom achieve scenic purpose.

They are concrete, rebar, Denny's restaurants, and Chevron gas stations. In their wake is a culture as homogenous as a herd of goats. They are bulldozed through mountain passes, in and around cities, through deserts and valleys on land inexpensive enough to acquire by eminent domain. They are cross-connected by cloverleafs and interchanges. They almost wholly obscure the point.

Freeway 580 across Altamont pass, elevation 1,362, cuts through rolling hills of brown grass, with rows of windmills strung up and down their flanks. Technology has found a way to harvest wind on a mega scale and convert it to energy. Sitting where it does, 65 miles east of the marine air off the Pacific and rolling into the sweltering San Joaquin Valley, Altamont Pass funnels bumper crops of wind. From the distorted scale of the freeway, the windmills appear distant and quaint, especially when immediate attention to speeding cars on the flanks is requisite for survival. Altamont Pass road follows the contours of the mountain itself. The two-lane road dips, climbs, and bends within view of windmills in real time scale. Human in car: small; windmill on ridge: large.

Freeway 580 traverses the pass without suggestion of the rock concert in 1969 which decommissioned the hippie generation. Altamont Pass Road runs past a truck and auto repair shop that is lost in time and intersects with Midway Road.

The killer rock concert in 1969 took place at Altamont speedway, three miles down Midway Road. Altamont was a watershed event in American cultural history. Traffic is always sparse in the area around the speedway. The terrain is deserted. The view belies the truth of 300,000 demented hippies boiling onto the foothills in full psychedelic regalia on a late fall day in 1969. The raceway reminds.

The Rolling Stones, for reasons more venal than philanthropic, were ambitious to stage a free concert in California. Woodstock had taken place four months earlier in August of 1969. Woodstock probably was filthy and deranged, but it is remembered as the bloom of the hippie rose: proof that indiscriminate sex and random drug ingestion could mix with rock and roll music to make things permanently groovy.

It was all bullshit. Nature asserted itself in time, hippie delusions notwithstanding. Indiscriminate sex led to psycho-sexual maladjustment, confused paternity, Herpes, and AIDs. Unmonitored drug

Steve Cassady

ingestion led to psychosis, criminal incarceration, serial killing and brains young turned into steamed broccoli. Rock music mixed in and choreographed.

    I was born two years too early to be a boomer. I failed to identify with the 1960s. I found the causes naïve, the music cacophonous, and the drug culture lacking both hygiene and sanity. I lived at the corner of Haight and Ashbury in the summer of love, 1967, but participated in none of it. I'd walk along Haight, and hear *Hello, officer*, from hippies believing themselves trenchant for penetrating my cover. I worked at Macy's at the time as a junior executive. I got the politics and didn't like either side.

    I wasn't surprised the world was in shambles. Emerson's signature essay: *Self-Reliance*. The signature line in *Self-Reliance: Vibrate to that iron string of self*. My grandfathers, father, and uncles gave me Emerson before Emerson did. I didn't repudiate the man, because I wasn't disillusioned in the 1960s. I had played that number a long time before. I was born into a patriarchy of few illusions and much cynicism. I rebelled from the crib. I trusted established authority from birth like a frog trusts a scorpion.

    Woodstock was a newspaper story. So was Altamont four months later. I didn't penetrate the significance of either until 12 years later while working to understand events leading to the murder of a young girl from Merced. I back tracked the story and found commons threads among people I knew. My friend Baron Wolman, the first photographer at *Rolling Stone* magazine, was backstage. My running buddy in NFL escapades, Michael Zagaris, was archetypal among the frenzy. Several of my English students at Merced College had attended as teenagers.

    One, a female, Kathy Driver, remembers being an aspiring hippie at 16. She drove to Altamont with a carload of friends. She was counter-culture costumed: peasant blouse, sandals, floral patches appliquéd on hip-hugger jeans. She remembers nothing else. On site less than an hour, she was drilled with a flying beer can and was dazed into a day-long stupor.

My best friend growing up, Bob Robertson, was a student at Berkeley, recently reborn into religion. He and some callow cohorts-in-Christ exercised futility at Altamont, distributing Jesus leaflets to drug-demented flower children. The Stones were not Billy Graham. Altamont was not a religious revival. Altamont was pivotal early 70's hippie madness. The Stones signature song: *Sympathy for the Devil*.

I researched the entire sequence. It was stunning how fucked up the whole thing was, and how far-reaching...The organizers wanted Woodstock reprised west coast four months later. The Stones figured to make enough on residuals to afford to offer a free concert. None of them accounted for the contrast in climate and conditions between Upstate New York in August and Northern California in December.

The short version of what happened: Mick Jagger foresaw the concert in San Francisco at Golden Gate Park. SF City Hall wrapped the proposal in red tape. The alternative was Sears Point Raceway in Sonoma County 50 miles away. Sears Point was a green light until December 5, the day before the concert. On December 5, Sears Point regulators, pulled the plug because its owners, the Odeon Corporation, rivaled the company that would film the concert. Neither Odeon nor the rival could cede video rights.

A plywood stage already had been built. At Altamont Pass, a man named Dick Carter, impresario of demolition derbies and 40-lap main event stock car races, had hired a grad student from Stanford to raise his business profile. The grad student connected with the concert people. They negotiated fast: Dick Carter offered his oval and 80 acres of hills for no charge other than free publicity.

Dick Carter got his free publicity. *Rolling Stone* ferried its entire staff to the site in a motor home on Friday night, December 5. *We went to interview the racetrack owner, Carter,* Baron Wolman said. *This was his big chance to make a killing. He was sleaze, a cheap promoter without the first idea who the Rolling Stones were, what rock music was, anything.*

We were sitting in his office under fluorescent tubes. It was starting to feel creepy even then. We went outside. All these campfires were lit--stoned, creepy people were wandering around. It was somber. These weren't our kind of people. There was a hard edge to everything. I don't know why it felt so different from any of the other festivals, but it did.

The trucks had been rolling since the morning of December 5. Crews, paid and volunteer, went to work. Portable generators groaned through the night. What had taken months to erect and test for Woodstock went up at Altamont in a little more than 20 hours.

By Saturday morning, December 6, the day of the concert, a stage had been set up, speaker scaffolds had been erected, the place had been wired, a medical tent had been raised, and convoys of chemical toilets had been trucked in—*about one-sixtieth the number needed,* reported *Rolling Stone* magazine, *insuring that people would use nearby fields and the sides of cars.*

Security fell to the Stones' road manager, Sam Cutler. Cutler had hired a London branch of the Hell's Angels for a concert at Hyde Park. Cutler contacted Ralph *Sonny* Barger, president of the Oakland chapter. Cutler struck a deal with Barger: premium access and $500 worth of beer for a squadron of Angels to protect the concert stage. Cutler misjudged badly. Significant differences between Oakland and London, between Sonny Barger and a SoHo Teddy Boy.

The concert started late. The sun set behind the hills at 4:30, and the place turned cold. 300,000 hippies were strewn across the fields deranged by drugs. The stage was built wrong, too low. Hippies stormed the parapets and climbed the stage. The Angels knocked them back. The thing went hostile.

At dusk, while the Stones were singing *Sympathy for the Devil*, the Angels swarmed a black kid from Berkeley, Meredith Hunter. They said later Meredith Hunter pulled a gun (in fact he had one: his last words, faintly uttered: *I wasn't going to shoot you)*.

Others said he didn't pull the gun until he was wounded. The Angels formed a stomping circle. They swung down on him with sawed off, weighted pool cues. An Angel with a blade gashed Meredith Hunter—three-quarters of an inch deep into his back and spine, where, an attending physician said, *there is nothing but big arteries.*

Baron Wolman hadn't stuck around. *I went to bed on Friday night,* he said. *The first thing in the morning I got up to look around. A lot more people had come in during the night. The first thing I saw was this black Doberman chasing down a wild rabbit and killing it, tearing it apart in his maws.*

I stayed around for a while, knowing more and more there was going to be trouble. You start with the Hell's Angels. But also, the stage. It was only chin high and located where people and their vehicles had easy access. No keeping the spectators away from the performers on stage. I only knew I didn't want to be there.. I left early that afternoon. I hitchhiked home, and I never hitchhike anywhere.

Altamont was the last crusade for disaffected 60's youth. Michael Zagaris was a classic among them.

Steve Cassady

Zagaris grew up as Beaver Cleaver in Redding California. He was a small town, Jesuit-educated sports head who harbored ambitions of becoming president of the United States. Zagaris was inspired by the election of JFK in 1960. He tasted politics first-hand in 1964 while a student at Shasta College.

He worked as a volunteer for the re-election of JFK disciple, Senator Pierre Salinger. *I would go around to places like Yreka, Weed, Anderson and Mt. Shasta City giving speeches. My parents put on a big democratic fund-raising dinner. Pierre showed up. I told him that night I wanted to be a page in the senate. He put his arm around my shoulder and said not to worry, lying through his teeth like all politicians do.*

Zagaris graduated from George Washington University in spring, 1967, with a major in Sino-Soviet relations, *because I wanted to negotiate the treaties with the Russians and the Chinese myself.* He returned to California, married his high school sweetheart, set up house in a San Jose suburb, and enrolled in the University of Santa Clara law school.

Zagaris evolved. *I knew from the first day of law school I didn't want to be there. But I still wanted to be president and saw it as the way to the White House— get a law degree, run for office, and on up the ladder. But other things were happening.*

I was doing well enough; I was number two in my class at the halfway point of the first year. But the Beatles were big, and their 'Sergeant Pepper' album had come out. I had learned the Beatles smoked grass. I learned it from their lyrics. I experimented with marijuana and dug it. I was into music and started to become, what, 'disaffected'?

Zagaris micro scoped his values but found nothing in focus. He was miserable in marriage. He strayed into affairs. He engaged his banker father-in-law in loud and bitter arguments. He resented time wasted in dank libraries studying obscure precedents within a system he was growing to loathe. He had long since stopped attending church. *I didn't think God was dead,* he said, *I thought organized religion was.*

It came to him in a rush in the late spring of 1968. *Gene McCarthy had come out for the presidency. I was reading Che Guevara. I was finding out what the world was all about. The Watts riot in 1965, Detroit in 1967, Martin Luther King just was hit in Memphis—all I could think was, 'this country is fucked, the world is fucked. More and more, the only things that made sense were the Beatles, the Rolling Stones, the whole hippie and music thing.*

When Bobby Kennedy came out for the presidency, I went to work on his campaign. Bobby didn't have that matinee-idol charisma like his brother did. But he was a person of substance. When he was killed in June, that was it. My ties with so-called reality, the middle-class American view—Sirhan blew them away.

Zagaris showed up for a contracts final still in shock from RFK's assassination on June 5. His professor took him aside and said, *Son, I'm sorry about what happened to Senator Kennedy. I know you're upset. But life goes on, and you're going to have to take the exam.* Zagaris said nothing.

He took his seat. He pulled from his pocket a baseball card of the SF Giants' pitcher, Juan Marichal. The card was one with the image of a player's face in a small wax ring in the upper corner. Zagaris peeled the ring and rubbed it with the edge of a coin, transferring the image to the top of the first page of a blue book. He sketched a dialogue balloon. He had Juan Marichal say, *Hey Michael, these ees all boolshit.* Zagaris filled that blue book and six more with an essay scathing America and its corrupt system of values. He did the

Steve Cassady

same thing with another baseball card the next day for his Torts final. *I left very pleased with myself,* he said. *Of course, my career in law was over.*

Michael Zagaris had been geeked for days in anticipation of Altamont. He said: *We piled into my Plymouth Duster—I had purchased it new eight days before—about Midnight Friday, myself, my first wife, several friends, and one guy I didn't know very well, some junkie from LA. We headed for Altamont—no one knew where the fuck it was. We loaded up.*

We had about three lids of grass, magic mushrooms, mescaline. Looking back, even putting it mildly, that was overkill. We got there in the middle of the night, totally blasted. We parked the car—abandoned was more like it—and started walking over these rolling hills with people who didn't know any more about where they were going than we did.

It was the hippie thing gone nuts. We passed campfires, hundreds of people around campfires, eight-track tapes going, people fucking out in the open, everyone smoking weed, people drinking from giant gallons of red mountain—real hippies, the kind you never see any more. They had dogs on ropes. There were dogs running loose in packs, barking, humping. People laughing that crazy laugh you hear when they're really fucked up.

They had a fence around the grounds, but it had been trampled over and cut with wire cutters. We went through the fence with about 300 others. We ran across this field. We thought we'd be the first ones to get a view. There must have been 70,000 people already there, some on the ground in sleeping bags, some wandering around crazed. We set up on the side of a hill looking down at the stage. It was early morning, that half-light just before sunrise. Even stoned, we were freezing cold. We took a couple hits of mescaline and smoked some more weed. We were going to save the mushrooms for later...

...The Angels were there, a lot of Gypsy Jokers, and another renegade bike group from San Jose I can't remember the name of. The Angels got all the publicity, like they were the only bikers there, or like the media thought all bikers are Angels. But I'll tell you—of the groups, the Angels looked the mellowest' I noticed at some point someone came along with a bunch of those gallon mayonnaise jars filled with pills.

They poured out on stage, and it was filled with whites, cross-tops: speed. Another had reds. The Angels, the Jokers, some others were scooping up handfuls of pills and washing them down with pulls from jugs of red wine. Even in my altered state, I remember thinking, 'I don't want to be around when all this shit kicks in.

The Angels were all swaggering around, shoving people. I remember these two Angels were on top of a bus near the stage, pissing off the roof onto crowds of people and laughing. People were getting uptight. Crowds were starting to press in. They had been tripping all night—it was getting toward noon. They wanted the show, it wasn't going on until two or two-thirty. People were getting restive. Fights broke out. A couple fights backstage were premonitions—the Angels were trashing people, kicking the shit out of them. Packs of dogs were getting into dog fights. People were crawling on the ground.

It all seemed ominous. I remember the contrast. Some beautiful hippies—I must have fallen in love a hundred times. But also some really evil looking dudes—real criminal types, the kind you imagine were expelled from prison for bad conduct. I saw those kinds the night the Stones played in November.

Steve Cassady

It was the first time in my life I ever saw people that heavy. I wondered where these people came from. I wondered what they did in real life, why I had never seen them, and where they went when they left. I shagged out of Altamont before the Stones finished playing, after the Angels had whacked that kid, Meredith Hunter. At rock concerts, they usually sweep me out with the last of the Dixie Cups, but this time, I remember thinking, 'We don't go now, we'll never leave this place alive.'

All around in the early 1970s a hard edge was forming. The outlaw 60's had been invaded by criminals who kill people. It was heard in music turned metallic and darkening in theme. It was seen in the headlines. Ronald Reagan and pork barrel republicans had coalesced with ACLU liberals to cut off funding for the nuthouses. The nuts hit the streets and were among us. Indiscriminate drug use was leading to drug psychosis and serial slaying. Charles Manson had lit the fuse for Helter-Skelter in August of 1969. Ted Bundy followed. In Santa Cruz came a trend of demented youth gone blood simple: John Linley Frazier, Herbie Mullin, and Edmund Kemper, III. The three, unknown to each other, accounted for 26 murders in 30 months. The early 1970s in America was a tremendously fucked-up period of time.

The line between outlaw and criminal, once broad and clear blurred and turned filament thin—especially among counterculture youth. *It was fallacious to think the Hell's Angels were our friends,* said Michael Zagaris after Altamont. *Hey, it was fallacious to think we were our friends. I used to think anyone with long hair who smoked grass was groovy—automatic, a brother. How could you lie and rip me off? You have long hair and smoke dope like me. Us against the Establishment. All the bullshit and clichés—I believed* them. *I thought it was my own personal mission to at once trash the system and be reborn into a new world where everyone was groovy and aware and smoked dope and told the truth and was real—and all the other Polly Anna bullshit that went along with it. Then there was Altamont, and the bubble popped.*

At Merced College in 1973, I had a student in English A class, Lee Turner. Turner was 19 then, with a big frame, long face and ice-blue eyes. He looked a little like Lee Marvin when Lee Marvin played the biker badass in *The Wild One*. Turner was 6-1 or 6-2 and weighed a well-proportioned 180 pounds. He had long hair, not always clean. Turner dressed like a thug: earring in one pierced ear, oiled black boots, jeans, Harley belt buckle, T-shirt affecting some counterculture logo. Turner routinely fell asleep in class, often with a commotion.

He would nod off and snore. He would sweep his books to floor with his forearm as he drifted off. I dreaded confrontation, but I had no choice. He was disruptive. I caught him after class one day. We stood outside the door on the balcony next to room V-110. I belied trepidation. I went at it hard. *You want trouble with me Turner?* I asked.

He looked surprised, almost hurt. *Not particularly, why?* I breathed relief and bore on. *Because you'll have it, you keep disrupting my class. I don't care if you don't come to class. I don't care if you do come to class and fall asleep. I do care if you make so much noise falling asleep or staying asleep that the class is paying attention to you and not to what we're doing.* I was grateful for Turner's response. He apologized. He said he worked graveyard at Foster's Farms in Livingston. He said he punched out at seven, and drove straight to English. He said he liked the class.

Steve Cassady

We were friends after that. Turner did well on assignments. I would ask for an exercise in descriptive prose. I asked for concrete, sensory detail. Turner wrote of metal trays clanging against jail cell bars or the lumpy gray of institutional oatmeal. Turner had been raised in Merced but left for Hawaii between his junior and senior years of high school. He had just been released from Oahu State prison. He did one-half of a 120-day sentence. He was 18 and had been convicted of a minor drug charge. He had been running with a couple of Polynesian thugs, Jesse James Bates and Earl Lum. Earl Lum was a bank robber and dubbed *The Robin Hood of Hawaii* by the *Honolulu Star-Bulletin*. Turner was given an early release on the condition he would leave the islands to attend college.

Turner was a raised in a loveless middle-class circumstance. He rebelled from same dramatically. He bought and sold motorcycles at police auctions and was riding a Harley panhead in those days. He wasn't using drugs, at least not heavily, but he was dealing. He was born in 1954, too late. He buffeted from innocence to awareness in the spiritual suffocation of the early 1970s. He said, *I had no place to hang my ideas.*

He formed a sour, alien rage he could not dispel before it warped him. Born sooner he might have be-bopped through the 1950s driving a cut-down Impala listening to Little Richard. He might have dissented through the 1960s in a psychedelic van saying *Right On* to Timothy Leary and the Chicago Seven.

As it was, he turned criminal—not completely, though. He always worked. He has a family and owns a home. He moon-lighted felony. He has checked in over the years. He is way too conversant with biker lore for me not to believe he is or was Angels-affiliated. Turner called me from County Jail in 1986. He wanted me to put 20 bucks in an inmate account in his name.

Bouncing Outside

He was doing ten days for a 502 in Winton. Turner said he'd repay me after he was sprung. He hinted of a darker purpose for being in town. I said, forget the 20 bucks—tell me the story. He did. It's a good story, heavily layered, but I can't print it. It drips with unlimited statute implications.

Turner was at Altamont. He was attending a private high school in the Sierra. His uncaring parents sent him away when they feared he was becoming a public school pot head. *We were the class hippies,* Turner said. *It's where hippies were congregating. We we're expected to go.* The story Turner told at school the next week was fantastic. He told of hitching a ride to stoner free love and wild rock music. He told of dawn-to-dusk psychedelic revelry.

He told pack of lies. He and his friends arrived late—years too late to be actual hippies—hours late to have heard any music. They roamed the weedy grounds above the racetrack area like stray cats after dark, frustrated, unable to connect. They rolled discarded rubber tires down the hills into zonked-out hippies in sleeping bags. They giggled when the tires hit, and the hippies shrieked. *I came back telling stories like I was one of them, a hippie,* Turner said. *In reality, I was a juvenile delinquent punk.*

Jerry Salley was a hippie long-hair teaching speech when I was hired at Merced College. I didn't pay much attention to him until I was excavating the Altamont thing in the early 80s. On Altamont and the stuff that followed, Jerry Salley was a resource. Salley grew up in Fresno without rebellion or complaint in a devout fundamentalist household. His father was a Pentecostal preacher. Jerry Salley grew up in the evangelical tent meeting generation of Marjoe Gortner. Politics in his household were as given as the notion of original sin. *Anyone raised in the San Joaquin Valley in a strict religious environment voted straight Republican ticket. 'Touch not the Lord's anointed,'* was the way his mother put it, citing scripture. We are a Christian nation, the dogma went: He who is president of our nation is president by Lord's will. She meant as long as a protestant republican was in office.

Salley was turned out in 1960 at Santa Barbara, where he majored in speech and minored in philosophy. In the 1960 election, Jerry Salley voted for Richard Nixon against the Roman Catholic John F. Kennedy.

Before the election, I remember going to a pastors' meeting. I was a youth pastor. They had a big prayer meeting, the gist of which was, 'Lord, please keep the Catholic out of the White House.' I knew leaving the booth after voting for Nixon I was wrong—religion was a stupid reason to vote for or against anyone. But I was still too ingrained.

Salley got his first lesson from a political science professor at the University of California, a doctrinaire liberal who hated Richard Nixon, knew why, and could speak to the subject—from the *Pink Lady* Helen Gahagan Douglas down to the Checker's speech. Jerry Salley stared straight into awareness. Education trumped creed. His own mind was working.

He found manifold flaws in material society and authority opinion. He discovered politicians lie and deceive, the military works from insane self-interest, and clergyman can be venal. He re-registered Democrat, embraced the Kennedy notion of Camelot and found, *lightning didn't strike me down because of it.* Salley grew his hair down to his shoulders and swapped Robert Q. Lewis black horn rims for gold rimless (Salley looked already like a thin Ben Franklin without the buckle shoes and white hose). He discovered dope—grass, speed, acid, and blow. He found they opened his head.

Jerry Salley turned radical, though within sedate liberal boundaries. He didn't drop out. He excelled in school and planned on working for a living. He stayed channeled in the 1960s until June of 1968 when he was teaching at Merced College. *A friend called on the night of June 5 and said, nearly hysteric, 'They shot Bobby.'* Salley's eyes were puffy with sleep. They started to water. He was silent for a minute. He said, *Go back to sleep, man. It's over.*

Jerry Salley crossed into the 70s as disillusioned as anyone. He escalated radical. He took more drugs. He mixed with students in drug use. He boinked women students. He saw the line between outlaw and criminal growing thinner. He saw one of his friends doing business with the Gypsy Jokers. *He knew what they are—a badass motorcycle gang that do a lot of drugs, eat a lot of reds and whites and get violent—really violent—but he liked them. Liked it. Liked playing with fire.* The Gypsy Jokers were big in Merced, Salley said, because they controlled drug traffic.

But at the same time, Salley said, *drugs were so plentiful that dealing has crossed into so-called respectable hands. Some ordinary guys. Girls too. We've had some great female dealers in this town. How I got into it myself, I never had to go looking. They came to me. My main man was a graduate student at Stanislaus State.*

He came to my office one day to ask about conducting an experiment in my Sociology class. His eyes were just barely open, he had trouble forming his words. I knew immediately he was a kindred spirit. We were into this conversation about a half-hour. He asked me if I wanted to burn a joint. That's the way it was at first. I've had students coming up and saying, 'You want this or this?' I had mescaline contact, heroin contacts, cocaine and speed contacts, pure opium contacts. Exotic shit for River City.

In 1973, Jerry Salley went on sabbatical leave from Merced College for half-pay. He wasn't looking to realize his academic potential. He went into business working blind for a consortium of Bay Area lawyers. The lawyers were buffered like mafia dons. None would venture within seven telephone digits of any deal they had set up. Jerry Salley couriered cocaine from southern California in smuggling compartments cut in the floorboards under the bench seats of gas-hogging 1960s Ford Galaxies and Fairlane 500s.

Jerry Salley was lured into his courier business at first because he needed $400 to buy his wife a Christmas present. He was attracted to it by curiosity over the depth of his sinful inclinations. Jerry Salley was a criminal dilettante—he found out how things cut when he was popped on an undercover sting. The prospect of paying the piper scared him shitless. He hired a slick San Francisco lawyer who bounced his charges on a technicality. Jerry Salley came within a gnat's ass of losing his teaching credential and voting privilege while serving serious time in state prison. Jerry Salley stayed counterculture, but he retreated hard from criminal complicity.

Basic post-60s hippie syllogism: drugs are cool; people who take drugs are cool; people against drugs are not cool; people denying us drugs are the enemy; therefore, people dealing drugs are our friends. Michael Zagaris found the syllogistic flaw while laced with pharmaceuticals at Altamont. Michael Zagaris was street smart and amended his naivete fast.

Jerry Salley taught logic and should have recognized it on sight. He blinded himself with counterculture dogma until the prospect of prison time opened the shutters. Lee Turner saw it for what it was, stepped over the line, and became a criminal himself. Most of the 70s young went at it like Mr. Magoo. Most never saw it and somehow still survived into adulthood, brains and psyches intact. Some didn't.

A girl named Denise Catlin moved to Atwater, California, near Merced, in 1973 after graduating high school in York, Virginia. Her dad was Air Force—he was transferred to Castle AFB. Denise had trouble making friends at first. She found a job, then another, before working at an earring stand on the Merced Mall. She met people through work. She went places in town. She met people at parties. She met a guy named David Estacio, a small-time dealer. They dated.

The Gypsy Jokers were in town dealing. A guy named Larry Hart was a Gypsy Joker from Santa Cruz. He was in town frequently. He ran with a SoCal cocaine trafficker named Clark Timmons, aka Dennis Crowley. Timmons was a big-time. Hart and Timmons had a Merced contact, an ex-con named Hubert, *Huck,* Hunwardsen. Huck Hunwardsen's wife, Pokey, met Denise Catlin and became friends.

Denise moved from her parents' house to a duplex downtown. She had a roommate named Sandra Battiest. Sandy Battiest said Denise was conservative for the times. *She was, I would say, less trouble than the kids of the people we know around the neighborhood. Denise was not a party girl, not like some I know. Oh, she liked to smoke a few joints, liked to drop a few beans. That guy Dennis she's running with—I know he's dealing coke, so maybe she'll do a line here and there...but that's about it.*

Denise met Clark Timmons at a party in Merced. She knew him as Dennis Crowley. She was introduced by Huck Hunwardsen. Clark Timmons was a big, strong, good looking guy. Denise Catlin crossed the thin line into the some serious criminal enterprise. She dumped small-time David Estacio, took up with big-time Clark Timmons, aka Dennis Crowley. In mid-May, 1975, 20-year-old Denise Catlin sent a chilling letter to her parents:

Dear Mom and Dad,

I'm doing fine. Really, I am. It might be a few years before I can see you again. But if you give out any information about me, I'll never be able to see you again. That means you can't give out any of my friends' address because they won't know anything, but they'll still get hassled for not knowing anything. They're going to tell you anything they can to scare you and make you talk. I don't have any idea what they're going to say, but they will say that they don't want me, it's the others, but that's going to be a lie. They want us all. But if they haven't tried to contact you, don't try and contact them. If by chance they don't know who I am, I can come home sooner.

But you can be assured that I am in the best of hands. They're going to treat me better than any FBI or cops will. And if they try telling you they might kill me, don't believe it. This is going to be very hard for you to believe but these are really good people, and I really love them. I have a few of our relatives addresses so if you move, don't worry, I'll always be able to find out where you are from them.

This weekend if you could I would like you to go to Santa Cruz to pick up a car I had to buy. It runs great, so you shouldn't have any trouble getting it back to Merced. Although it does need a new brake light. It's completely paid for. Title will be coming in the mail soon. License number NICK 144—65 4-door dark green Chevy Bel Air. Also, I put a necklace on layaway at Toppers in the mall. I owe $208 on it, so just put $5 on it for now, and I'll send $200 to get it out and $100 to pay off doctor bills. Would send you the money now, *but I would rather you know it's coming instead of taking a chance of you never getting it. So, I'll send that sometime this month. Also, if they should confiscate my things, please try and get them back. That's where you will know for sure they know who I am. Don't show them this letter. Just get the car and throw this letter away. Please! And just remember what I said.*

Miss you and will love you always.
Denise

P.S. Don't be scared cause I'm not. In fact I'm even happy.

Denise sketched in a map near the Hitching Post Motel on Soquel Avenue in Santa Cruz where the Chevy Bel Air was parked. Her parents never saw her again. Less than two months later, her boyfriend Clark Timmons, aka Dennis Crowley, led her to a wilderness site in the Deschutes National Forest near Bend, Oregon. Timmons distracted her while a complicit criminal named Floyd Forsberg, shot her in the back of the head with a 9 .mm pistol. He shot her because he believed she couldn't withstand interrogation in the event of capture. Floyd Forsberg was afraid she would implicate him and his criminal co-conspirators.

From Freeway 580, nothing hints of the Altamont concert of 1969 and the linking events that followed. Freeway 580 is congested commuter traffic and high winds. Three miles over a hill, an obscure racetrack on uncrowded two-lane Midway Road, throws recall into the path. Back roads will do that. They will take you where you're going, maybe not as fast in all cases as the freeway, but just as surely and much more meaningfully. They show where you've been. They revive connections that freeways have severed.

I found this out during my outlaw run of the 1970's. I redoubled my knowledge in the mid-1980s when my sister was dying of melanoma. I was driving

Steve Cassady

a Mustang GT convertible by then, eight cylinders screaming under the hood. I was tortured by grief and tagged by existential rage. I knew the back roads already, and my anodyne was pure V-8 adrenalin surge. I reasoned that northern California roads pre-freeway were organized as a set of grids to transport goods to market and people to towns—that most roads funnel into the cities and connect with each other. I made the connections and returned to where I began.

I crisscrossed the grids for diversion at high speeds while my sister sunk into cancerous decline. Once while visiting my parents, I woke up early one Sunday and took off at first light for Santa Cruz to see my brother. Salinas to Santa Cruz door-to-door is mostly city streets and two-lane roads, 116 out Market Street to Castroville, through Moss Landing, picking up three-lane Highway 1 through Watsonville, Aptos, Soquel and into Pasatiempo, where my brother lives. 39 miles, and I nailed it house-to-house in 39 minutes flat.

It had to be a record. In my mind it was, until I mentioned it to my brother. My brother said he left the hospital in Salinas in his 1957 Porsche Speedster one night and was home 32 minutes later. My brother is a mechanical engineer; he can do the math. Driving 39 miles in 32 minutes across that route means at least 15 of those miles had to be taken at speeds greater than 100 miles per hour. My brother is a maniac. He got a ticket on his bicycle as an adult. While peddling down a steep hill near his house, he hit 45 in a posted 25 mph zone and was zapped by a town cop at the bottom of the hill who had him on radar. I remember as teenagers my dad always admonished us to slow down. He never did himself, and neither did we.

The back roads have beckoned often over time. Cop-free, and uncongested, they have always come across to me as nature did for Emerson, ...a *mutable cloud, which is always and never the same.* Now in a third phase they were leading me to water and this Gestalt: as much as the back roads can take me to my destination, they can take me simultaneously to my roots. And this: the roads are pre-dated by the rivers. The rivers were there first, and their roots run deeper.

Somehow it all connects.

Steve Cassady

3. Alameda: The Raiders

...Life is not a matter of holding good cards, but sometimes playing a poor hand well.
--Jack London

Some enthusiastic bureaucrat had called August 11 athletic director's meeting in Lemoore on the southwest side of the San Joaquin Valley. Lemoore sits as the only civilization in a sand swept void near where the government allows the disposal of toxic waste. On August 11, the outside temperature sizzled 104 degrees. The Central Valley is a breadbasket as fertile as Eden. Nothing grows in Lemoore except dry-ground crops—cotton and tumbleweed.

Lemoore is Dogpatch. AD meetings are crashing bores trumped up as useful activity that degenerate fast into anecdotal exchange. I have never solved a problem specific to my department based on insight acquired at an AD's meeting. My grandfather on my mother's side was the Finn, Uuno Railo. In his time, Uuno Railo was the fastest Finn alive. He ran a 10.8 100 meter in 1907, a record that stood in Finland for 28 years. 10.8 was the fastest 100-meter Olympic time until *The Chariots of Fire* guy, Harold Abrahams, ran a 10.6 in the 1924 Olympic Games in Paris. Uuno Railo's best time in the 200 meters was 22 seconds flat. Uuno Railo could run like a striped-ass ape.

Uuno Railo represented Finland in the 1908 Olympics in London but ruptured a thigh muscle in the time trials. He returned to Finland. In 1910, like all healthy young male Finns, he was obligated for conscription into the Russian army. My grandfather thought for himself. He thought about the Red Army.

Bouncing Outside

He considered forced marches in Siberian snow. He said, u*p yours, Boris, I'm going to America.* He sailed for Southampton and sailed steerage to Ellis Island.

He couldn't speak a word of English when he landed. He made a nice life for himself before dying young. I am imbedded in my profession. Whatever I have achieved, I have achieved without group thought. At a state-level sports administrator's conference in Palm Springs one year, I was loitering outside a breakout seminar titled *Thinking Outside the Box.* One of the event coordinators asked if I was planning to attend the session—it already had started. I said, anyone attending a seminar to learn how to think outside the box already can't do it. Meetings hold no imperative. I never knew my Finnish grandfather, but DNA tells. I go my own way. I bagged the meeting in favor of a cool place to paddle. I trekked the back way toward Alameda and the Oakland Estuary.

Uuno Railo had an affinity for water. All Finns do. Finland is all about snow, melted snow and birch trees. Finland has 190,000 lakes, 180,000 more than Minnesota. Uuno Railo keeled over hoisting anchor in a row boat in San Pablo Bay in the Carquinez Straits while fishing with his brother. He was 47 when he died; my mother had yet to marry my father. The Carquinez Straits run freshwater flows from the Delta through San Pablo Bay and to San Francisco Bay and through the Golden Gate into the Pacific. I wrote a book about the Golden Gate Bridge. The Carquinez Straits are formed by the delta confluence of the Sacramento and San Joaquin rivers. The Merced flows into the San Joaquin. The Merced is my home river. Rivers run deep. Things connect.

I ate breakfast in Patterson, at Mil's. I cling to rules for eating on the road—no chains, no off-ramp restaurants. I won't eat anyplace that has a version in

Merced. I like beaneries and diners, downtown USA coffee shops. I always look for the same mythic place: the unpretentious counter in Edward Hopper's painting, *Night Hawks*. Mil's comes close. So does Ole's Waffle House in Alameda and Bette's in Salida. They offer common man, short-order food and waitresses that don't grind fresh pepper or hover. They feature waitresses that call you *Hon,* pour coffee, take an order, serve the food, and drop the bill on the table. .

I took the back way to the Bay Area. I left I-5 at Patterson Pass Road turned right on Midway through dry brown hills, abandoned farm equipment and defunct windmills. I drove past the Altamont Raceway to Grant Line, to Old Altamont Pass Road, through and wind farms and over the summit.

I hit the 580 freeway at Vasco Road in Livermore, 23 miles from where it would connect to 880 and on to Alameda. From 580, the 238 freeway Y to 880 at Castro Valley was bottlenecked. It usually is—no matter the time of day or day of the week.

I slipped the bottleneck by staying right on 580 as it hooks toward San Francisco. I exited on Foothill in east Oakland which merged with MacArthur Boulevard. I took MacArthur to 98th Avenue, downhill to the freeway 880 on-ramp. 880 to High Street, left on High under the BART rails through the unsightly waterfront warehouses of industrial Oakland, over the tan drawbridge into Alameda, a tidy island town fronted on the east and south by the Oakland Estuary, north and west by San Francisco Bay.

Alameda once was a navy town. Now it devotes itself to the development of parks, shoreline, marinas and beaches. Alameda Point on the north end was a 2,800-acre military installation, the Alameda Naval Air Station, now decommissioned—comprising a third of the island's area. I turned right to Grand, another right to the Grand Marina. The marina provides an uncrowded boat launch on weekdays, available free parking 75 feet from the water and a good public bathroom. I put in five minutes later. It was 68 degrees outside. The Grand Avenue Marina sits directly across from Coast Guard Island and the four high-endurance cutters stationed there, the Sherman, the Morgenthau, the Munro, and the Boutwell.

    I could paddle north toward Jack London Square with the skyline of downtown Oakland in the foreground, past the giant shipping cranes, past Pier 3 and the USS Hornet, famous for the World War II Doolittle Raid, the 30-second over Tokyo bombing of Japan, to Alameda Point, and into the bay. Or south, down the estuary along the backside of shoreline houses, under three drawbridges, toward San Leandro Bay with the Oakland Airport in view to the southwest, and the Oakland Coliseum to the northeast. I chose the estuary. Under the second bridge, the sight of a restaurant called Pier 29 triggered a recall.

    In the football season of 1974, I went to Pier 29 with Marv Hubbard after an Oakland Raiders game. Marv Hubbard was a fullback beset by contradictions. He was six-foot one, 240 pounds. He lived for gridiron collisions but had a thinker's brain. He was from upstate New York, a hamlet called Red House.

    Marv Hubbard developed formative notions in Appalachia while engaged in Saturday night bar fights. He had trouble understanding why Californians wanted to prosecute for activities considered recreation in Red House. Hubbard went Cornell University on a skiing scholarship and excelled academically. Marv Hubbard didn't always walk along the center aisle.

    In the bar at Pier 29 in 1974, Hubbard engaged in an argument with a strong-minded woman of some stature and looks. The strong-minded woman was outspoken in the *I am women, hear me roar* tradition. She was mostly disagreeing out loud with everything Hubbard had been saying to everyone but her. Hubbard's Appalachian upbringing had yet to factor in a place for the liberated female.

At one point, the woman claimed to be a channel swimmer. She was wearing a butter soft brown leather coat. After hearing her Gertrude Ederle/Florence Chadwick credentials, Hubbard bet she couldn't swim across the estuary to Alameda and back. She sneered. The estuary is about 150 yards wide, child's play. Hubbard asked, "In your leather coat?" She bit on the challenge. The bet was made, for how much I don't exactly remember, maybe the price of the coat plus a hundred dollars. The bartender held the stake. She left, presumably for the water. The bartender gave Hubbard back his money, and we left. The Raiders of the seventies were a different breed.

In the summer of 2004, a man named Bob Brown, nicknamed "Boomer" was inducted in the Pro Football Hall of Fame in Canton, Ohio. Bob Brown was a Raider in the 1970s. He called himself a gypsy right tackle. He performed when players tended to stay with the same team the duration of their careers. Bob Brown moved around. He was an All-America offensive tackle from Nebraska drafted by the Philadelphia Eagles coached by Joe Kuharich. He was smarter than most—he graduated from UN in four years with a degree in biology—and more articulate.

Bob Brown seldom kept his thoughts to himself. Management seldom was endeared. Philadelphia fired Joe Kuharich, and Bob Brown voiced dissent. He moved to the Los Angeles Rams, where George Allen liked to control things. Bob Brown resisted control. He moved from LA to the Raiders, where winning on Sundays trumped preoccupation with control. Offensive linemen are typecast as passives giants. They wall off floods—blitzing linebackers, onrushing D-tackles and ends. Bob Brown was temperamentally disposed to deliver punishment, not absorb it. Bob Brown was big for his time, 6-4, 295 and completely physical, a nasty competitor. Bob Brown characterized himself as *subtle as a sixteen-pound sledge.* He didn't wait for the pass rush. He went looking for it.

Bob Brown moved around because he was big, black, outspoken, and demanding. He said, "If the Chinese would pay enough, I'd slap a Sampan sticker on the side of my helmet and play for the Yangtze Sailors." He said, "When I go see the Wizard—and I call all general managers 'the Wizard' because they live in Oz—they tend not to like what I have to say."

Bob Brown wanted quarterback money. He reasoned quarterbacks can't earn quarterback money knocked on their ass. He was paid to protect the quarterback from the best rush ends in the league— Claude Humphrey, Carl Eller, Deacon Jones—and as long as he could do that he should be paid like a quarterback. Bob Brown was clearly moved at his induction ceremony. The years had settled him. He knew his place in football history and loved the game and all it meant. But he had no sentiment about such things in 1973. He said, "When I can't keep those guys off the quarterback, the Wizard will get rid of me— because I'm a pain in his ass."

One day in training camp, 1974, a rookie was coming out of the mess hall at the same time Bob Brown was lumbering toward it. "What's for dinner, rookie," Bob Brown asked? "Pork chops, Mister Brown," said the rookie. Brown turned about face. "Where you going, Mister Brown," asked the rookie, "food's good, they got plenty more." The big man said, "Bob Brown don't eat the big rat."

Steve Cassady

Bob Brown was prescient. When his performance slipped, the Raiders cut him. He didn't suffer fools gladly, and the fools retaliated. Bob Brown's induction in the hall was probably 20 years beyond when it was due. Bob Brown played for three teams, but he was a Raider at heart. He settled in Oakland in a high rise near Lake Merritt. Lake Merritt is fed by the Oakland Estuary. John Madden said Bob Brown brought a defensive lineman's mentality to the offensive line. Bob Brown: "Pro football fans pay good money to see violence in great abundance. I owe it to them to be an asshole for three hours every Sunday afternoon."

I insinuated myself into the Raiders' circle sideways. When I first moved to Merced, I had been where things were happening. I was in Los Angeles in school during the Watts Riots of 1965, in San Francisco, living on the corner of Haight and Ashbury, during the hippie incursion in the summer of 1967. Merced was a small valley town, population 26,000, with no headline drama. Insightful teens called it "Merdead." Merced couldn't grip me. Its best action was subterranean in depths I had yet to plumb.

The surface all was static stability—white bread and four-door Chevrolet sedans. Merced had four TV stations from Fresno worth of reception obtainable with a UHF antenna. Merced's nearest urban presence was Fresno, 50 miles away. Then and now, Fresno is my idea of shit city, USA—a bad valley town sprawling past its edges, culturally and architecturally unredeemed. Fresno's nightly news was arson blazes, gang violence, and domestic disturbance.

Merced was a better valley town because there was less of it. I cocooned on work days. I became good cook, a dropdown from both parents, because Merced had few joints that weren't Mexican, Chinese or a chain. I like Mexican and Chinese food, but not exclusively on alternate nights. I hate chains.

Merced was proximate to everything, however, and my contract obligated me only to 175 teaching days of year. The job paid enough to purchase a horribly unreliable 1967 Porsche 912. When not on the job, I tended to bounce my Porsche to the outside.

Harry Blauvelt was the sports editor of the Merced Sun-Star. I had never written anything beyond papers for grades in graduate school and a master's thesis on the Shakespearean overtones in William Faulkner's first Yoknawpatawpha novel. I approached Harry Blauvelt and offered stories written gratis in exchange for *Sun-Star* press credential access to the San Francisco Giants. Harry said okay.

Harry Blauvelt had quirks. His father was a petroleum nabob, the chairman of the board of Continental Oil. Harry was east coast by way of Ponca City, Oklahoma. He had been kicked out of prep school, Andover Academy in Massachusetts, for "an accumulation of minor offenses." His father told him he had to enlist in the army. Harry didn't figure out until sometime during his military hitch that parents cannot make their children join the service.

He went to Tulane University but never finished. He claimed to have graduated from Yale and played football for the Eli's along with Calvin Hill. He said he tried out as a punter for the New York Giants. None of that happened. Much of what he claimed was lies.

Harry was a prodigious liar but an extremely competent newspaper man. He had a house in San Jose, where his first wife lived, bought when he was working for the newspaper in Livermore, which eventually would fire him. Harry had trouble with authority figures. He found work in Merced and commuted home to San Jose on weekends. During the week, he lived like a recluse a couple blocks off Main Street, downtown. He lived with a slew of cats in a ramshackle second-story Victorian apartment with no air-conditioning.

He liked my Giants' features once I taught myself how to write them. I wrote stories on Bobby Bonds, Al Michaels, Dave Kingman. I took my *Sun-Star* credential to Dodger Stadium in Chavez Ravine and wrote about Tommy Lasorda and Steve Garvey. Baseball season was winding down and Merced was still Merced. I went across the bay to Oakland and secured press access to Raider games through PR director Tommy Grimes.

I got to know Tommy Grimes. He told me inside truth. He told me how Al Davis, who started as a coach, assimilated ownership of the team. He said when Al Davis was the commissioner of the old AFL, he had to review all league contracts. He scoped what Joe Robbie had been doing in Miami. Joe Robbie had been a minority partner with the Dolphins, but the managing partner. Joe Robbie set policy.

Smaller shareholders, the one and two percent people, lost interest in minority football ownership, mostly because Joe Robbie's policies didn't treat them very well—meaning they couldn't get their kids on the sidelines or into the locker room. Joe Robbie began collecting their mom-and-pop shares until he had more than anyone, meaning more stockholder votes, even though he wasn't the majority stockholder—because nobody was. With something like 23 percent ownership, Joe Robbie had ironclad control of the Miami Dolphins. They eventually named the Dolphins' stadium after Joe Robbie.

The AFL merged with the NFL in 1966 mostly because of Al Davis' guerilla tactic of raiding the NFL for its marquee quarterbacks. The new combine wanted

Bouncing Outside

a diplomat not a guerrilla fighter as commissioner and retained NFL boss Pete Rozelle. Al Davis returned to Oakland and began to wrest control of the Raiders by aligning with one general partner, Ed McGah, squeezing out the other, Wayne Valley. Al Davis became managing general partner, meaning he set policy like Joe Robbie, and he accumulated more shares than any other partner. He was the Raiders' Czar.

The Raiders idea of PR was different from most. Al Davis cared only about winning on Sunday and how much money he could leverage to afford players who could win games for the Oakland Raiders. Attitudes trickled down. It didn't matter to the Raiders if you wrote for the *New York Times* or a shopper's weekly. If they liked you, you were in. If not, you were shunned. I represented no threat to their stronghold.

I wasn't a beat reporter prying for scoops and working for a paper that anyone read. I wrote what I wanted in obscurity about a game that fascinated me. I followed my own scent. Most NFL teams trained on college campuses and roomed in dorms. The Raiders co-opted entire wings of a resort motel in Santa Rosa, the El Rancho Tropicana. The El Rancho had acreage in back. Al Davis fenced in the equivalent of two adjacent football fields for a practice facility.

I was broke half the time during the summer. Any day from mid-July to early August, I'd call Tommy Grimes and wind my Porsche up the valley, across the Delta through the wine country to Santa Rosa. A room would be waiting. I ate free at the media and coaches' section of the mess table. I hung around the two-a-days and whiled away late nights in the lounge picking up this and that. Al Davis once asked, "and you do this because you love football?" I answered, "Yeah, mostly." But what I loved was the vagabond life. The game was cool, the periphery was cool, but peripatetic motion through towns and cities, avenues and boulevards, everywhere the thing could take me—that was way beyond cool.

John Madden's endorsement was an E-ticket. The Raiders were playing the Cincinnati Bengals one Sunday in 1973. The Bengals were coached by the legend, Paul Brown. They were scrapping to become more than an expansion team. The Raiders trailed by less than a score in the fourth quarter, four minutes and some to play. The Raiders stalled, fourth down just inside the Bengals' side of midfield.

Madden sent in the punting team. The Oakland Coliseum, always noisy, erupted with ignorant derision. Upstairs, some media members groaned. The Raiders won the game with the clock running and no time for another play. Halfback Charlie Smith took a Kenny Stabler toss and swept right end behind blocks by Marv Hubbard, right guard George Beuhler and Boomer Bob Brown for an eight-yard touchdown.

In the press briefing afterward, I lingered until the room was empty. Madden was flopped in the interview chair holding a diet coke, looking drained. I asked if he minded a question or two more. Madden looked up, apparently unaware anyone had stayed behind after the press conference. He said, go ahead.

I said: I get that you won. I get that you won after giving up the ball behind by a score with four minutes left. I get that the fans were booing the punt. I get that your idea was better than theirs because you won the game, and mostly they were just drunk and loud. I don't get why. Madden seemed relieved to deconstruct a positive rather than defend a bad call.

His explanation: "It was fourth down. I didn't want to give up the ball, but I can't be an emotional idiot just because the fans will boo. We just proved through three tries we couldn't make a first down. Why would the fourth down be more successful? We have Ray Guy, the best punter in the league. He will bury the Bengals inside their own 20.

"I have all three timeouts plus a clock stoppage at the change of possession. I have confidence in the defense. I know Paul Brown. With a short lead inside his own 20, he won't pass, because an interception loses him the game. I have confidence in my run defense. If we stop the run and call time out after each down, we can get the ball back in 15 seconds and still stop the clock after the exchange. Their punter is not as good as Ray Guy. We'll get the ball back in better position, with a fresh set of downs to go in for the score. As for the scoring play, nobody sweeps in that situation, because sweeps take too much time and tend to get thrown for losses. It would be the last thing they'd expect, so that's what we did."

I wrote the story in copious detail. It was headlined "Anatomy of Winning Decision". I showed it to Madden the next week. He thought it was deep. He said the tendency is to rip with headline negatives and walk away. The story opened a door. I took road trips with the Raiders, the first one to Cleveland. I had no money as usual. The whole trip cost me 65 cents out of pocket, for newspapers, plus gas to the Oakland Airport and airport parking. The Raiders picked up the hotel tab and all meals in the hotel restaurants.

I taught English classes at Merced College during the week. I followed Raiders' games on weekends. I was in Oakland for home games. For road games, I flew in the DC-8 team charter to San Diego, Kansas City, Seattle, Denver, New England, Philadelphia. I traveled to Pittsburgh for the AFC championship in 1975 when Russell Kellum was the navigator. I traveled to Super Bowl XI against Minnesota at the

Steve Cassady

Rose Bowl in January of 1977, the first of nine Super Bowls I worked.

In 1973, I was on the team charter to Kansas City. I flew white-knuckled. I was assigned a window seat but traded for the aisle. I didn't feature spending three hours looking out at a five-mile void between me and the ground, only riveted sheet metal between me and the big fall. The DC-8 lumbered through menacing early winter Midwest skies. Across the aisle, a guy was reading a book, *Fear of Flying,* by Erica Jong.

I looked over at him and mentioned he was reading what I was living—a conversational icebreaker. We talked. The guy's name was Baron Wolman. He was photographer and publisher. Baron Wolman was eclectic. He had been the original staff photographer for *Rolling Stone* magazine. He took pioneer pictures of rock-and-roll. He had witnessed Woodstock and survived Altamont. He shot the icons, Janis Joplin, Jimi Hendrix, Jefferson Airplane, the Grateful Dead. He cashed in his start-up *Rolling Stone* stock and founded a magazine called *Rags,* focusing on the gilded denim 60s fashions. He had published a black and white photo book titled *Profiles.* It captured in feature and form an artistic variety of bare female tits.

Baron Wolman wanted to publish a photo book with essays on pro football. The publishing arm of the NFL, NFL Properties, was run by a man named David Boss. David Boss was an artist and photographer. He knew Baron Wolman and recommended him to Al Locasale of the Raiders. Al Locasale had an unrevealing title with the Raiders— "Executive Assistant". Al Davis tended to confer titles like McDonalds. Everyone has a badge. Everyone in the Raiders' front office had a title, most of them nebulous. They worked out among themselves who did what.

Bouncing Outside

Al Locasale had been Al Davis' major domo since the early days of the AFL. Al Locasale was Higgins in *Magnum P,* the turnkey. Among his chores, he guarded the doors of the stronghold, keeping intruders at bay. The week before, in the airport at San Diego, I asked Al Locasale if he had room on the charter to Kansas City. Locasale took a long time wielding his authority. He denied my request with some attitude attached. I mentioned it to Madden.

I said a simple no would have worked. 20 minutes later, Al Locasale found me at the newsstand and told me what time the KC charter was leaving the next Friday. The next week I asked Madden what he said to Locasale. He was reluctant to admit he said anything, but I persisted. He said: "I told him, 'what the fuck, Al. You take every freeloader in the Bay Area on these trips. We finally get a guy who works and you want to leave him behind.'" Madden trumped Locasale, and I made the KC flight. David Boss put Baron Wolman through the door guarded by Al Locasale. Baron Wolman was looking for a writer. I was looking for something beyond writing free stories for the *Merced Sun-Star.* It all connected.

The result was published the following year, during the playoffs. It was called *The Good Guys.* We had invented the title late one night at training camp in Santa Rosa while talking with Al Davis. It was just after Al Davis slipped and admitted part of the reason for the Raiders' color scheme was to inspire dread the same way the SS did in Germany with black shirts. He said he was color blind—that was part of it. He said the silver came from the Detroit Lions, a dominant NFL franchise in the 50s. He said the black came from West Point, *the Black Knights of the Hudson.* He might have been posturing about the Nazi thing, but it came through. He wanted the Raiders to be frightening. We

Steve Cassady

promoted intentional irony: black shirted misfits and thugs called the good guys.

In mid-December, the Raiders had just beaten Miami 28-27 in the first round of the playoffs when Kenny Stabler hit Clarence Davis with a late-game touchdown pass. I saw destiny. I foresaw a hot market for *The Good Guys*. Clarence Davis had maybe the worst hands in the NFL. He was surrounded by at least four defenders. Stabler was scrambling left and threw from his knees as he was being knocked to the ground by a relentless Dolphins' pursuit. He never should have thrown the ball. The game was among history's best, nicknamed the *Sea of Hands*.

The Miami press corps dressed in their south Florida polyesters and white loafers looked out at the gray cement walls of the Oakland-Alameda County Coliseum. They looked at black-shirt Raiders. They looked at black-clad fans that had yet to become the caricature ill-mannered, foul-mouthed buffoons they are today (that came after the return from the move to LA). The writers looked at the gray overcast sky, and the seagulls that perched on the light poles like vultures. One of them said, 'It looks like the end of the world out there.*"* It had to be the Raiders' year.

The following week they lost at home to the Pittsburgh Steelers, 33-14. Terry Bradshaw picked them apart, throwing to Jon Stallworth and Lynn Swan, handing off to Rocky Bleier and Franco Harris. The Steel Curtain defense with Mean Joe Greene, Jack Lambert, and Mel Blount stopped them cold. My destiny idea was dumb-shit naïve. The Steelers stomped all over it. The Steelers went on play Minnesota in Super Bowl IX. The *Good Guys* market went cold, but the book became a bona fide.

At *PRO!* Magazine, published by the NFL Properties in Los Angeles, publisher David Boss and

Bouncing Outside

editor John Wiebusch took notice. Wiebusch flew me down to LA for lunch and commissioned my first magazine cover assignment. The story featured John Madden. It took an NFL coach through his game day regimen. Baron Wolman shot the cover picture. Madden's wife Virginia said the story cut so close it gave her chills.

The next year, a photographer, Michael Zagaris, approached me in the media room at the Coliseum. He was complimentary about the book. Zagaris was a long-haired bald guy wearing Beatle boots and a wide-brimmed Borsalino fedora—he was extreme in appearance and manner. I liked the compliment, but I found Zagaris weird. He was another rock photographer who shot sports. Zagaris was already a legend in rock photography. He had snapped a picture of Lou Reed spiking heroin into his arm hinge at a concert back stage. On the Friday night, before Super Bowl XI, I ferried Michael Zagaris and his not-wife, pregnant with their son, Ari, from the airport Marriott to the Super Bowl party in the Pasadena convention center.

I don't know how he got back to the hotel. I ditched him in the parking garage. His patter was constant, politically charged, and apocalyptic. He ranted about republicans. He analyzed hot spots in world events and forecast certain nuclear holocaust. He said, A lot of people will fry. His consolation: "But I'm a survivor, I won't be one of them."

First impressions registered him deranged. That was at first. Later, we became great friends and great collaborators. I calculated deeper. I figured it this way: Zagaris worked the edge on the sane side of crazy. I worked the edge from the crazy side of sane, and the thing connected at maximum RPMs through a decade of fast-lane escapades.

Steve Cassady

The Raiders cultivated and exploited the half-way house hospitality of their bad guy image. They took in misfits and the misfits produced. Ted Hendricks played linebacker in Baltimore and Green Bay before becoming a Raider. Ted Hendricks once rode a horse into practice at Santa Rosa. Ted Hendricks said, "In other places I've played, I was considered 'colorful'. Here, I'm just one of the guys."

I saw the late John Matuszak for the first time on a charter to New England in 1976. Matuszak was 6-9. He was walking up and down the aisle during a flight from Oakland International saying hello to people. The plane was still in lift-off, practically vertical. Matuszak didn't seem to notice. He wore a three-piece light tan suit, and tortoise-shell tinted glasses. He had a beard, and sported a white guy's Afro. The whole tableau was mismatched. The Hall-of-Fame center, Jim Otto, working off some obscure title in the Raiders' front office, had to escort him by the elbow to a seat. Matuszak went willingly. He didn't care. He was completely out of it.

Matuszak was emblematic but not typical. The Raiders had core guys with solid stuff they couldn't thrive without. Those guys didn't generate stories. Guys like Matuszak did. He was a first-round draft choice out of the University of Tampa. He had just joined the team after rolling out in Kansas City and Washington. Matuszak had an issue with authority and Quaaludes, among other things.

Paul Wiggin, when he was coaching the Kansas City Chiefs, once was called to the training room at Arrowhead Stadium, four floors below his office. The trainer was babbling. Matuszak had brought his girlfriend into the training room for a nude romp in the whirlpool tub. The girl friend covered her showgirl tits when Wiggin walked in. Wiggin was insulted. "She's in a room full of men, and she covers up when I come through the door?" The Chiefs trained at a religious college in Liberty, Missouri, William Jewell University. Matuszak brought his dog to training camp. Matuszak shared some pharmaceuticals with the dog. The dog OD'd and died.

Matuszak once gave me and an *Sf Chron* writer named Jack Smith a ride from the Raider practice field near the south tip of the estuary to the Edgewater Hotel on Helgenberger Road. Matuszak noticed a bill board advertising batteries. Robert Conrad was the pitchman. On the billboard Robert Conrad was pictured with a battery on his shoulder and dared anyone to knock it off. I remember the ad as pointless.

Matuszak wanted to knock the battery off Robert Conrad's shoulder. He said he didn't like that kind of guy. He didn't seem to notice it was a billboard, not Robert Conrad himself issuing the challenge. The late Jack Tatum once explained how the Raiders turned misfits into a productive team. He said, "Some teams like to control guys; some guys don't like to be controlled. The Raiders don't care about control. They only care how you play." Once at Santa Rosa, I passed a room where the defensive backs were meeting. It included Willie Brown, a future hall-of-fame inductee, and Skip Thomas at corners, George Atkinson and Jack Tatum at safeties. Bob Zeman was the coach.

Bob Zeman was conducting the meeting. Not one Raider DB was sitting in a chair. Some were lying on the ground, some were standing. One—probably Skip Thomas—was lying down on the floor with his feet opposite Zeman and the film projector. Those guys were loose in protocol, but they could play on Sunday. They knocked the shit out of people.

The Raiders got their Super Bowl victory in 1977, a 33-14 stomping of the Minnesota Vikings. The game was pure Oakland Raiders. Willie Brown at age 34 intercepted a Fran Tarkenton pass and returned it 75 yards for one touchdown. Jack Tatum hit Minnesota receiver Sammy White so hard Sammy White's helmet flew off his head one direction, and his chinstrap another. Gene Upshaw and Art Shell at left guard and left tackle buried the Vikings pass rush. Clarence Davis rushed for 137 yards. Kenny Stabler hit all open targets. Fred Biletnikoff set a record for reception yardage and was named game MVP. John Madden jumped for joy after the Raiders' first score but not very high. John Madden was a great coach but a crappy jumper.

John Madden was 31 years old when Al Davis picked him the coach the Raiders in 1969. In 1979 he was 42 with an ulcer bleeding into his intestines. The doctors could treat the ulcer with Tagamet, but they said the ulcer wouldn't go away until the cause went away. The cause was coaching. Madden had worked in the shadow of Al Davis' mythic rule. Some said he was Al Davis' puppet. Al Davis has had puppet head coaches. John Madden wasn't one of them.

Nobody wins like John Madden being somebody else's bobo. John Madden's career winning percentage was .739—second only to Vince Lombardi. Madden was west coast when media attention stayed east of the Mississippi. He had fame but not celebrity.

Celebrity would come with national TV exposure via Miller Lite beer ads and broadcasting. John Madden was a king-hell football coach, and he had met his goals. John Madden was named to the Pro Football Hall-of-Fame in 2006 and should have been inducted sooner. Madden coached against 10 of the 20 coaches elected before him. Madden's record against teams coached by Hall-of-Famers: 36-16-2, a .685 winning percentage. He had his super bowl ring. He had won a world championship. He had won more games than

Vince Lombardi. He had won 100 games in 10 years. He retired and awaited his celebrity.

John Madden, despite his slovenly appearance was a natural for broadcasting. His childhood friend John Robinson told him never to turn *smooth*. He didn't turn smooth, but he was always smart. John Madden missed nothing. He noticed most color commentators flew off the cuff and didn't work very hard. He was the first to prepare for games all week watching the all-22 coaches' films, all players in the frame at once. From the booth, he had all-field visions. He could deconstruct the play in workingman's argot. He innovated the Telestrator. Once on a train, a blind man told him he could follow a game clearly through Madden's television commentary.

He looked at his job as becoming the viewers' eyes and articulating what they saw, why it happened, and what it meant. CBS loved him. After the Miller Lite ads, he attracted product endorsement. He thought he had a product endorsement shelf life of maybe 18 months. He went strong until retirement in 2010. His biggest problem was travel to and from his assignments. He couldn't fly commercially. Team charters were never pleasant experiences for him, but he could get up and move around in a team charter.

In a charter, he could direct the pilot to evade turbulence. He said he was claustrophobic; commercial flights suffocated him. After a game in 1979 he left a flight from Tampa when it stopped at Houston and took a train home. He evolved into a tricked out personal bus. The answer early on was Amtrak. He had fame but not yet celebrity.

On Amtrak he still could move without being swarmed by gawkers gone fan simple because of celebrity status. That would happen but not for the first few years. Madden's early Amtrak journeys were idiosyncratic. They warranted editorial attention.

At *PRO!* Magazine, John Wiebusch called in 1981 and commissioned a story on John Madden's train travel. I wasn't sure what Wiebusch had in mind. I never asked. I dropped in on Madden in his office in Danville. He said he was headed out in a few days. I would have guessed Wiebusch would want me tag for one leg of a trip for minimal expense, say from Oakland—actually Martinez—to Reno.

I had other ideas. Madden did too. He said, do it right, go the whole way. He was scheduled in New York for three days of production meetings with CBS—this was the first year he would be teamed with Pat Summerall. From New York, he would deliver the kickoff breakfast address for hall-of-fame weekend in Canton, Ohio. Oakland Raider George Blanda would be inducted, along with two Green Bay Packers, Willie Davis and Jim Ringo, along with Morris "Red" Badgro. Red Badgro was deceased. He played for the New York Yankees, the New York Giants and the Brooklyn Dodgers in the *Hupmobile* era.

From Canton, Madden would broadcast a preseason game in Seattle between the Seahawks and the San Francisco 49ers. I calculated the itinerary. The trip would log 16 days and span 8,000 railroad miles. I was sold. I said, "I'm in."

I had some experience on Amtrak. The summer before, I was talking on the phone, I don't remember to whom. I mentioned I'd never been to New York. I hung up thinking. I'm sitting around the house bored in a boring town, making a pathetic statement about never visiting the most famous city in America. I lived a ten-minute walk from the Amtrak depot. I don't report to work for six weeks. I walked over and bought a ticket to New York, departing the next day.

Bouncing Outside

I was gone nine days. Three days across the country, three days, two nights, rambling around the city, three days back. I packed a lot in. I saw the Statue of Liberty. I took a Circle Line boat tour and saw everything from Grant's Tomb to the Brooklyn Bridge. I took subways. I took the A train. I walked along Park, Madison, Fifth, and Lexington Avenues. I went to the tops of the Empire State Building the World Trade Center, now known as *ground zero*.

I saw *42nd Street* on Broadway with Jerry Orbach in the lead. I ate a Nathan's hot dog on the boardwalk on Coney Island. Nathan's has superior hot dogs; they serve French fries in drink cups. I ate Italian food at Patsy's, Luca Brasi's favorite restaurant. Luca Brasi is the assassin in *The Godfather*. I ate Manhattan clam chowder and signature Oyster Stew at the Oyster Bar in Grand Central Station.

Train travel is mystical. A passenger train is a moving hotel that keeps the vastness of a vast country in proper scale. Airplanes compress time and deny scenery. On a train, I *saw* the country while recording the flow of past into present. Intercontinental tracks were laid in the 19th century and haven't moved since. Trackside terrain hasn't changed.

Mountains still are high, water wet, and prairies flat. Amtrak cuts through the Sierra, traverses the desert and prairies, parallels rivers, and crosses lakes. Cities and towns are laid out the same, but demography has altered. Prosperity has fled to the suburbs, deteriorating urban blight riding its slipstream. Train tracks run through what the country used to be when the tracks were laid. Amtrak runs 79 miles an hour through the trashed-out backyards of bygone America.

The Zephyr from Oakland takes two days to reach Chicago through Nevada, Utah, Wyoming, Colorado and Nebraska. The Lakeshore Limited from Chicago to

Steve Cassady

New York takes a 24-hour day to wind through Indiana, Ohio, Pennsylvania, and upstate New York.

Existence in Amtrak ebbs and flows. Surge and fall with the rhythm of ebbs and flows, and train travel is total escape. I rode Amtrak before cell phones, when I couldn't be made to dial a phone, answer a phone, or work when I didn't want to. Those who resist the rhythms are always angry. They complain about the noise, the food, the faulty heating or air. They look at their watches and wonder if the line to the diner will ever subside, when the next layover will finally arrive, and why the train is always late. They don't get it. If they're worried about trains being late, they should travel by airplane, bus, car, or foot.

We once waited 11 hours in Ottumna, Iowa, for a train that was late. That was in the NFL strike year of 1982. The Burlington line east of Colorado was on strike as well. Trains in motion finished their run; everything else was shut down. We were trying to get home. We caught the last one to Denver. Trains don't always run on time. Deal with it.

That first trip we ground to a halt somewhere in Montana. An eastbound freight train had highballed around a tricky bend and whipped off the rails. It tore up a half-mile of track and sent 24 twisting cars careening across a grassy meadow. We were on *The Empire Builder,* train #7, heading from Chicago to Seattle. Amtrak's solution was the trade destinations with train #8, the eastbound *Empire Builder.*

Number 8 had been waiting already 18 hours at Culbertson, Montana for the exchange. We off-loaded at a speck on the map called Bainesville and carried out own luggage to busses which ferried us to Culbertson. Culbertson is a treeless and dusty prairie hamlet. Madden had read John Steinbeck. Steinbeck wrote about the grandeur of Montana's big sky country in

Bouncing Outside

Travels with Charley, but he wasn't talking about Bainesville or Culbertson. We lay over at Culbertson for three hours waiting for #8 to convert into a westbound train. We hung out in the Stockman's bar with day time drinkers and played machine poker.

Madden bought drinks for the house. He consulted the bartender; he wanted to phrase it right. He said, *Set up the house!* He said he'd always wanted to do that. The house wasn't all that crowded. The tab: $6.50.

One hard-core drinker on crutches grabbed his coffee-drinker girlfriend and ushered her out. He hobbled back in ten minutes later with a buddy who drank more than coffee, especially when someone else was running a tab. One guy said he'd find some Indians. They called for the passengers to return. We ordered ham sandwiches to go from a downtown diner. The waitress asked, "Everything on them"? One local said, "Around here, you ask for everything you're gonna find a sheep turd on your plate."

I called John Wiebusch when I returned to Merced. He wondered where I'd been the past two-and-a-half weeks. He arched an eyebrow over my expense claim. The bean counters at NFL Properties approved everything except for three nights at the Essex House in New York. Apparently, I had appeared on their radar. They said, "We're not paying for Steve Cassady's vacation." They didn't comprehend their bargain.

I went first-class all 8,000 miles. I had a sleeper berth. I had worked the Amtrak PR people—Amtrak comped most of it. Amtrak wanted to gravy train John Madden's incipient celebrity. John Wiebusch is from Minnesota—he is Midwest understated. His highest accolade: *I like it; I like it a lot.* Wiebusch liked the Madden train story a lot, heavy expenses and all. He gave it feature treatment under the title *Pullman Coach.*

Steve Cassady

He ran it eight pages on buff-colored paper with exceptional illustrations by F. Bruce Dean.

Madden offered me a job after that. He was contracted for a five-day-a-week, two-minute daily radio commentary on an RKO feed out of New York. RKO saw him as a radio NFL Andy Rooney. Madden never ran out of things to say, but had trouble with the transmission mechanics. He tried ad-libbing, but it hadn't worked. He tried scripting it beforehand but didn't like writing. His new idea: for a grand a month, he'd tell me his take on a topic.

I'd retail a script and send it to him. He'd perform the script, and the show was done. I jumped at it, especially the grand a month part. It was easy work once I decoded the challenge of prose style. I couldn't sound like me. I had trouble sounding like him. I stripped the phrasing bare, and let him sound like himself by using his own inflection.

It took me 45 minutes a day to write the script. Logistics was a bigger issue. We started in the Barney Rubble era of electronic communications. We talked by dial-up phone from wherever he was and I was. I took the information, wrote the script, and called it in to a typist, often his wife.

In 1982, I was in Washington, D.C. at the Library of Congress, looking to see if anything I wrote was in their stacks. I found only one entry, my book on the Golden Gate Bridge. I found a slew of books written by my Uncle Ralph. He had been the Director of Business and Economic Research at UCLA. Uncle Ralph wrote heavily footnoted stuff about arcane subjects like the barter system in ancient African cultures. I admired Uncle Ralph's body of work, but his stuff is unreadable except to marketing scholars.

I found something else: card catalogues were out. Stack information was accessible only on computer screens. Two years earlier, I was walking through downtown Oxford, England, running low on cash. I passed a stately stone bank. I noticed PLUS system logo next to the ATM on the wall. I thought, why not? I pushed in my card, punched out the PIN and watched British pounds come snicking out. I saw the handwriting in Washington and connected it to the money machine in England. I was already behind. I bought a primitive computer, learned to use it, equipped it with a modem, and found it a better way to send the radio scripts. I wrote in an oversized font and blipped them via modem through prehistoric e-mail.

The easiest system involved being the same place as Madden. Teaching English to unwilling college students was grating on me. Merced was grating on me. I met with Madden. He mentioned an autobiography Random House was contracting him to write. I trumped up a sabbatical request.

Sabbaticals are unique to education. Every seven years a college teacher is eligible for a year at half-pay, or a semester at three-quarters, for the purpose of academic/intellectual renewal. The college gains putatively from the instructor's replenished enthusiasm and knowledge. My sabbatical request somehow was approved. I had a year at half pay. The rub was selling to the Board of Trustees in a report at the end. I planned no academic activity. But I had a year to work out that small detail. For the 1982-83 sabbatical school year, I rode the rails with John Madden.

The autobiography crapped out. I worked it for a while but failed. I knew Madden too well. His voice and personality were too stylized in my head. My own was too ingrained. Everything I wrote came across unauthentic, neither him nor me. Nothing I wrote sounded as good as him telling it. His best stuff was anecdotal and spontaneous not linear or chronological biography. I work my craft assiduously. My writer's voice is my own. Autobiography demands assimilation of the subject's voice. I went tone deaf on the project. With a briefcase full of bad drafts, I copped to the truth: autobiography was not my métier, unless the auto was I, and the biography was mine.

Random House gave the project to Dave Anderson of the *New York Times*. Anderson's book with Madden was a best seller, but I didn't care. I had stayed true, and Amtrak still comped me. I was pulling in half-salary from Merced College. I was writing regular for *PRO!* I was earning a grand a month from Madden for the radio show. I wasn't supporting anything but restless whim. I rode out the tour.

We headquartered in New York and spent time in Dallas, Washington, and Philadelphia. CBS wanted Madden and Summerall on the marquee games in big market cities. Train travel's innate weakness: depots were built for 19th century travel, city to city. They all were in the middle of town. New York wasn't a problem. Subways and cabs were all over. Manhattan is only 13 blocks wide. Everything is within walking distance of midtown. Nobody in his right would drive a car in New York. Everywhere else, surface transportation was necessary.

I'm from California. I decode logistics by automobile. Acquiring a car honed a capacity for challenge. I could rent one, but that was like giving up. I invented other ways. Madden had figured early in his train travels that New York to Dallas by train requires an extra day because the train runs down through New Orleans instead of across to Texas. He could save a day by driving to Meridien, Mississippi from Dallas, and picking up the New York train. The same way on the return: taking the New Orleans train to Meridien and driving to Dallas. My first time on the Meridien run, we were in Dallas on a Saturday night for the third preseason game, Dallas versus Houston.

At the final gun the CBS production crew was hustling toward the airport. Sandy Grossman, the producer, had rented a Lincoln Town Car. He said, "I'll go with (director Bob) Stenner. You guys can take my car." Madden had already been to Meridien. He said it was a six-hour drive. We left at midnight. He had the number six right, only it was 600 miles not six hours. We drove all night through Texas, and Louisiana. The sun rose in Vicksburg, Mississippi where we stopped for a breakfast of ham, eggs, and red-eye gravy. I'd driven the whole way.

I was rummy, looking for distractions to stay awake. I noticed a Hertz decal on the windshield. It read: *Please return to the greater Dallas area.* We were three states away, leaving greater Dallas at a clip of 85 mph. Madden's solution: At the Meridien Amtrak stop, he gave the trainmaster ten bucks and the keys and told him, "After the train leaves the station, call Hertz and tell them they have a pickup."

Another time in Meridien the following December, we actually turned in a car. We'd come down from New York, rented a car in Meridien, bought a jumbo pack of Popeye's chicken and drove 600 miles to Dallas, stopping only for gas. We were scheduled for 10 days in Texas. Madden said, "I won't need the car, you can keep it." I saw every sight proximate to Dallas. If greater Dallas had better scenery than the school book depository, I would have toured more.

At the end of ten days, we drove back to Meridien. The rental car bill was 1300 dollars, a huge sum in those days, something about excess mileage. Madden said we could have bought a car for less. He didn't care. He thought it was funny. He put it on his CBS American Express card. CBS didn't care. They were flush. They only cared that receipts matched expenditures. Other than that time in Mississippi, I don't remember a time in 18 months we actually turned in a car at a Hertz office—it was always what Madden called, *a dump job*.

The third week in November, CBS had the Thanksgiving Day game in Detroit. The night before, the production crew was treated to a full turkey dinner. For entertainment, somebody in the crew ordered in a pair of strippers, what they called "interpretive dancers". Thanksgiving eve in Motown: Squanto by way of Gypsy Rose Lee.

After the game, as usual, the production crew hit for the airport. Our train didn't leave until late. We had a rental car. We drove from the Silverdome toward downtown looking for an open restaurant. We found squat. Downtown Detroit was dead to the world on a holiday. We toured urban decay. On Michigan Boulevard, we found an open White Castle. Uninspired fry cooks and counter clerks worked behind bullet-proof plastic windows.

The place smelled of fried onions and stale grease. Winos crept inside to stay warm. Thanksgiving Day dinner, 1982: a half-dozen belly bombs and a soggy bag of fries. We went across the street to a place called "...Bar" for a beer. I couldn't figure the full name. That section of neon was burned out. We drove downtown, dumped the rental with the Amtrak trainmaster, and rode the rails to New York.

The NFL went on strike the first half of 1982. CBS didn't want to broadcast games played by scabs. We stayed busy while the network scrambled for alternatives. One week we did a D-III football game in Ohio. Another, a pool shoot in Atlantic City between Willie Moscone and Minnesota Fats. Moscone was authentic. Fats was a blowhard who bored Moscone.

Bouncing Outside

Moscone had heard it all before, but I found Fat's stuff fresh. Willie Moscone made shots. Fats ran one-liners past the audience. He delivered in W.C Field's nasal intonation: *I've had women that make Raquel Welch look like an onion.... If you could lay all my victims end to end, I could walk across them from here to Rangoon.* One week, Madden's agent secured a $50,000 fee from a consortium of mid-western lawyers.

The lawyers were rubes. The agent anted way high. The lawyers bit as though it were a bargain. Attorneys in the Midwest had just been permitted to advertise. The consortium sent him some ad copy to study. Their stuff was terrible. They were new at advertising. They came across as ambulance chasers with Madden as a shill. We cleaned up the concepts. That's what ad people called them, *concepts*. Madden loved to talk about their *concepts*.

Madden never exactly introduced me when we traveled. He did by name, but never by function or title. People we met made their own assumptions. I worked it. I didn't dress any better than Madden. I could be a bum or an eccentric important guy. I gave no clues. We were met in Denver by the spokesman lawyer, Norton something and his high-school-age son, Norty. Norton was beyond hospitable. He housed Madden in a luxury hotel suite. He secured limo arrangements to and from the filming.

Norton finished attending to Madden. He said to me, "And what will you need?" I thumbed off a list. I went for it. I said, "a room, an IBM Correcting Selectric…and a car." Norton, said, "No problem, you can stay at the same hotel as John. I'll have the girls at the office deliver a typewriter to your room, and… you can use Norty's car." I was set. I didn't have to leave the hotel to write the radio scripts. For three days, while Norty bummed rides or sat home, I spun his whip around the Mile-High City.

The phone rang in my room in the Essex House in New York one day. The voice said he was looking for John Madden, and was told I was traveling with him. I said I didn't know where he was. The guy asked if I would like to have lunch. I was hungry. I met him and another guy downstairs in the coffee shop.

They bought lunch and said they wanted to show Madden some advertising concepts. They asked if I would look them over. They had no idea who I was, and I never said. I scoped their presentation. I told them I didn't like it, but it had promise. I tweaked it this way and nudged it that. I reshaped the whole thing. They sat back, pleased. They left happy they had a viable concept. Madden would never see it. He had ditched them on purpose. I told him: all my hard work, down the drain. He thought my act was funny. I could see why characters had thrived with the Oakland Raiders. The head coach enabled them.

The 1982 season ended with another car episode. The strike had ended at mid-season. The Super Bowl was in Pasadena at the Rose Bowl, the Miami Dolphins versus the Washington Redskins. I was working on an NFL properties credential, writing Madden's radio scripts, and collaborating with Michael Zagaris while he shot Super Bowl color. On game day I drove an NFL rental car to the Rose Bowl. I was way early.

I had a parking pass for Lot B. Every lot was empty. Lot B wasn't clearly marked. I guessed the location of Lot B. After the game, I saw nothing but buses where I had parked the car. A parking lot security guy said the car was probably towed. The tow lot was in the northwest part of the general parking area. It was cordoned off by sawhorses and yellow caution tape. I worked around the back until I saw the car. I slipped into a shadow and under the tape. Only one guy in a yellow windbreaker guarded the entrance. The entrance was two sawhorses split a car-and-a-half wide. I fired up the car and squealed out between the sawhorses.

I could only go left, up the hill onto surface streets toward the 210, the Pasadena Freeway, the only uncongested post-game route. The tow truck had done me a favor; in fact, had pulled me out of traffic. The 210 is the long way from the Airport as the crow flies. But the crows all were stalled traffic down below. From the 210, I beat most everyone else to the Airport Marriot. I don't know if the yellow jackets wrote down the license plate. I didn't care. He'd have to take it up with either Hertz or NFL Properties.

I had been working for Properties all along. I wrote good stuff from places writers had no access. For the *Good Guys,* Madden had let Baron Wolman and me into the locker room pre-game. He said it would the greatest thing we'd ever seen. He said, everyone has only one thing in common—they're all scared to death.

He was right. We heard Fred Biletnikoff throwing up. We saw George Blanda on his locker room milking stool, smoking, staring into space. We listened to the late Gene Upshaw jabber non-stop to nobody listening. We felt ashen fear converting to game-face resolve.

We had whites-of-the-eyes access to pro football, and I sought more. By 1981, I had moved across the bay to the 49ers' camp. The Raiders weren't fun anymore. Madden was gone, and the Raiders were planning their defection to LA, with symbols of big-time disconnect predating the move. Kenny Stabler and Jack Tatum were playing for the Houston Oilers. Jim Plunkett was the new quarterback, Tom Flores the coach. The Raiders would return 15 years later. But they would return in shambles with a disgusting fan base. Thomas Wolfe was right.

Steve Cassady

A few years earlier, John Wiebusch had sent Michael Zagaris and me to Marysville/Yuba City—two towns on either side of a bridge across the Sacramento River about 70 miles north Sacramento on highway 99—for a story on semi-pro football. Billy Wilson, the old 49er split-end coached the San Jose Tigers. They were playing the Twin Cities Cougars at Marysville High School. I met Zagaris at the Amtrak stop in Oakland, and we drove to Marysville. Semi-pro football was primitive. Billy Wilson didn't care how close we got. His team couldn't even dress in the locker room. Marysville High chained it shut in response to damage occurring in the previous game.

The home team Cougars drove to field already dressed. The Tigers formed a circle with their cars, turned on the headlights and dressed in the circle. We mingled with players and coaches during the game. Lighting was bad, decorum worse—late hits, vicious clips, constant trash talk. Play was flawed—rosters filled with big-league dreamers with small-time bodies, skills, character, or brains. Bob Hoskins, the old 49ers defensive lineman, coached the defense.

Bob Hoskins would die too young of Hodgkins disease, at that point in remission. A disgruntled linebacker came off the field after being replaced. He was tearing off his jersey and shoulder pads. He was yelling, *shit, hey those coaches be showing favoritism against me.* Bob Hoskins spoke basso with James Earl Jones gravity. He said, *I've got five kids at home. I don't need any more out here. Sit down.* Zagaris took short glass photos in dim lighting. He caught images that cross referred a passion for the game with the frustration of a futile quest. I caught the same stuff and scribbled trenchant quotes. We nailed the story.

The 49ers stunk as a team and an organization in the late 1970s. Ed DeBartolo was the new owner. He was learning on the job and making mistakes. Al Davis had recommended Joe Thomas as general manager to Eddie DeBartolo. Al Davis took a finder's fee he should have had been embarrassed to keep. Joe Thomas was a disaster. He was as paranoid as Captain Queeg. He thought everyone was scheming for extra portions of strawberries. He fired a winning coach, Monte Clark and hired no-name replacements that wouldn't buck his authority. He made bad draft choices. He spent big money on washed-up veterans. He had a plan. He drafted tight end Ken McAfee out of Notre Dame to block the edge so free agent O.J. Simpson could turn the corner. The plan sucked. McAfee was a stiff. Simpson was washed up.

    Eddie D finally figured it out. He canned Joe Thomas and hired Bill Walsh in 1979. By 1980 Walsh's genius flashed intermittently. Until it came out for good the 49ers were a dream for us: pro football up close—wide open access because nobody gave a shit. In 1980, on a 49ers team charter back from New York, I gained grudging permission from Bill Walsh to enter the locker room at half-time of an upcoming game. I told him he could approve the story before it ran. He did. The game was against the New Orleans Saints. The 49ers were behind 28-7 after two quarters.

    I expected red-faced profanity over sub-standard effort and sloppy execution. It was anything but. The staff talked calmly. The staff grease-penciled Xs and Os adjustments on white boards with the position groups. Walsh gathered them as a team. He said, boiled down, 'The next 30 minutes of football will go a long way in determining the direction of this football team and your career." Walsh said later a coach can berate a veteran team. He said a young team trying to find its way would only buckle. He said a young team needs to be built up not broken down.

Steve Cassady

New Orleans kicked a field goal to forge ahead 31-7. On the next possession, Joe Montana, in his second year, not yet established, hit Dwight Clark on a crossing pattern, and the 49ers burst into prominence. They tied the score in regulation and won it overtime 38-35. At the time, it was the greatest comeback in NFL history. The 49ers Super Bowl dynasty was conceived with the hiring of Bill Walsh and drafting of Joe Montana. It was born in the second half of the comeback against New Orleans. It was slapped into action with the NFC championship game of 1981 when Joe Montana hit Dwight Clark in the back of the end zone in *The Catch,* which sent the 49ers to Super Bowl XVI in Detroit. I saw it all up close. Timing is everything.

In Oakland, Tommy Grimes had moved from public relations to the football side. He had some title in player personnel. Earlier in 1981 I approached him about tagging along during a scouting trip. He said fine. We went out one Sunday early in August. I picked up him up at his house in Alameda, not two miles from where I was currently paddling.

We flew from SFO to Atlanta. En route, Tommy Grimes was studying a printout from BLESTO (BownsLionsEaglesSteelersTalentOrganization). BLESTO is a subscription scouting combine. The Raiders were well known for their refusal to join. They led on that they generated independent scouting information. I mentioned it to Tommy Grimes. He only smiled. I read the smile—pure Al Davis: 50,000 dollars to join a combine or 500 to bribe a BLESTO clerk with access to the Xerox machine?

We flew from Atlanta to Knoxville on a DC-8 and rented a car. We visited the University of Tennessee. Johnny Majors was the head coach. Johnny Majors barely gave us the time of day. He came through the coaches' lounge. He was polite. It was obviously he

Bouncing Outside

couldn't care less about a scout from the Oakland Raiders. The lounge was roomy. It smelled of SEC booster money, new leather furniture, new carpets, and fresh paint, all in orange and white. Johnny Majors said we were free to watch film but that practices were closed. We watched SEC prospects on film, a tight end that could catch who had lower legs too skinny for drive blocking; an offensive lineman with pancake blocking strength but questionable feet.

Tommy Grimes wanted to see the UT kicker in person. He drove us to the stadium. Kickers are hard to scout on film. Kickers tend to practice by themselves in the stadium. He and his kicking coach apparently weren't told that practices were closed. We watched the whole workout while bullshitting with the coach, George Cafego, a UT hero from the 1930s.

Grimes liked the Tennessee kicker. We went back and watched film from the year before. Grimes pointed out a linebacker. He like the way he hit but not the way he reacted. The linebacker had been drafted by the 49ers in the fourth round would start on Bill Walsh's first Super Bowl win over Cincinnati five months later. He washed out fast after the Super Bowl. He had a bad cocaine habit. Cocaine was big in the NFL players in the early 1980s, rampant with the 49ers. Hip people thought cocaine was harmless because it made them feel good. They were full of crap. Cocaine ruined lives and didn't discriminate in favor of NFL players. The linebacker wasn't the only 49ers whose pro football career dissipated up his nose.

We went to an NAIA school the other side of town, all-black Knoxville College. Knoxville College was red-dirt poor and ran three-a-day practices in ragged, reeking uniforms with mismatched socks. Knoxville College yielded no prospects, but NFL scouts for teams that win don't leave stones unturned in their territory.

Steve Cassady

NFL scouts fear pro bowl players unearthed from remote schools playing for opponents in their division. Knoxville College since has discontinued football in favor of intramurals. We took a propeller plane to Johnson City and visited East Tennessee State, coached by ex-NFL assistant Bernie Miller.

    East Tennessee played on turf inside a 13,000-capacity dome. Bernie Miller told stories about coaching under Bill Peterson with the Houston Oilers. Bill Peterson was notable for malaprops. He told his Oilers team once: *Men, I want to focus on one word and one word only—Super Bowl.* Bernie Miller once was an assistant with the San Francisco 49ers under Dick Nolan. He had some players worth writing reports on, none that ever made it to the NFL.

    East Tennessee was division 1-AA. East Tennessee since has addressed its budget problems by discontinuing football. We drove to Division II Carson-Newman College in Jefferson City. Scouts from Atlanta and Denver came into the film room mid-reel. We all watched more film without colluding. We talked to more coaches, PR guys, and trainers. A scouting trip is tedious, but a scout cannot yield to tedium. Make-or-break footage on a prospect is always on the next reel. That's the myth. The guy he dismisses always makes the Pro Bowl for another team.

    We broke the tedium one night after dinner by crashing an Arthur Murray Dance Studio graduation party. We saw it full swing through a plate glass storefront window in a strip mall and went in. We stood out. The only males in the room not wearing a tuxedo, puffy shirt, and patent leather pumps. The hosts were gracious. Their names were Ross and Freddie. Freddie must have been short for Frederica. Freddie offered us wine, and we stayed until the evening was old enough to return the motel.

Bouncing Outside

In the spring of 1983, the year John Elway was coming out from Stanford, the Properties editors and I approached all 30 teams to gain permission for me to enter the war room on draft day and write about it. We offered out-front concessions. I would camouflage the team's identity. I'd let them read the copy before it ran, implying veto power over sensitive intel inadvertently revealed. Some teams snorted at our audacity. Some said they'd get back to us but never did. Some said they'd consult their staff and told us no a few days later. 29 teams refused one way or another.

The St. Louis Cardinals said yes. I was versed in Cardinals' history. I wrote their NFL encyclopedia entry in 1976 when I was contemplating a job offer from Properties and was working a two-week stint in the office in Westwood. The Cardinals were the oldest team in NFL history. They started as the Chicago Normals in 1898. They were longtime inept.

They had one only one championship, in 1948, when they beat Philadelphia behind Pat Harder, Charlie Trippi, Paul Christman and Marshall Goldberg. The Cardinals had good years in the 1970s when Don Coryell coached them and Neil Lomax was the quarterback. Jim Hanifan was the Cardinals coach in 1982. I watched Hanifan as a kid when he played for Cal. My parents were Cal grads. My father pole vaulted for Brutus Hamilton.

My dad organized a team of ushers for Cal home games when I was in grammar school. Ushering was easy. Cal stunk, the crowds were sparse. We stayed in the south end zone, which never was crowded. People who sat in the south end zone always sat in the same seats. They knew how to find them. We wore usher's arm bands while we sat on empty seats and watched the games from kickoff to final gun. Jim Hanifan was an end who played both ways. Jim Hanifan was from

Steve Cassady

Southern California. He knew the baseball coach from Merced College, Butch Hughes. I connected with Jim Hanifan. He greased me into the war room.

In 1983 the NFL conducted a 12-round draft, competing with the USFL, which was signing players like Steve Young and Herschel Walker. To thwart the USFL, the NFL conducted the 12-round draft in one day—didn't want second-day talent defecting to the USFL if they weren't picked in the first six rounds. The draft is intense. It makes or breaks NFL franchises. I held back. I didn't want to obtrude.

The Cardinals are owned by Bill Bidwell. His father, Charles Bidwell owned the team dating back to the 1920s. Bill Bidwell is synonymous with the Cardinals' suspect performance, a reputed cheapskate who won't pay for a winning NFL operation. The Cardinals reputation is laughable.

Bill Bidwell has a cherry nose and wears bow ties. My dad and my Uncle Paul wore bow ties. I felt an affinity when Bill Bidwell came into the room carrying boxes of donuts. Bill Bidwell taunted the coaches and player personnel people. He had a sneaky sense of humor that broke ice all through the room. Bill Bidwell worked the phones. I didn't care about Bill Bidwell's tightwad reputation. I liked him.

Larry Wilson was the general manager. Larry Wilson, nicknamed *Wildcat,* was an archetype 1960s NFL tough guy. He was 5-10, 165 and hit with everything he had. He invented the safety blitz. Larry Wilson is as genuine as a 20-dollar gold piece. George Boone was the director of player personnel. George Boone looks like Joe Don Baker when Joe Don Baker played Tennessee sheriff Buford Pusser in *Walking Tall.* In the movie Buford Pusser whacks peckerwood bootleggers and pimps with a hickory stick. George Boone looked like he could do the same.

Bouncing Outside

The Cardinals had a shitty draft in 1983, if a draft is judged by the first-round pick. They selected a receiver from Tennessee, Clyde Duncan, whom Tommy Grimes had watched on film and written up but not recommended. Clyde Duncan never pissed a drop in the NFL. In the war room, I held back maybe an hour. These all were my kinds of guys, the scouts included. I waded in without fear of obtrusion.

I involved myself in the whole process. I checked the board. I read the reports. I pulled up a chair for discussions. A guy from Merced was drafted in the fourth round by Buffalo, Tony Slaton, a center from USC. Tony Slaton had a good career with the NFL, mostly with the Rams. The Cardinals didn't rate him very high. They thought he had a soft upper body.

The draft day started at seven am. By two the next morning when it was winding down, they gave me a say on the final pick. I weighed in for a big offensive guard from Georgia who had a surprisingly good vertical leap. Fat guy that can jump—a good reach. The Cardinals took him—not on my vote alone—but we all whiffed. The fat guy never made the team.

I went back to my hotel with a view of the Arch outside the window. The architect for the Arch was a Finn, Eiro Sarinnen. I felt a bond. The skies were unfriendly. I had flown in on a very expensive ticket. The Cardinals' permission came late, and the only last-minute flight available from SFO was first class, maximum fee. I slept through the rest of the night and woke up to TV news announcing tornado alerts for the Midwestern region. I made some decisions.

The room was secured by an NFL Properties credit card. I booked it for another day. I was Amtrak-conditioned. No way would I fly through a tornado. I ran a deal with TWA and cashed in my return flight for an open-end round-trip ticket to New York redeemable sometime. I checked the Amtrak schedule for the next available train headed somewhere interesting in a western direction. Seattle looked good. I could afford to disappear into the northwest for a week or so. Properties would want to know about the war room story, but they didn't need to know about my ticket exchange. They could wait for their report. They had before. I went back to Busch stadium.

Jim Hanifan, Larry Wilson, and George Boone took me to lunch at a redneck bar and grill, the hotel Scoville, in East St. Louis, on the other side of the river. They invited me back next year's draft (I went again in 1984 and squeezed out another story). I hung out for a day in the hotel with its view of the Arch. I signed for meals on the league's card. The NFL milks the public without shame for maximum profits. I felt no guilt pirating an expense account.

The scouting story and the war room story both were anthologized in a NFL Properties publication called *A Game of Passion.* John Wiebusch edited the anthology. The book included big name writers Andy Rooney, Don Delillo, Ray Bradbury, and Gay Talese. Some of the best known sportswriters were included: Mickey Herskowitz, Will McDonough, and Jim Murray. Also included, as coincidence would have it: John Madden with a chapter from the autobiography written with Dave Anderson.

When I sold my sabbatical tale to the Merced College Board of Trustees in the fall of 1983, I opened with a story from the road. We'd been three days cross country, Martinez to New York. We hit Manhattan on the Lakeshore Limited, #48, through Buffalo, Albany, and along the Hudson past West Point. We detrained at Grand Central Station. Madden stayed at the Parker Meridien, a 5-star on west 57th. I was up the street on 57th, on the 14th floor of Holiday Inn, a real dump.

Bouncing Outside

Trains have washrooms but no showers. Three days on a train, and all that matters is feeling clean again. I was soaking in a hot tub in my hotel room, smoking a cigar, a Palma Fina maduro. The phone rang. Madden.

He asked, "Is your hotel on fire?"

"I don't know, why?"

"I got the news on," he said. "There's a hotel fire, I think it's yours."

I said, "Hold on, let me check."

I wrapped a towel around my waist, stubbed out the maduro, and looked into the hallway. It was filled with smoke, fire hoses snaking around, fire fighters milling in pig snout gas masks, hard hats and yellow slicks. I went back to the phone.

I said, "Yeah, it's my hotel."

He said, "You want to have lunch?"

I said, "Where?"

He said, "Wolf's."

I said, "Soon as I can get out of here."

I dressed and threw everything I cared about into my briefcase and ventured into the hall. I asked a fire guy how to leave. He said, *Walk down the stairs, you should be fine.* I managed to descend the 14 floors of steps without tripping over fire hoses or expiring of smoke inhalation. I went to lunch reeking.

I found out later, the fire was started during a drug transaction on the 15th floor. Testing the goods, somebody was careless with the flame. The Holiday Inn is a fireproof hotel, meaning if no oxygen is let into a room unaffected by fire, the fire from another room cannot penetrate. Without a rush of oxygen, the fire inside a room contains itself. The drug dealers didn't know about fireproof hotels. One of them broke out a window in hopes of finding a fire escape; another opened the door. The fire shot through the open door into the hallway, and the room went up. The one who tried to escape out the window didn't find a fire escape. He jumped. He ended up dead on 57th street.

I told the Board I was an instructor of American literature. Ernest Hemingway said all American literature in some way emanates from Mark Twain and *Huckleberry Finn.* I said *Huckleberry Finn,* among other things, was a picaresque account of life on the road. I question Hemingway's assertion. Emerson predated *Huckleberry Finn.*

Emerson wasn't on a raft along the Mississippi with a Negro slave named Jim. He was riding his spirit through the flow of Transcendental thought. A hobo hits the road without an unpinning of philosophic purpose unless he is Woody Guthrie. Emerson obsessed about search for meaning. So did Mark Twain, Jack London, and Jack Kerouac.

I told the board: "As much as I could, I wanted to replicate Huckleberry Finn's life on the raft." I said in my year away I had traveled maybe 100,000 miles across America. I had been to 46 states. I missed only one of the Dakotas, Alaska, Vermont, and Maine. Traveling mostly by train, I encountered America face-to-face. I crossed the Mississippi on foot, by car, train, plane, and limousine. I said I could weigh in with new experience and new awareness that would only enrich my teaching. The more I talked, the more I sensed the Board was buying it. I more I talked, the more I realized I was buying it.

I wasn't scamming a sabbatical. I actually had hit a seam of meaning: America on the road as a spiritual search. I had just hit it from an odd angle. Maybe not odd at all, upon further reflection, just my own, which, according to Emerson, is what it is all about.

The whole spree came surging back during a long paddle through the Oakland Estuary on a cool afternoon in August when once again I was supposed to be elsewhere. The elsewhere had zero meaning. Paddling the estuary meant everything.

It brought me places that connected past and present. Emerson called it the *Oversoul*. The transcendentalists tapped the Oversoul for truth. Paddling the estuary turned on the spigot. Athletic directors' meetings in Lemoore in 104-degree heat could only clog it with dregs.

I felt vindicated.

Steve Cassady

4. Lake Tahoe: Renrob, Part I

...a noble sheet of blue water lifted 6300 feet...walled in by a rim of snow-clad mountains that towered aloft 3000 feet higher still...I thought it must surely be the fairest picture the whole world affords.
—Mark Twain on Lake Tahoe

In the summer of 1990, I spent three weeks in Italy on a coaching junket teamed with a guy named Don Rowe. Rowe looked like Alan Ladd, if Alan Ladd had big shoulders and stood 6-2 instead of 5-4. Don Rowe was 55, a SoCal juco football coach and big-league baseball gypsy. Rowe coordinated the offense for Golden West College football in Huntington Beach. During various and frequent leaves, he coached pitchers on the staffs of the Philadelphia Phillies, Milwaukee Brewers, and Kansas City Royals.

Don Rowe entered baseball backwards. He was a quarterback at Compton JC in the late 50s when he and his buddies heard about triple-A tryouts at Gilmore Field in Hollywood. Gilmore Field was the home of the Pacific Coast League Hollywood Stars.

Rowe and his buddies were sports junky rogues. They went to the tryouts hoping to steal equipment for their Sunday pickup games. Scouts in attendance were dazzled by his left arm. They signed him to a minor-league contract. Don Rowe was seduced by chump change money paid to minor-league prospects at the time, a few hundred a month. He didn't realize his signature forfeited amateur status. He was surprised to discover he was finished in college football.

Rowe was a left-handed pitcher who had cups of coffee in the big leagues. He pitched long relief for the worst team in Major League history, the 1962-63 Mets managed by Casey Stengel. He still holds a major league record for futility: longest string of innings pitched without a win, save, or loss: 54 2/3. Rowe asked to be sent to the minors in 1963. He tired of Casey Stengel's eccentric old man act. He thought triple-A life in Alabama was a better deal.

We were working through the European baseball federation teaching Italians the game of baseball. It was a scam, at least for me. The former baseball coach at Merced College, Butch Hughes, was employed as a pitching coach for the Italian national team in Parma. Six months prior, he had seen a group of Cuban coaches working with some local players. He found out the Cubans were coaching on tour. He knew the Italians were ambitious to elevate their level of play in time to compete with other European national teams for the 1992 Olympics.

Butch Hughes asked the head of Italian baseball, a pezznovanti named Aldo Notari, why Italy wasn't using American coaches. Aldo Notari said he tried; the Americans weren't interested. Butch Hughes said, *I'll get you American coaches.* Butch Hughes enlisted six including me. I had never coached baseball in my life. At the time, I was starting my third year coaching women's softball at Merced College.

Butch Hughes worked with Italian baseball on our assignments. He knew us all. He was fearful neither Don Rowe nor I could get along with anybody else, so he grouped us together. Our tour was cushy. We had more free time than work time. We spent a week in Modena in the Po Valley, a week without work in Parma, and two weeks in San Remo on the Italian Riviera. Every minute we weren't coaching, we drove the Autostrada in rented cars. The Autostrada is a race track—the only place I've ever driven where other drivers honked at me for driving too slow.

We toured Florence, Venice, Milan, and Rome. We went to topless beaches in Nice and Cannes in the south of France and gawked like dumb Americans. We drove round trip one day from Parma, Italy, across the border into Switzerland, across the Alps to Lichtenstein because we wanted more border stamps on our passports, unaware that Euros no longer stamped passports at the borders.

We ate lunch one day at an outdoor café overlooking Lake Como on the Italian-Swiss boundary. I scoped the view. It mesmerized. I took in rippling blue water with white-tipped Alps in the far horizon. I had traveled nine time zones from home in cars, trains, and planes on someone else's dime. I was sitting in an outdoor café on Swiss border. I stared across the water. I hipped to an ethnocentric flash: *Lake Como at the foot of the Alps is breathtaking, but Tahoe is better.* I grooved in the irony. I'd traveled halfway around the world to see something that comes in second to a spot four hours' drive from my house.

At 8,000 feet elevation in the Sierra Nevada Range Lake Tahoe is one of the most exhilarating pieces of scenery on earth. Lake Tahoe is also a tourist's nightmare. Lake Tahoe is ringed by picturesque two-lane roads, highways 50, 89, 267 and 28 on a circumference of 72 shoreline miles. 50, 89, and 28 and 267 are rush-hour crowded at all times they aren't snowbound. Lake Tahoe is all natural splendor and gridlock—75,000 tourists in a typical summer. I went into the crunch one summer in late July on a two-day family vacation. I towed along my CLC long boat.

As with all mountain lakes, Tahoe is buffeted by winds. As with all lakes, Nature mandates. Wind and waves come when they want. Worse: power boats rile

Bouncing Outside

proliferate wakes. Kayaking in Lake Tahoe generally involve docking fees and long waits in line. The prettiest and most protected area of Lake Tahoe is a horseshoe cove, Emerald Bay, punched through the southwest shoreline some 10,000 years ago by glacial imperative. Emerald Bay is not accessible by motor vehicle. Hikers can reach it by trekking a downhill mile from the road along the high rims above.

Hikers are not profuse. A one-mile vertical ascent separates the sheep from the goats. Limited campsites sit among the evergreens on the west side of the bay, but they sit well above the shore. Boats find can reach Emerald Bay from marinas and beaches on the other sides of the lake, but no one drives straight in. I had seen Emerald Bay overhead from Inspiration Point on highway 89. I marked it as a destination. I was angry over its inaccessibility.

I put in at Baldwin Beach two miles away and was quickly repelled by waves, wakes and winds. I took on water trying to enter the boat. I aborted immediately. I schlepped the boat back up the orange-sand beach and strapped it onto the trailer. I drove around, soliciting misinformation from locals. I stumbled onto Fallen Leaf Lake at the end of a long one-lane road the other side of highway 89 from Lake Tahoe,

Fallen Leaf Lake is three-and-a-half miles long, a mile-and-a-half wide and gorgeous. Mountain peaks rim its horizon. Evergreens rise from the shore in dense stands. The occasional deciduous alder peaks through, the only type of tree that could account for the name of the lake, unless the lake was named for reasons unrelated to leaves falling from surrounding trees. Pine needles fall at Fallen Leaf Lake. Leaves don't. I paddled all afternoon in Fallen Leaf Lake.

I broached Emerald Cove the right way at first light the next morning. Locals told me winds kick up as early as 10 am. They said the town doesn't wake up until 11. I wanted to be off the water by 10. I was waiting at the gate to Baldwin Beach when it opened at 6:30. The lake was flat and calm. I hugged the shoreline and paddled nearly two miles to the mouth of Emerald Bay and turned in. It was 50 degrees and crystal clear—sky and water. I could see the bottom of the lake through dark green water.

    Except for the dip of blades into the water, the morning was soundless. I went fast, no wind, no current, as fast as I've ever paddled. The information board on Inspiration Point says the bay is three miles long. Paddling was so smooth, it felt like one mile. Fannette Island sits on the middle of the bay, a granite formation rising to a 150-foot-high knob that sits in the middle of Emerald Bay as a bird and wildlife sanctuary. In the near horizon, a waterfall cascades down the snow-capped granite peak.

    I amended yesterday's anger. Emerald Bay needs seclusion to remain pristine. I turned wide around Fannette Island and went back up toward the lake itself. I exited Emerald Bay at a compass heading of 34 degrees North by Northwest. Straight ahead six-and-a-half miles I could make out the town of South Lake Tahoe: beaches and marinas straight ahead, the town itself to the west, the high rise casinos across the Nevada line to the east. Carving left to a compass reading of due north I could see the north shore outlined in the misty horizon 22 miles away, Carnelian Bay and Kings Beach on the California side, Incline Village across the border on the Nevada side.

    The town of Incline Village, Nevada, prompted recall. Mid-April, 1974, a property manager named Roger Tracy rented a house at 1020 Apollo Way in Incline Village 2.5 miles up highway 431—the road to Reno over Mt. Rose—to man calling himself Ed

Haycock. The house was built with redwood and set back from the road as part of a sparse neighborhood. It had a wide deck that overlooked the lake, and sat on a two-acre plot rising through the evergreens. Ed Haycock was 34 years old. He said he lived in Sparks and had a situation. He said his father and mother had just divorced after thirty-some odd years of marriage. Haycock said he wanted to make it as easy as possible for his father to get over things. He said he wanted a rental *back away from everything* where his dad could walk into the forest, *where it would be, you know, quiet for him.* The house rented for $350.

Haycock left a $100 deposit on a six-month lease. He reappeared in Tracy's office the next day with a white-haired gentleman he introduced as his father. Haycock paid four months' rent on the Apollo Drive house. Roger Tracy would have no reason to interrupt the elder Haycock's grieving seclusion until two more months' rent was due in August.

Except for the part about living in Sparks, Ed Haycock told Roger Tracy a pack of lies. Ed Haycock's real name was Curtis Ray Mickelson. He was an escaped federal fugitive. Mickelson had been incarcerated at McNeill Island in Tacoma, Washington, in 1968, a 22-year term for bank robbery. In January, 1973, he escaped on a rubber raft he had fashioned from inner tubes. Mickelson was a body-builder and very powerful. He had to be. He had fabricated a bad raft; it deflated, and he swam the half mile from McNeill Island to shore.

Sonic alarms from the island were signaling escape. Mickelson was jailhouse shrewd—he knew the sonic alarms had directional beams. He fought the instinct to run away from the noise, the direction the alarms were prodding him. He ran into the noise and came across a stray dog. He befriended the dog and walked away with a credible cover—a man and his tail-wagging dog strolling along a country path.

Mickelson disappeared, surfacing eventually in Sparks, Nevada. He lived with a Korean blackjack dealer, Kim Haydock at 2137 Rizzo Street. Kim Haydock's husband was in the Navy. Neighbors said he was rarely home. Mickelson rented the Apollo Drive place as a safe house for planning and getaway from a bank robbery he and two others would execute in Reno in September of 1974.

His accomplices were Edward Thomas Malone, 54, his so-called *father,* the white-haired guy that wanted to walk in the woods, and Floyd Clayton Forsberg, 33, a badass bank robber from Oregon. Mickelson, Malone, and Forsberg all had been incarcerated at McNeill Island. When they robbed the bank in Reno, they took out $1,000,044—at the time the largest cash bank robbery in U.S. History.

The FBI file tabbed it *Renrob*. *Renrob* ramified into subsequent crimes including jailbreak, money laundering, drug trafficking, and murder. *Renrob* crossed state lines into California, Oregon, and Washington. It mainlined into Merced and was bubbling subsurface in the mid-1970s with no one but local FBI knowing it. I was following the Oakland Raiders around America at the time. I was oblivious to *Renrob* like everyone else in Merced.

Nothing about it made the papers until the final episode, a misinformed 20-inch story plus sidebar. The kidnapping of Patty Hearst was simultaneous, the latest *Crime of the Century,* FBI file name *Hernap*. The Patty Hearst story rivaled Watergate, the energy crisis, and the fall of Saigon as 1970s impact stories. It paralleled the Merced phase of *Renrob* in eerie ways.

I came to *Renrob* in 1981. I met a retired FBI agent, now an almond farmer, named Tom Walsh through a former football coach at Merced College, Roger Imbrogno, who had coached Walsh's son, Dan. Tom Walsh wanted to reinvestigate *Renrob*. The case was all loose ends in his mind. He was retired from the FBI with little to do but harvest nuts.

I met him at a coffee shop on Main Street. He was mid-50s at the time and shopworn. Tom Walsh had silver gray hair parted on the side. His face was lined and creased, tanned like a farmer's. He laughed a little off-key at things that weren't all that funny and stayed on the laugh a little too long. His eyes were gray-green and a touch unforgiving. I snap-judged: I wouldn't want to be interrogated by Tom Walsh.

His son Dan played football that way. Dan Walsh was undersized, 5-10, 200 pounds, and purely ferocious. Playing at Hayward State, Dan Walsh once recorded 18 ½ tackles against Santa Clara playing with a sprained ankle. At Hayward State, head coach Tim Tierney brought in famous sports psychologist Tom Tutko from San Jose State to evaluate his players. Tutko reviewed his findings with Tierney. Tutko reached the Ws. He asked about Dan Walsh. He asked if Dan Walsh were the kind of guy who would fake the answers. Tierney said no, he'd answer straight. Tutko told Tierney he'd be wise to keep Dan Walsh busy. I knew: the apple didn't fall far from the tree.

Over crullers and coffee, Tom Walsh told his story. He told about the bank holdup and a subsequent jailbreak. He said the Merced phase involved known associates of Floyd Forsberg after Forsberg was apprehended for the bank robbery and had escaped from the Washoe County Jail. He said a local girl was involved. She was 20 years old at the time. Her name was Denise Catlin. She was a year older than Patty Hearst. Patty Hearst was kidnapped in February of 1974 and held underground for 591 days by an inept

Steve Cassady

band of revolutionaries led by a guy named Donald DeFreeze who called himself Cinque.

Cinque was a derelict who had been incarcerated most of his adult life. In prison, he developed a taste for convict hooch fermented in cell block toilets. Inmates make it from raisins and call it Pruno. On the outside Cinque drank plum wine from half-gallon screw-top jugs. Patty Hearst was captured by bank video camera holding an automatic weapon while her captors held up the Hibernia Bank in San Francisco for $10,600. Patty Hearst was a kidnap victim turned bank robbery defendant. Denise Catlin abetted a jailbreak by a bank robber, who, with two accomplices, robbed the first National Bank of Nevada of $1,000,044. Tom Walsh thought Denise Catlin was victim more than accomplice. He felt bad he couldn't extricate her during the Merced phase of *Renrob*.

He explained FBI protocol. He said a single agent never follows a case throughout its leads once those leads leave the office of origin. He said a case is assigned to the agent who first picks up the phone when the crime is reported. An agent named Tom Dempsey answered the phone in Reno the night of September 27, 1974. It was Dempsey's case in Reno.

The bureau assigned a lead to Tom Walsh when known associates surfaced in Merced. *Denise was in my area,* Walsh said. *We were the only ones who dealt with it from her angle.* In California, the case tripped through Merced, Santa Ana, San Diego, Santa Cruz, Willits, and Fort Bragg. In Washington, the small town of Amboy in Cowlitz County. In Oregon, Portland and ultimately, Bend. Tom Walsh said no one agent or office had total focus on the whole picture.

Tom Walsh wanted to back track the scene of the bank robbery and jailbreak, tie it to the Merced phase and the final phase, which took place in Bend, Oregon.

He wanted to fit all pieces of the puzzle into a coherent picture. His motives weren't clear. He said maybe a book. I thought as much he liked the idea of returning to harness. I liked the intrigue of it all.

I said, *let's go*.

Tom Dempsey was retired and living in Carmel. His partner in the Reno investigation, John Norris, still lived in Reno. We visited both. I contacted the court reporter on the various trials, Alan Bunnell. Bunnell charged five cents a page, and I walked away with 75 dollars' worth of trial transcripts, 1500 pages. We visited the Washoe County Jail. The spokesman at the WCJ was not forthcoming on jailbreak details. I sketched the story to a former student, Lee Turner. Lee Turner was an occasional criminal. He put me in contact with a federal fugitive named Marlon, who had spent time in the Washoe County Jail.

For the cost of McDonalds' cheeseburgers and fries at the Santa Rita off-ramp in Pleasanton, Marlon and his drug-dealing girlfriend Carolyn filled in background gaps. I obtained permission from Denise Catlin's father to impersonate him for purposes of contacting the Freedom of Information Office in Washington. The FOI was supposed to redact every name beside Denise Catlin's in the thick set of files they sent. They did a sloppy job. Other names showed through sufficient to form what amounted to a master file. Over time—with the help of documents Walsh already had—we reassembled the whole thing.

It wasn't the full book Tom Walsh had imagined. It was instead an episodic account of criminal enterprise without redemptive values—without heroes or moral. It spoke to degeneracy in America at time, the post-1960s, when American culture was spawning degenerates in abundance. It began after Mickelson broke out of McNeill Island. He surfaced in Sparks with the blackjack dealer, Kim Haydock.

Mickelson bought a 1974 Mercury Cougar in Haydock's name. He would drive her to work every day and hang around the casinos in downtown Reno. Kim banked at the First National. Mickelson went in with her one morning. He was struck by the proximity the casinos along Virginia Street, Harolds, Harrahs, The Silver Slipper. He scoped it as fat with gambling money. He cased it solid—floor plan, hours of operation, and schedules/shifts of employees.

Ed Malone, his mentor at McNeill, was paroled to Los Angeles in the spring of 1974. He joined Mickelson in Nevada, when Mickelson, using the name Ed Haycock, rented the Apollo Way house in Incline Village. Malone said it was dumb to rob a bank in the town where you live. Mickelson agreed, and they planned it anyway.

They needed another accomplice. Mickelson ran with a weight-lifters clique at McNeill. Floyd Forsberg was part of the same clique. They both had worked on the prison farm. Forsberg was a short-timer at McNeill; Mickelson had 17 more years to serve. They had hatched Mickelson's escape plan together.

Mickelson hid out with Forsberg's girlfriend, Deeta, for a few months after he broke jail. He pulled two bank jobs, one in Oregon and one in Phoenix before heading to Sparks. Forsberg was on parole by then. Mickelson and Malone met him at the Stardust in Las Vegas near the first of April and asked him if he wanted in on a bank job in Reno. He did.

The planning was meticulous, but the Apollo address was a weak link. Roger Tracy commuted from Reno over Mount Rose on highway 431. He'd drive by 1020 Apollo every so often. The last two months of rent was due; he saw neither Haycock nor his father nor any outward sign they were around. He secured the owner's permission to check. Inside, Tracy found no staple food, just lunchmeat and cheese in the refrigerator. He saw slacks and shirts hanging from the closet but no wardrobe or luggage.

Tracy noticed something furry leaning against the electric baseboard heater. It was a man's wig with a burn spot from the heater on the side. In the closet he saw a police scanner for monitoring law enforcement frequencies. On the kitchen table he found an unfolded forest service map of the Sierra wilderness. On that map were red pen marks tracing a route from 1020 Apollo to a street in the village where a murder-suicide that authorities termed *drug-related* recently had occurred.

Tracy contacted the sheriff's substation at Incline. He left them with Ed Haycock's name and the address in Sparks that Haycock had given as his own—2137 Rizzo Street. That was Sunday, August 18. On Monday the 19th, Haycock called and said his father was vacating the house and he'd turn in the keys the next day. Tracy heard nothing more for two weeks.

On August 31, a deputy sheriff phoned to ask for access to the house. The deputy said they had turned the map with the red pen marks to the DEA. The DEA in turn requested the sheriff to dust the house for fingerprints. The deputy told him the DEA had also checked the Rizzo Street address but Haycock had not turned up. The sheriff's print technician lifted only one usable print couldn't match it with a name. Later they could—Floyd Forsberg.

The First National Bank was located in the lobby and basement of a four-story high-windowed stone-gray building. When Mickelson cased the bank, he saw a stand of elevators leading to the offices in the top two floors, and, he discovered, to the basement. He took the elevator down. Right across from the elevator alcove he saw a locked glass double-door leading into the safety deposit area. In one stint in federal penitentiary, Mickelson had enrolled in a correspondence locksmith course from the Bell Saw Institute. When later he was arrested, the FBI confiscated his kit of burglar tools containing 87 instruments. Mickelson figured to break in by cutting his own key.

Malone had flown up from Los Angeles. They chose June 22—the day of the Reno Rodeo Parade. He and Ed Malone dipped into the entry alcove that separated the bank lobby from the elevators that carried passengers to upper office floors of the building itself. They punched B and rode it down. Malone stood guard by the elevator door. Michelson took his tool kit from a gym bag and went to work. Within seconds he had picked the lock, and the opened the door. He worked quickly with confident moves. He unscrewed the doorplate bolts, removed the lock, and replaced it with a dummy lock from his gym bag.

He reassembled the doorplate and shut the door. *Three to five minutes the operation took, no more,* he said. He and Malone exited the bank. They walked a few blocks west to the Fireside Motel, where they were checked in. They went into their room. Mickelson spread the tools and materials on the paisley bedspread and toiled like a watchmaker for one solid hour. The lock was old; the tumblers fell loosely into Mickelson's hand when he removed the cylinder.

Exact reassembly was impossible. Mickelson improvised. He left in two tumblers and threw away the remaining three. He took a blank, made an imprint, and cut his serrations for the two tumblers, an easier task than if all five tumblers had been in place. He replaced the cylinder, tightened down the spanners and inserted his new key. The lock clicked open. He repacked his bag, and retraced the route to the bank, into the entry, down the elevator to the basement. Ed Malone stood guard. Curtis Mickelson removed the dummy lock and reinstalled the original.

Their entrance accounted for, they planned for the escape. Mickelson rented a garage unit in a mini-maxi storage complex in Reno. He rented it under the name of Ray Chase. Mickelson called it an *all-the-way-through* unit—it would fit two cars and had rollup doors padlocked on either end. They would use the garage first for storage—stashing clothes and guns—later for cars they would steal. Mickelson had master keys for Dodge vehicles. He had done this before--his MO revealed the preference for Dodge vans—and it would help the feds to nab him.

He and Malone went van hunting in California on August 16, Friday. Malone, then back in Southern California, flew to San Francisco. Mickelson drove the 1974 Mercury Cougar registered to Haydock to San Francisco. He was meeting his girlfriend—not Kim—Marilyn Burgess, and her young daughter Tracy. Marilyn and Tracy were flying down from Washington. They all would drive the 90 miles to Sacramento. Mickelson and Malone conferred on robbery plans that night. The next morning, Saturday, August 17, Mickelson dropped Malone at the Greyhound depot so Malone could take the bus back to San Francisco for his return flight to Long Beach.

Mickelson, Marilyn and Tracy toured Sutter's Fort—the museum commemorating the discovery of Gold in California. At noon, they met Floyd and Deeta Schulze Forsberg, who had been married the day before in Oregon. They spent the day as tourists. That night, Mickelson drove Marilyn and Tracy to the airport for a flight to Reno. Floyd left Deeta at their motel. Mickelson and Floyd trolled for a Dodge van.

Steve Cassady

They targeted dealership lots but spotted the right model Dodge in the parking lot of the California State Department of Motor Vehicles. Mickelson found the master key for the van and turned over the ignition of the second one he tried. They returned to the motel in the DMV van and the Cougar. They checked out and headed east. Forsberg drove the van. Mickelson and Deeta followed in the Cougar. They hit Reno about three a.m. They stashed the van in Sparks, in the Nugget Hotel parking lot. They did not want to enter the storage garage in a stolen car. Mickelson dropped Floyd and Deeta at a downtown hotel. He returned to Rizzo Street in the Cougar.

At dawn they reconnoitered—picking up the van and driving it to the Telegraph Street garage, where it stayed behind padlocked doors until the day in September they would need it for the Reno bank robbery. That was Sunday, August 17, the day Roger Tracy invaded the house on Apollo Way looking for Ed Haycock or his father. They left for Incline unaware it was no longer a haven.

The plan was to rob the bank in the Dodge van, switch to a four-wheel drive vehicle that Forsberg was supposed to steal in Oregon. They would drive it to Hunter Lake Road, over Mount Rose on 431 35 miles to Incline, to Apollo Way, where they would have stored their other vehicles. Mickelson's scanner was fixed with crystals for the Sparks and Reno police and forest service frequencies.

When a call went over the Reno-Sparks frequencies, the Sparks frequencies would get it, Mickelson explained. *On a scanner, if it's moving you miss calls. The way I had it rigged, I had a chance to get it on three frequencies.*

They abandoned the escape to Incline that same Sunday, when they noticed that Roger Tracy had entered the Apollo Street address. Mickelson cancelled the lease the next day and returned the keys—two weeks before the DEA would seek a connection between the map with red marks found at Apollo Way and the *drug-related* murder-suicide they already were investigating. None of the *Renrob* bandits was connected to the Incline investigation.

It was pure coincidence, but it prompted a DEA investigation of the Rizzo Street residence. Kim said detectives were around asking for an Ed Haycock. Mickelson had no idea why *detectives* were so close. But by then, he wasn't especially worried. No one could tie him to a robbery yet to happen. He was guilty only of being a federal fugitive.

Most of the details had been attended to already. After meetings in June and July, the bandits had acquired a shotgun, an AR-180 semi-automatic rifle, one .357 magnum, and two .38 caliber pistols. Forsberg and Malone bought a dozen sets of handcuffs. Forsberg winked at the curious clerk and said, *kinky sex.* They bought three pairs of Big Mac coveralls and three pairs of crepe-soled desert boots. They acquired rubber Halloween masks with old-woman's faces they would daub with makeup so the features appeared more normal. They stowed everything in the Telegraph Road garage. Forsberg left with Deeta. Mickelson took Marilyn Burgess and Tracy to Oregon in the Cougar. They laid low until it was time.

They reassembled in Reno on September 11, a Wednesday, and checked into the Vagabond Inn. According to plan, Forsberg would fly from Portland to Sacramento on Friday the 13th, rent a car, and drive it to Reno. Deeta would drive down and meet him there. Ed Malone had read Chamber of Commerce brochures matching potential robbery dates with diversionary events. They wanted to hit the bank early evening of the 13th, during the Reno Air Races.

On Friday, Mickelson saw an unmarked car with a buggy whip antenna in the Vagabond Inn parking lot. He called the Forsbergs at their motel and aborted plans. He, Malone, Marilyn Burgess and her daughter Tracy drove west to California before heading north to Oregon on Highway 5. The Forsbergs went the other way, driving east to Elko, then north through Idaho back to Portland in Deeta's Plymouth Valiant. Forsberg was traveling under the identity of Douglas Bentley Schulze. Douglas Bentley Schulze was cited outside Winnemucca by Nevada state patrolman James L. Bagwell for speeding in Deeta's Valiant.

They set a new date: September 27, coinciding with a Shriner's parade through downtown. Mickelson stole a gold and white Buick off a dealership lot in Beaverton, Oregon, the Tuesday before. He walked in near closing time. He found the Buick with keys in the ignition, pocketed them and left.

He drove it off the lot late that night. The car still had protective soaping on the windshield. He drove it to the Royal Inn near the Portland airport, where he met with Forsberg and Malone. They cleaned the windows in the motel parking lot and fitted the Buick with stolen Washington plates.

The three of them and Marilyn Burgess and her daughter drove to Reno. They hid the Buick in the mini-max garage on Telegraph road. Forsberg checked into the Peppertree Inn as Douglas Bentley Schulze and waited for Deeta to drive from Oregon in her Plymouth Valiant. Mickelson went to the bank to see if his homemade key still opened the basement door lock. It did. He took Malone and Marilyn and Tracy to Quincy, a hamlet in the Sierra across the California line off highway 395 where they rented a cabin in the woods. That was Wednesday, the 25th.

Two days later, Friday at 5:30 p.m. they all met in Forsberg's room at the Peppertree. They drove in two cars to the Telegraph Road garage. Forsberg and Malone slipped on their coveralls and desert boots. They put on gray baseball caps and added sunglasses. Mickelson, still in Levis and a purple shirt, backed the Buick out of the garage. Forsberg and Malone followed in the van. Forsberg drove. He was jumpy. He scraped the side wall of the garage on the way out.

They drove downtown along Glendale. They turned at Sierra, then again at Court. Forsberg parked the van on Court, a half-block from where Mickelson drove the Buick into the second-story garage of the Sierra Inn. Mickelson parked the Buick. In the shadows of the garage he put on his coveralls.

He attached his police scanner to the pocket of a hunting vest he wore underneath. He strung the cord under the shoulder of the coveralls to his right ear. He walked to the van, took the wheel from Forsberg, and they drove away. From Court, they went across South Virginia to Center, and up Center. Mickelson turned left on Second and drove by the alley in which they would park the van. At Virginia he turned right. He passed crowded downtown foot traffic, casino pedestrians strolling under the neon arch blinking out *The Biggest Little City in the World.*

Mickelson was a little whacked, subject to fits. Mickelson couldn't find an empty parking spot in the alley. He flamed out. He slammed his hands on the wheel and cursed. Forsberg crawled between the front seats. He blasted out aggressive moods of his own. Malone calmed them down. *We got time,* he said to Forsberg. To Mickelson: *Do it again.*

They circuited four times until a Chevy van pulled out from a spot. Mickelson slipped the DMV van into the vacant slot. They piled out wearing coveralls, caps, and sunglasses. Mickelson carried two large green duffle bags. Forsberg carried a blue duffle containing handcuffs and leather thongs. They had side arms wedged inside pants belts under their coveralls. It was 6:10 p.m. The bank closed to normal business at 5:30 p.m. The bandits took the alcove lobby elevator to the second-floor lobby. On the way up, they noted most of the employees were still in the bank.

Forsberg and Malone stayed out of sight on the second floor. They stayed in the shadows. They were wary of easy ID's. Forsberg was noticeably tall. Mickelson was a fugitive. They sent the Malone back down the elevator. They watched the employees. The employees were bent over book work in the shadow of an open vault. They looked up to watch the Shriner's parade outside. The bandits feared parade watchers coming within view of the robbery inside.

Malone came back and said, *Now!* They rode the elevator to the basement. They scanned the glass door: no one in the safety deposit area. They donned their old-woman Halloween masks daubed with makeup. Mickelson slid his homemade key into the lock, twisted, and heard the tumblers click.

He opened the door with gloved hands, and the three of them slipped through. They gave themselves code names: Mickelson, *General;* Forsberg, *Captain*; and Malone, *Tiny.* The others stayed below. Mickelson went up the stairs to check the bank lobby. Everything normal. The bank manager, Herb Brown, sat at his desk talking on the phone. Mickelson perked the scanner. No indication Brown was talking to the police. Mickelson went down and signaled. It was just past 6:25. They drew their weapons. Operations officer

Bouncing Outside

Robert Franz and his assistant, Mari Kay Bennett strolled past the bookkeeping area, past the teller cages, through the main lobby, into the foyer, and toward the stairs to the basement. They descended the stairs. They were checking the safety deposit vault before setting the time lock—their last duty of the day.

At the bottom of the staircase, Curtis Mickelson wearing blue coveralls, desert boots and Halloween mask, bolted from behind a partition and stuck his gun in Mari Kay Bennett's ribs. She screamed. He said, *Scream again, and I'll kill you.* She gurgled consent and stared incredulous. The man holding her at gunpoint was slightly taller than her five-eight, and his eyes were blue. He wore a plastic earpiece with a wire running inside his coveralls. She thought it was a hearing aid. Five feet behind stood two other bandits, also wearing coveralls and masks.

Frantz thought it was the Reno police staging a test. Reno PD announced two weeks earlier they were changing holdup procedures. They talked about trial runs. Frantz thought it was a trial run until he saw *the inside of their guns. It looked like three cannons. I looked into the cylinders of the pistols. I could see live bullets.* The three made Bennett and Franz lie face down on the marble floor. The blue-eyed man was called *General* by the others. *General* told Mari Kay Bennett: *You know the man on the phone upstairs—Go tell him what's happening, that you're being robbed. I'm listening to a police scanner. You set off an alarm I'll know it, and I'll kill you.*

With *General* trailing her Mari Kay Bennett rose. She walked jelly-kneed up the staircase, across the lobby over to the officer's platform, through the swinging gate. Herb Brown was still on the phone. *What is it?* he asked. His eyes rose. He saw *General* slipping in behind Mari Kay Bennett, holding her at gunpoint. He saw *Captain* behind Robert Franz. *Captain* was jamming Robert Franz' right arm into a chicken wing behind his shoulder blade. *Captain* had a big-bore revolver pushed against Robert Franz' head. General hissed, *Get off the fucking phone, or we'll blow her head off.* Herb Brown cradled the phone.

The bandits gun-pointed the other three employees into the vault. They ordered the employees by gesture to lie face down on the floor, their hands behind their backs. O*kay,* General yelled, W*ho has the keys to the money drawers?* Robert Frantz said, *We don't have the keys to get in there.* The one called *Captain* whipped around to Frantz. *We're not here to fuck around,* he said, *Now, open this vault or we'll kill you.* Mari Kay Bennett volunteered knowledge: two sets of keys required—one in the supervisor's desk.

Robert Frantz admitted he had the other. *General* ordered Bennett and Frantz to rise. *Captain* and *Tiny* worked handcuffed the others. They lashed their ankles with rawhide thongs. *General* escorted Bennett and Frantz to the supervisor's desk. He brought them back to the cabinet type locker inside the vault where the reserve cash was kept. Frantz opened the cabinet. *General* handed him a blue duffle bag. He told Frantz to hold the bag and motioned Mari Kay Bennett to fill it with money: *Everything five's and up.*

A buzzer rang when the bag was half-full. *Who's that,* General asked. *Probably Gail, my friend, a teller,* said Mari Kay Bennett. *She said she was coming back by. General* said, nodding at Robert Frantz: *Captain, take him and see. Captain* and Frantz returned with a frightened teller, Gail Anderson, and another employee, Walter Wilk, a janitor who had been in back. By then Mari Kay Bennett had cleaned out the reserve vault, filling one duffle and half of another.

Bouncing Outside

Captain wanted to break into the cabinets. Mari Kay Bennett told staccato lies. She told them she didn't have the keys. She said that something was in the cabinet that wasn't. She told them they already had over two million dollars. *Captain* said, *Goddammit, don't give me any shit! What's in there? General* broke in and overruled: *Let's go—we've been here long enough.* They made Bennett and Frantz lie face down with the others. They cuffed and bound them. *General* laid empty money sacks under Mari Kay Bennett's head as a pillow. They left.

Mari Kay Bennett said she heard them leave through the back door. She heard one of them ask, *Who the hell are you?* She assumed they'd run across armored car driver Gary Cessna. They returned with Cessna, made him lie down with the others while they cuffed and bound him. They left for good a little less than a half-hour after they had entered.

The bandits struggled to carry bulging duffle bags out the door to their stolen DMV van. The bank employees, all nine of them, were face down on the marble floor inside the vault. Mari Kay Bennett found her handcuffs loose. She worked her wrists free, untied the thongs around her ankles and scampered up to push the silent alarm. She walked to the nearest phone and dialed the Reno police. Because bank robbery is a federal crime, Reno PD immediately called in the FBI. Tom Dempsey was a 20-year bureau veteran, took the call. *Renrob* became Dempsey's case. He dialed SRA (senior resident agent) John Norris at home.

The Reno robbery was big. Three unidentified bandits had escaped into the night with $1,000,044 of federally insured money. At the time it was the largest cash bank holdup in U.S. history. Awaiting Dempsey and Norris at Second and Virginia Streets were loose strings of leads that would take them nowhere but 48 hours of pointless legwork.

They learned from witnesses, two hunters named Dwight Reeve and George Moritz, that the three robbers had fled in a green Dodge van. Reeve and Moritz had been strolling south on Virginia Street and peered inside the bank through the high rectangular window closest to the corner of 2nd Street. They saw men in coveralls wearing strange masks walking into the vault. *They're either doing some weird exterminating,* one of them said, *or the place is being robbed.* Reeve and Moritz turned the corner and hustled up 2nd to the alley.

They saw the van and noted it had frosted windows. They saw the three men in coveralls. One had black hair combed back along his head--his facial features somewhat flat. They noticed nothing distinctive about the second man. The third *appeared to have either white or graying and thinning hair that was combed back.* They said all three were Caucasian.

The information sent sheriff's patrols combing the back streets of town. They found the van at eight o'clock p.m. wiped clean and abandoned in the parking garage of the Sierra Inn near the Washoe County Jail. It bore hot Nevada plates. It had been stolen from a DMV lot in Sacramento. *Son-of-a-bitches stole it from Ronald Reagan,* said one of the deputies.

In June of 1974, a month after six of their comrades had been incinerated in a shootout with the FBI and LAPD swat teams, the three surviving members of the Symbionese Liberation Army fled from Berkeley California to the east coast. The three survivors were Bill and Emily Harris, aka *Teko* and *Yolanda,* and Patricia Campbell Hearst, aka *Tania.* They hid that summer in a secluded farmhouse near

Bouncing Outside

Scranton, Pennsylvania, rented for them by movement radical and sports activist, Jack Scott.

By September of 1974, they were restless from inaction. They wanted to renew the cause of violent overthrow in the San Francisco Bay Area. They were completely full of shit and dangerous because of it. Bill and Emily Harris posed as the establishment couple they really were and traveled west by Amtrak. Patty Hearst rode out in the back of a U-Haul van driven by Jack Scott. Scott chauffeured her to Las Vegas, Nevada. Jack Scott kept her one nervous night in his parents' Vegas apartment.

The next morning, he paid two days rent for a small motel room off the strip and sneaked her in. The most famous fugitive in America waited behind drawn curtains for SLA sympathizer Jim Kilgore. Jack Scott had been told Kilgore would escort Patty Hearst, aka *Tania*, to San Francisco via Greyhound bus. The evening of the second day, Jack Scott returned to his parents' apartment to unwind.

He slouched on a couch in front of the TV. On a local channel, he watched the movie *Bonnie and Clyde*. The local channel broke in with a news flash. Jack Scott cinched. Jack Scott fully expected the screen to fill with Tania's face. He anticipated an announcement that Patty Hearst had been captured or killed. He ebbed when he saw the dateline Reno and heard the bulletin: the First National Bank of Reno had been robbed by three unidentified perpetrators.

In the stolen Dodge van, Curtis Mickelson saw the two hunters taking down their license number, but he didn't speed away or panic at all. He crossed 2nd, moving slow, driving through the alley behind the Cal-Neva lodge. He picked up the police calls on his scanner. He figured at least three cars were responding. He was certain it would be five minutes at least before they could reach the scene and assimilate enough information to put out a call on the green Dodge van. Enough time. At the garage behind the Sierra Inn, they moved quickly.

Malone and Forsberg changed from their coveralls and shoveled the duffle bags into the trunk of the gold and white Buick. Mickelson had shed his robber suit and was in the driver's seat of the Buick. Forsberg left the garage on foot. He headed downtown to the Peppertree Inn, where he was registered with Deeta under an assumed name. Malone slammed down the trunk and jumped in the Buick.

Their plan was simple. They eluded a dragnet by driving roundabout to Sparks before one could be formed. They avoided it later by not leaving town that night. Once inside the mini-max garage on Telegraph Road, they opened the duffle bags. They dumped the money on the floor and divided it into imprecise piles. They stuffed the piles into one large duffle bag for them and a smaller one for Forsberg. They didn't bother to count. *We figured we were awfully well off, that's all,* Michelson said later.

They went back to Howard Johnson's in Sparks. They called Forsberg and told him his share was waiting in the garage. The next day Mickelson and Malone drove to the mountains on the Mt. Rose highway near Galena Creek. They didn't use the Buick. They had obtained a blue Chevrolet through one of Malone's friends from Los Angeles, a fellow named Gus Hernandez. Gus Hernandez had driven the Chevrolet from Southern California, left it at Howard Johnson's, and flown home.

The bank money was in plastic bags under the back seat of the blue Chevy. They previously had dug a hole on a slope above the creek and buried some truck tire inner tubes. They exhumed the tubes. They cut incisions and transferred some of the money from the plastic bags into the inner tubes. They sprinkled in baking soda to absorb moisture. They glued the incisions. Mickelson reinterred the tubes. Malone shoveled on loose dirt and patted it down with the back of the spade. They had planned to bury more in another remote spot near Galena Creek, but they saw a couple backpackers on the access road. They took no chances. They drove back to Howard Johnson's and checked out. They left the same afternoon for Las Vegas.

At the FBI office downtown, Dempsey and Norris spun wheels. They were feeling pressure. Washington pressured Las Vegas. Las Vegas sent in the bank squad and pressured for fast results. The bank squad pressured Dempsey and Norris. They speculated inside job: the bandits had come in through a locked door to the safety deposit vault; they had been given the keys to the cash drawers. They put all nine employees on the black box and all of them passed. They dismissed inside job. The bank squad called in more help. 20 agents were working on leads. *With all that Brass, our biggest job was trying not to look stupid,* said Tom Dempsey. Dempsey and Norris sent out teletypes on every aspect of the MO—coveralls, Halloween masks, green Dodge van.

They checked the owner of the stolen Nevada plates. They checked with the DMV in California. They tore off teletype messages from other agencies listing possible suspects. They answered phones. They checked possible suspects against known whereabouts and cross-referred them to local KAs. They built stacks of names: *50, 100, 150, I was losing track,* said Dempsey. *We had possibles, we had theories, we had agents calling every five minutes suggesting perps they thought* could *have done it. .*

Steve Cassady

On Monday night, September 29, Norris answered the phone. It was an agent assigned to the Portland, Oregon, Division, Regis Boyles. Regis Boyles was vacationing in Cleveland when he heard about *Renrob*. Norris knew Boyles and didn't like him.

He thought Boyles was calling to gloat. Boyles said, *Tell me about the holdup, I think I know who pulled it.* Norris recited MO litany: time of day, method of entry, handcuffing and binding of employees with thongs, stashing them in the vault, the desert boots and Dodge Van. Boyles said: *Yeah, that's him. Curtis Ray Mickelson. He broke out of McNeil 18 months ago—he was doing 22 years.*

We're looking for him for two vault jobs I know goddam well he pulled. There's someone else you need to look up: Floyd Clayton Forsberg. He was in the farm with Mickelson at McNeill. He's on parole. We think he helped Mickelson escape. We think his girlfriend, Deeta Schulze, harbored him.

Norris called Portland. Portland read the file and confirmed Regis Boyles' opinion. They added information on Deeta Schulze Forsberg. Deeta was 54 years old, 20 years older than Floyd. Floyd had been dating her daughter when she fell for him, abandoning a straight life with her alcoholic husband.

Portland said the Forsbergs were unusually close. Portland said they suspected Deeta of harboring Mickelson in Oregon for three or four months after Mickelson's escape. *They said that's when he pulled those vault jobs Boyles was talking about,* said Norris. *One in Portland with a guy named John Eldon Burkhart and one in Phoenix they think with Deeta. They made Mickelson for those jobs, and they've been looking for him as an escaped federal prisoner. They said find Deeta, and Floyd will be in the next room.*

Bouncing Outside

Tom Dempsey broke in. *He's here. He's been spotted. We got a note on that guy, the one Boyles is talking about, Mickelson.* Dempsey dug into a stack of file folders. He fished out a slip and read it aloud. *Curtis Ray Mickelson, alias Curt Mickelson, Curtis Ray Nickerson, Butch Mickelson, Mike Mickelson. 35 years old. Blonde/Green. 5-11/ 150. Arrests for bank robbery, burglary and auto theft dating back to 1954, when he was 15.*

Dempsey read the whole file. Several months earlier, an informant had stopped at a red light in Carson City. He recognized the driver of a Mercury Cougar in the next lane, a Korean *entertainer* named Kim. The informant knew her from the casinos and clubs around Reno and Sparks. He locked in on her passenger. He recognized him: *Butch Mickelson, a reputed bank robber.* Mickelson's M.O fit the Reno bank job. Agents ran Kim's Cougar registration for Rizzo Street Address. They canvassed Rizzo Street. Neighbors ID'd mugs of Mickelson. They knew him as Michael Ronnigen. The feds rented a nearby apartment. They watched 2137 Rizzo through a high-powered telescope but came up empty.

Through Mickelson's file, they came up with name of Ed Malone. Malone was 54 years old and wore glasses. He looked like Dennis the Menace's next-door neighbor, old man Wilson. As a young man, he trained for the seminary. He was bounced for homosexual proclivities and turned to a long career in bank robbery. In 1968 he was sentenced to McNeill for holding up a savings and loan in Southern California.

At McNeill he met Mickelson, and the two bonded. Prison officials didn't think Mickelson was a fruit. They read it as father-son surrogacy. Malone had been paroled in the spring of 1974. By summer, his parole officer could not locate him. Operating assumption:

Malone was white-haired *Tiny*. He had violated parole to reunite with his protégée and rob the Reno bank. Mickelson, Malone, and Forsberg went to the top of Dempsey's and Norris's list: they knew who they were. They had to find them and prove it.

They had robbed the bank on September 27. Their identities were broadcast on September 29. On September 30, a Monday, federal agents spotted Floyd Forsberg in Portland. They were in no hurry to pull him in. They wanted to establish guilt. They wanted to lurk in his shadows, tail him close, mark whereabouts, monitor his mail and spending habits, interview his associates. Forsberg was shrewd. He made the surveillance early and turned hostile. He took pictures of agents tailing him and the cars they drove. He jumped from the curb onto the hood of one agent's car and yelled in front of witnesses the agent was trying to run him down. *I wish we would have,* the Portland SAC, John O'Rourke told John Norris, *We may have missed our best shot at him.*

The feds pressed on. Sometimes, agents are subtle and employ advanced technology and technique. Sometimes they aren't. Sometimes, they brace known associates and relatives, threaten them with accessory arrest and turn them with bribes. They found Forsberg had retained a Portland lawyer named Terence McCauley two days after the holdup.

They found out because McCauley tipped them. McCauley thought Forsberg was a killer and wanted no part of him. Forsberg had retained McCauley with a $5,000 cash payment in five dollar bills. They found that Forsberg had opened bank accounts with cash deposits under assumed names, $500 here, $750 there, $1,250 elsewhere. On October 24, they called Terence McCauley and set up a meeting with Forsberg that day in McCauley's office.

Forsberg claimed an alibi. He said on Thursday the 26th, he and Deeta drove her Plymouth Valiant from Portland to an area near Seaside, Oregon. He said they camped in the Seaside area that night. He couldn't recall specifically where. He said the following day, Friday the 27th, they drove from the Seaside area south on Highway 101 to Lincoln City, where they ate dinner in a main street café. That night, he said, they drove north 50 miles to Netarts and camped.

He said on Saturday the 28th, they drove south from Netarts and developed car trouble, something with the electrical system. They headed inland to Eugene and returned to Portland direct via Interstate 5. He said they tried visiting Deeta's daughter, Mary Schulze, in Eugene. He said Mary wasn't home but they talked to her landlord. He said he tried the car again, and it seemed to run fine, so they drove back north, along coastal Highway 101.

They drove to the point where 101 intersected the Sunset Highway. He said the electrical problem recurred, and the car broke down. From the Sunset Highway, he said he hitchhiked back to Portland, rented a car from Avis and returned to where the Valiant was parked. He said they got it running again and drove two cars back to Portland. He said he brought the Valiant in for repairs on Monday, September 30. September 30 was the day after Forsberg retained Terence McCauley with a cash payment of $5,000 in five-dollar bills.

The agents listened patiently, two of them. They both thought they were hearing a line of crap. One of the agents, Stan Renning, said: *We don't believe you, Floyd. We think you were in Reno on September 27, robbing the First National Bank. We think you did it with Curtis Mickelson and Edward Malone. We think when we check your bullshit story, we can prove it. We can put you away for 25 years for this job, federal time. You won't like that, Floyd.*

Forsberg said nothing. Renning went on: *Floyd, the bank has put up a reward of $50,000 for information leading to arrest and capture. You roll on the other two, Mickelson and Malone, and the government is prepared to grant you immunity from prosecution and make you eligible for that $50,000 reward.* Renning paused for a weighty interval. *What do you say?* Forsberg told Renning to shove the deal up his ass. Renning said, *That's all for now, Floyd. We'll see you again.*

The agents took days to deconstruct Forsberg's story. They found from Deeta's employment records she hadn't worked from September 26 to September 30. They found from car rental receipt that Floyd had rented an Avis car on September 28, Saturday night, and kept it for one day and 16 hours. They found he had taken the Valiant in for repairs on Monday, September 30. They marked the repair story.

The service manager at Roy Burnett Motors said they took in the car on September 30 but the party was unable to wait. The party took the car and left. The service manager voided the ticket. The story started to smell. The landlord in Eugene confirmed Floyd and Deeta had shown on September 28, looking for Deeta's daughter, Mary.

The agents gripped that Floyd and Deeta could account precisely for the time between Saturday the 28th and Monday the 30th, but the period between Thursday the 26th and Saturday the 28th[th] was vague. *Camping on the coast* couldn't be proved unless a restaurant or gas station customer remembered them. Floyd was spieling lies: he and Deeta actually took the trip to the coast, but a week previous.

Bouncing Outside

They took it paying cash, no incriminating receipts. Forsberg was dealing: it if came to agents checking, maybe the waitresses and attendants would remember them and *think* it was a week later. Forsberg's alibi wouldn't crack unless he was made in Reno for that same time, and the feds in Nevada couldn't place him at or near the scene. Forsberg's alibi held; agents couldn't arrest him without more. The day after the interview in lawyer McCauley's office, he and Deeta ducked from view. No one—trailing agents, Floyd's parole officer, his sister, Deeta's daughters and son-in-law, her employers—could say where.

Agents stayed busy. They watched Forsberg's lawyer and Deeta's relatives. They saw no signs themselves, but they worked relatives and associates. Finally, around Christmas, they high-lowed Deeta's son-in-law, Bob Youngs. They threatened to arrest him for harboring; they offered him $2,500 to roll.

Youngs took the money. He said Floyd and Deeta had been in New York for five weeks. They had returned briefly then gone to Southern California to launder some money through a *guy in Orange County Floyd knew about, Hooper or Hopper, his name is.*

He said he heard they were back now, under cover somewhere in Washington State. He said they were moving around, laying money on Deeta's relatives to hide them. He said they had given him a large sum of money to put down on a remote piece of property near Amboy, Washington, in Cowlitz County near the Oregon border in the wilderness area between Columbia River and Mount St. Helens.

He said that Deeta bought a Ford Bronco in the name of Janet Craig. He said she had a post office box under that name in Amboy. John Norris in the meantime had placed Forsberg near the scene. He cross-checked his stacks of files and found the DEA report on the Apollo Way address from late August. He matched the fingerprint found on the toaster with his suspect. It matched Forsberg. He interviewed Roger Tracy. Roger Tracy IDed Mickelson as the man who called himself Ed Haycock and rented the unit for his *father.* He IDed Ed Malone as the father. He flashed Forsberg's mug. *Recognize him? Sure do,* said Roger Tracy. *That's the man who stayed in the place.*

You're certain.

I'll never forget that face. We had some complaints about him. He was a fitness nut—he jogged around the property all the time. But that wasn't the bad part. Some of the neighbors—we got good tenants around here, quiet, you know—complained 'cause this guy was having parties at night, making a lot of noise.

I went to see him, to be nice, you understand. I told him we got some older folks who like to turn in early, who appreciate peace and quiet. He practically slammed the door in my face. He cussed at me and told me not to bother him. He glared at me. You know, he has black eyes that go right through you. I don't mind telling you, I left the place scared.

Incline was proximate to Reno. Mickelson rented 1020 Apollo, and Forsberg stayed there prior to the robbery. It was thin circumstance, but combined with the small- bills cash Forsberg had been laying all over Oregon, it was enough to secure a warrant. On January 3, 1975, under a hard rain at five p.m. Floyd and Deeta Forsberg rolled up in a Ford Bronco to the post office in Amboy. Surveilling FBI agent Thomas Manning watched them leave with a handful of envelopes. He tailed them loose to two-lane road 503. He watched them head west while he radioed the Cowlitz County Sheriff's office in Kelso. The call was patched to patrolling sheriff's deputies, who fell in behind the

Bronco just east of Woodland. Forsberg saw his rearview mirror fill with flashing red and blue lights.

Agents interrogated Forsberg in the Cowlitz County jail. They had established suspicious spending patterns. They had worked it out with his parole officer, David Looney. Looney casually asked about whereabouts and income fed to him by FBI agents. In custody, they went through the whole routine—his five-week disappearance, how he could afford a new house. Forsberg trotted out a version.

The feds showed him a counter version transcript of his conversations with Looney. *The son-of-a-bitch was lying,* Stan Renning told Tom Walsh, *because he said one thing to his parole officer and another to us. We should have had him in a pickle. But I'll tell you what, we didn't get a virgin when we got Floyd.*

We couldn't break him. We asked him about the last week in September, and he gave that bullshit story about camping on the coast. We asked him about being in Lake Tahoe, and he denied it. We told him we had a positive ID. We'd catch him in lie after lie, but when we'd face him with it, he'd just dummy up and smirk. We couldn't get any kind of confession, but finally the U.S. Attorney said charge him anyway. We shipped him to Nevada on circumstantial evidence for the bank job, and for generally being such an asshole.

Mickelson and Malone meanwhile were in custody in Southern California. They had left Sparks the night of Saturday, September 28. They drove south to Las Vegas in the blue Chevrolet supplied by Malone's friend from Los Angeles, Gus Hernandez. In Las Vegas, they separated: Malone flew back to LA: Mickelson stayed in Vegas.

After a week in Vegas and a few days in Phoenix, Mickelson screwed up big—he dropped into Southern California, where the feds were bracing his KAs. He drove the blue Chevy across the desert and abandoned it in a parking lot at LAX. He contacted a friend and paid the friend $30,000 for two 1975 Chevrolet Monte Carlos registered to the alias of Michael Ray Kelly.

Under the same name he rented an apartment in Newport Beach, 4819 Bruce Crescent. He sent for Marilyn Burgess and Tracy. They lived quietly as the Kellys for a month-and-a-half. The feds turned a female informant in November. The informant said Mickelson and Malone were in Newport Beach. She said they had '75 Monte Carlos purchased from a Newport Beach dealer named Bill Rennick. The information checked. Bill Rennick was a Mickelson KA, though not a criminal.

Agents surveilled Rennick's house—1807 Irvine. On November 22, local police on patrol spotted a '75 Monte Carlo in front and called it in. From Long Beach, two federal agents rolled on a stakeout and were told to keep things loose until SAC from Los Angeles could arrive with a SWAT unit. The agents saw the front door open on their third pass. They saw a man stroll out and wave to a man who remained on the porch.

Mickelson, said the agent driving, *the other guy must be Rennick.* A car was parked at the curb. The curb had been empty their last pass. *The car…Malone…with a woman and a kid.*

The agents breached their instructions. The driver screeched the car sideways within inches of Malone's Monte Carlo. The agents bailed out fast. Mickelson saw them, and adrenalin hit. He tensed with his weight on the balls of his feet. His hands drooped to belt level. The agents drew down on him, yelling out *FBI* and telling him to throw up his hands. The car dealer had stepped down from the porch and was scudding left across the lawn toward a hedge separating his house from the one next door.

One agent moved toward the driver's side of the Chevy. He hammered back his .38. He held it tight in both hands and pointed it at Ed Malone's left temple. The other agent rushed Mickelson, watching the car dealer in his periphery. Mickelson's hand snaked toward his right hip. The agent swarmed him. The car dealer turned pale and fell to his knees. Ed Malone sat in the driver's seat of the Monte Carlo, both hands on the steering wheel, eyes straight ahead. Tracy looked big-eyed. Marilyn Burgess let out jerky, wet screams.

Mickelson went limp. He submitted when the agent jumped him. The agent frisked and cuffed him. At the click of the cuffs, Mickelson threw a fit, flailing his legs and shoulders, bleating gibberish. More agents had arrived. They shoved Mickelson into the back seat of one of the unmarked bureau cars. Two of the incoming agents left with Mickelson for the Orange County Jail in Santa Ana. Mickelson's fit abated ten minutes into the ride. An agent named Sidney Pruitt read him his rights. *I know my rights as well as you do,* Mickelson said. *I'm calm now. I'm ready to talk.* He said, *You got me. You want the bread now, don't you?*

You talking about the First National Bank in Reno? Pruitt asked.

You know that's my job, Michelson replied. He went on to list his terms. He said the money was buried in three separate locations. He said no one could find it without him. He said in return for cooperation he wanted assurance that Marilyn Burgess would not be charged with any federal violations.

You know we can't deal, Pruitt said, *But we'll tell the U.S. Attorney what you want...Floyd Forsberg the third man on the job?*

Forsberg and I don't get along at all. His part in this was strictly business.

Do you know where Forsberg is?

No.

At the booking, Mickelson beckoned Pruitt and his partner to his cell. He refined his offer. He marked off the terms on his fingers. *Tell the U.S. Attorney I can return $800,000 if (1) if Ed Malone and I serve our sentences together, and (2) if Marilyn doesn't get charged with no federal crimes.*

Forsberg would do the same when he was caught 45 days later in Woodland, Washington. Forsberg would tell agent Thomas Manning he received about a quarter of the bank proceeds. He offered to testify against the others and return all but the 100 thousand he had spent up to that point. Manning read it as bullshit, a con offering information to test the case against him, spilling information that couldn't be used in court.

After a night in jail, Mickelson amended. Pruitt interviewed him again. Mickelson said he would tell the feds where $500,000 in bank loot was hidden. He said an additional $250,000 to $300,000 was buried in a location in the hills near Reno.

He said he would ante up the buried money only if he himself were not buried at sentencing. He said he was convinced no physical evidence existed to place him or Ed Malone inside the Reno bank. Any case would rely on testimony by perpetrators rolling on each other or confessing. He conceded that bank money would constitute evidence against him. He said he should be permitted to plead guilty under Federal Rule 20 to a charge of receiving stolen property, because that is all that said evidence would prove.

Mickelson told them of the apartment on Bruce Crescent in Newport Beach. He said he lived there with Marilyn Burgess and Tracy as Michael Ray Kelly. He signed a consent-to-search form. He said the agents would find the money hidden in three spots. He said $120,000 was stuck in an A/C vent in the hallway;

$40,000 was buried beneath the cable television box outside the garage door; and the remainder was stashed behind the refrigerator.

He said his .45 automatic was hidden behind the bedroom dresser. They terminated the interview with Pruitt asking how large a share Forsberg had received. *He got what he earned,* Michelson said. *I planned that thing so careful...so no one would get hurt. Some things happened in the bank I'm not proud of, screw ups. Those were Forsberg's.* He said Forsberg *screwed up* several times. He restated that Forsberg's role was *strictly business.* He said he trusted Forsberg but didn't like him. He iterated: the feds could never place Ed Malone or Frosty Forsberg in the Reno Robbery and said again he should be allowed to plead guilty to a charge of receiving stolen property.

The agents committed to nothing. They held the high cards. The biggest bank job in U.S. history was solved with routine and relentless detection. Significant money would be returned. The bandits were behind bars. The feds didn't have to deal. Evidence couldn't place the bandits inside the Reno bank. A case would depend on one or more of them rolling on the others, but they had months to work that angle.

I paddled north for a mile or two then angled back southwest to the orange sands of Baldwin Beach. It was not yet ten in the morning. Power boats were taking to the water. The waves were beginning to chop. Time to leave. I formed a new plan for the day. I would stash the boat trailer and hit the road before South Tahoe comes alive at 11. I recently had a factory rebuilt V-8 dropped into my 35th anniversary black Mustang ragtop. I had them install Flow Master exhausts. The car sounded good. It roared with authentic leonine Ford V-8 sound, like my father's 1949, 1954, and 1957 Ford V-8s.

Steve Cassady

I was jazzed to unleash all 280 horses top down on uncongested mountain roads. I wanted to backtrack the Reno phase of *Renrob*. I gunned through the gears on South Lake Tahoe Boulevard and crossed the state line into Nevada and followed highway 50 above Lake Tahoe until the junction with highway 28. I cut down 28 into Incline Village and turned right at the junction with 431. Two-and-a-half miles up 431, I found 1020 Apollo. I loitered a bit.

431 is the highest year-round passage through the Sierra—it peaks at 8,900 feet. At the summit, Reno is visible in the hazy brown horizon. Without traffic the trip takes 30 minutes. 431 descended down the dry side of the Sierra through the Galena Forest where upscale residential construction intrudes on the high desert landscape. 431 cuts into 395 toward downtown Reno.

I followed an intuition at the I-80 junction of 395 and turned east toward Sparks. I exited at the last Sparks off-ramp and cut over to what looked like a main surface road toward downtown Reno—Greg Street. I found what I was looking for within two miles, Telegraph Road, with a storage garage complex at the intersection of Greg.

It's been refurbished and franchised, something called Public Storage, with a high-rise sign in contemporary purple and orange colors advertising an 800 number and storage units with catchy orange roll-up doors. The modern overlay didn't cover the fact that it was the *all-the-way-through* unit that Curtis Mickelson rented to stash the stolen cars and disguises used in the *Renrob* holdup.

I hit downtown Reno along Mill and parked in the second floor what used to be the Sierra Inn parking garage where the robbers stashed the stolen DMV van. The whole thing is a parking structure now. I walked over to Virginia Street. The First National Bank isn't gray any more, it is sand-colored, the same as an expanded Harrahs to which it connects on all sides and is now a Japanese steak house and Sushi bar.

The high rectangle windows that the hunters George Moritz and Dwight Reeve looked through to see *Renrob* in progress in 1974 have been reformed smaller. I turned the corner up 2nd Street to the alley where *General, Captain, and Tiny* dragged out duffle bags filled with bank swag. Harrah's expansion overtook the alley as well. I bagged a cheap meal across the street at Cal-Neva discounted to attract gamblers. I hung around Reno most of the day reviving the feel of a bank robbery in progress.

I like Reno better than Tahoe or Vegas. It is grittier, more authentic, a better place to hang. Virginia Street has turned seedy in the last 30 years, but it's still Virginia Street in the heart of downtown Reno. Tahoe and Vegas are like degenerate gambling theme parks. Reno is like degenerate real.

In the early 1970s I worked my way through graduate school parking cars in San Francisco at the 840 Sutter Garage. My boss was Larry White. Larry White was from Reno. He always worked parking lots—always as a boss. In Reno, he handled collections from the ticket machines. One day he collected $20,000 and succumbed to the casinos.

Larry White had a bit of drinking problem. He pissed away the whole $20,000 playing black jack and throwing down shots of Johnny Walker Red. He made no excuses; he told it straight up to his bosses. They considered him otherwise a model employee. They let him work it off until the 20k was repaid.

Larry White moved from gambling temptation to San Francisco, working for the same company. Larry White's is a Reno story, not a Tahoe or Vegas story. I stayed in downtown Reno all day. I went back over the

Steve Cassady

hill to Tahoe at sundown knowing I'd tied up recall of the Reno phase of *Renrob*. I would be home in two days. I was energized. I wanted to paddle local waters and put the rest of it back together.

    The Merced phase awaited an alpha state revisit.

Bouncing Outside

5. Lake McSwain—Renrob, part II

> *...The enemy is anybody who's going to get you killed, no matter which side he's on.*
> --Joseph Heller,
> from *Catch-22*

The Merced River originates in Yosemite National Park at the crest of the Sierra Nevada at 11,000 feet. It roils sharply downstream through Red Bud, Bagby, and Briceburg, all the way to New Exchequer Dam at 867 feet. New Exchequer Dam, located just above Merced Falls, repels the natural flow and forms Lake McClure. Lake McClure offers manifold recreation opportunities: camping, boating, fishing. Lake McClure is spacious and wind-blown. It is hospitable to houseboats, powerboats, fishing boats, and jet skis. It is an aversive place to paddle a kayak.

Six-and-a-half miles below McClure, McSwain dam at 400 feet elevation creates a forebay for McClure in which paddling conditions improve dramatically. Lake McSwain starts as a wide mouth of a lake at the Marina and boat launch near McSwain Dam. It narrows into an actual river a few miles upstream and hits black water 45 minutes into the paddle.

The Merced River as Lake McSwain flows through protected brown hills dotted with stands of oaks and pines. Cattle graze on the hills and drink from river. Deer venture down to the water line to drink. Fish jump for insects, and the water ripples concentric. Ducks and Osprey land on the water and skitter on the surface. Lake McSwain caters to campers, day campers, and fishermen and enforces a 10 mph no-wake zone. Most anglers fish off the bank near the campsites. Boats are few on weekdays, mostly trollers. Early morning and late evening on weekdays, the dam-to-dam paddle is a solitary and tranquil two-hour forty minute flatwater run.

I access McSwain via county roads in 45 minutes from my house. Lake McSwain has become my home base paddling venue. I've paddle Lake McSwain dam-to-dam on my birthdays. I paddle McSwain spur of the moment on summer evenings. I went two days after returning from Tahoe and reflected during all 10 miles the Merced phase of *Renrob*.

I wanted alpha state authenticity—a home town paddle for synthesizing a home town story. I was working through the contrast of *Renrob* and crime in Merced that made the local paper at the time. What was showing on the surface versus what was festering below. 1970s crime in Merced was small-time stuff: a set of tools stolen from the back of pickup truck; a pedestrian stabbed when the assailant was irritated the victim had no cash; a water pump, air compressor and power saw taken from a storage yard.

Aberrations were cartoon material. A man named Victor Burnham was convicted and sentenced for spousal rape. Victor Burnham broke new ground as a spousal rapist. He did his wife against her will by proxy. He brought in friends and acquaintances and held her at gunpoint while they did her. He had his German Shepherd do her. At trial, Victor never disputed the charges. His attorney could formulate no defense beyond the feeble—his client's constitutional rights to unusual connubial expression.

The jury wasn't moved. Victor Burnham was sentenced to 13 years. We had a Klansman in town in the 1970s, Larry Mettert. Mettert drove a dirty white van without windows hiring out for odd jobs. I engaged him once to roto-till my back yard. He was a skinny white guy with vacant yellow eyes and a sunken chest. Looked like he was fighting off malaria. Larry worked like a coolie. He had a woman with him who stifled in the van with the window cracked open while he worked—his wife, daughter, and girl-friend, captive—it wasn't clear. He tilled himself into a flowing sweat. He ate dust and broke up hard pan one sweltering afternoon. He denied himself even a single break for water. He charged 25 bucks.

Larry's work ethic trumped his politics. One day he brandished a shotgun at an integrated school bus. He yelled epithets. He railed crude racial slurs. Larry Mettert couldn't fathom his own irony. He was arrested—he hadn't mapped out much of a disguise or getaway. In court, the judge sentenced Larry to 180 days in the country farm, sentence suspended upon the condition he surrender his weapons.

Larry Mettert feared the state would confiscate his arsenal in violation of a citizen's second amendment right to keep and bear arms. He sputtered illiterate protest until the judge slapped him with contempt. The judge said he could make him serve time. Larry rejoined: *Those animals in Applegate Park zoo—not a one is safe if I go to jail, and my dogs don't get took care of.* The judge considered Larry's point. He said with a pound of the gavel: *You, sir, are a mean and vicious man. 180 days, probation disallowed.*

I had my own Klan exposure. The *Sun-Star* reported an upcoming Klan rally. I never hassle over wardrobe. Standard then was drawstring pants, running shoes, aloha shirt, dark glasses with oversized rims. My second vehicle at the time was a Kawasaki 400. My hair fell below my ears. I wrapped a white bandanna around my head, and rode downtown for ham and eggs at the Dutch Tavern and a look at the Klan gathering. The rally was seriously uneventful.

Dour pedestrians, single or in groups of three to six, loitered around 18th street between M and N. Some were carrying five-packs of sodas: a six pack with one can missing, so the owner could use the plastic loop as a holder. Nothing was happening. A guy sidled up and said, *I know who you are.* I seized the moment: *If you know who I am,* I replied, *you know why I can't say anything.* He nodded. He said, *I know you're undercover.* I nodded. *What's going on here?*

He pointed out that a San Jose Klan chapter was checking the Merced group for possible affiliation. He pointed out his guys, a dozen of them, driving six to a car making passes around a two or three block circuit. They drove gray big-boat GM sedans, Oldsmobiles I think, with buggy-whip antennas.

The pedestrian Klansman pointed out the opposition, the Hispanic and black groups with the five-packs of soda. He said the soda was frozen. If a riot ignited, they'd use the plastic loops as handles and swing the frozen five-packs as a weapons. The guy gave me a card with a 408-phone number and two-color red and black text in a Third Reich font.

It said: *You Are Being Recruited by the Ku Klux Klan.* I thanked him and vowed to change whatever made him believe I was a potential recruit. He faded into the crowd. Minutes later, I ran into a *Sun-Star* reporter and relayed all the information the Klansman told me. She asked how I knew. I said, *I'm a trained observer.* I don't know what a trained observer is—I heard James Garner use the tag in a *Rockford Files* episode. The next day the *Sun-Star* ran the Klan rally story under the reporter's byline. She attributed facts to *Steve Cassady, a trained observer.*

Even the FBI in Merced had clown-show components. Merced in the 21st century with a population of 80,000 and growing has no FBI field office. In 1975, with a soporific census of 26,000, its residency staffed with five agents and a stenographer. Tom Walsh explained why.

When he first was assigned to Merced in the early 1960s, the bureau had divided the state of California into San Francisco and Los Angeles. Merced was the northern-most outpost of the LA Division. Tom Walsh ran a then two-man office. Modesto reported to the San Francisco Division. Modesto, because of gerrymandered division boundaries, had jurisdiction over Yosemite Park and Mariposa.

In 1966 or 1967, Washington made a new field division in Sacramento and changed the boundary lines all around. Yosemite was accessible an hour-and-a-half up highway 140. Merced became part of the Sacramento Division and was assigned Yosemite Park. Yosemite Park is a federal reservation. The FBI can assimilate any crime on a federal reservation and make it a federal case. Tom Walsh said: *Every crime in the park was a federal crime, and they had their own magistrate. Every arrest, no matter how it was adjudicated meant for statistics for us.* Statistics were high-yield ore for G-men in the 60s.

In Washington in the 60s, J. Edgar Hoover strained to defend his anachronistic fiefdom. The FBI went hard on communists but the fear of domestic communism, never much of a threat, had crapped out after McCarthy. They went sneaky after civil rights and got caught wire-tapping The Black Panthers and Martin Luther King Jr. The FBI denied the existence of organized crime when it was obvious after the Appalachin convention in 1957 that the mafia was as entrenched in the culture as US Steel.

Steve Cassady

The FBI made no inroads into civil disobedience, revolt by youth, and proliferation of narcotics. Congress, the national press, and the public were storming the castle walls. Rumors had Hoover as queer with his long-time companion, number two FBI administrator, Clyde Tolson. Rumors had the mafia holding photos of Hoover with Clyde Tolson. Rumors had Hoover hanging on because he collected damaging information on politicians up to and including presidents. Hoover was getting old and feeling big time pressure. Hoover had the political ideals of a brownshirt. Tom Walsh said: *He was accountable to the people in the White House and Congress who could pull his charter. Them he wanted to dazzle with arrest statistics. The rest, if they got too loud, he'd see they were audited for ten straight years*

Hoover rolled his shit downhill. He pressed the divisions for compelling stats. Hoover especially liked big drug arrest numbers. Tom Walsh said: It *didn't matter many cases ever were prosecuted—the arrest statistics were something he could use to show we were solving domestic problems.*

Division rolled Hoover's discontent down to the field offices. Revolt by youth and rampant drug use were high profile national worries. Tom Walsh saw the bureau redistricting as a gift. He rolled Hoover's agenda to the burnouts from the 60s that had not yet remobilized into the establishment.

They came from Haight-Ashbury, Berkeley, and Los Angeles. They squatted in the Santa Cruz Mountains, Mendocino, and the Sierra, including Yosemite Park. *We were having a hell of time justifying two men in the Merced office,* he said. *After we assumed Yosemite, I parlayed it into a five-man operation. Four were kept busy because of Yosemite*

Park. The FBI has no narcotics jurisdiction. But we did have crime on a federal reservation.

When a crime of any kind is committed on a federal reservation—and it is not covered under federal law—we could assimilate authority and make arrests. We had a gold mine. Washington wanted statistics. We gave them statistics. We pinched every hippie we could find in Yosemite carrying so much a single seed of marijuana. Yosemite was a cesspool then—hippies were scattered all over the park living out of their vans, all of them holding. We were shooting fish in a barrel.

One time, we arrested so many hippies, I needed a bus to bring them in. I rented an off-duty school bus and hired a driver. We damn near filled it up. We handcuffed the hippies to the seats and drove them to the Mariposa jail. From 1967 to 1974 and 1975 our office supplied about 25 percent of the arrest statistics for the entire Sacramento Division.

Tom Walsh supervised a stenographer and four agents: Mel Shannon, Denny Hughes, Herb Davis, and Jerry Hicks. The Merced office was inflated to scam arrest statistics with hippie sweeps of Yosemite Park. When the Reno case hit on Friday night, May 2, 1975, Tom Walsh was happy it was. Jerry Hicks had taken the call from Sacramento ASAC Walter Weiner.

Facts were sketchy, but the brief was simple: Six days earlier, *Renrob* bank suspect Floyd Clayton Forsberg escaped from the Washoe County jail with the help of a male and female accomplice. The female was thought to be Forsberg's wife, Deeta, who had jumped bond in Oregon three days earlier.

The male was thought to be an ex-con named Clark Gable Timmons from Orange County. Timmons had a KA in Santa Cruz named Larry Hart. Timmons and Hart both had a KA in Merced named Hubert *Huck* Hunwardsen. Weiner had a local phone number for

Hunwardsen. The agents were to locate Hunwardsen and brace him for any information they could secure on Floyd Clayton Forsberg, Deeta Schulze Forsberg, Clark Gable Timmons, and the man from Santa Cruz, Lawrence Field Hart.

You sure of the address? Tom Walsh asked. Technically, it was Hicks' case, but Walsh was the senior man. Walsh would lead the full-staff maneuver. Walsh was stalling. The address bothered him. Walsh was familiar with that stretch of Gerard Avenue, a two-lane county road running north-south across Merced in the outskirts from highway 99 to J-59. J-59 was the country road extension of J Street, now called Martin Luther King Jr. Boulevard. MLK fronts the Merced County fairgrounds. Gerard Avenue was rural. It featured open fields and a dotting of small truck farms and businesses run out of rusty tin buildings—pick-and-pull Rottweiler junkyards, tire warehouses, sheet metal shops. Gerard avenue was rundown but not seedy; it was semi-respectable. It didn't profile as a bandit neighborhood. Walsh was bothered.

You sure about the address, he asked again?

Hell, yes, I'm sure, said Hicks. *I checked number with the city directory. That's the place. Look for yourself. It's there in the book.*

I felt bad, Walsh would say later, *from that moment on. Not scared, exactly, but something wasn't right. If you want to know the truth, I thought we were going to get shot that night, and I never felt like that.* Walsh detained his staff trying to outwait his apprehension. He had them check weapons, map logistics, review steps. *Hunwardsen,* he blurted suddenly, *I know that guy. I used to buy eggs from him. He's a chicken farmer, an old man.*

Walsh had heard about Hunwardsen's egg business from a dairy farmer acquaintance named Larry

Bouncing Outside

Migliazzo. He dialed Migliazzo's number. Migliazzo affirmed: Hunwardsen was an honest, hard-working old man who had to scratch like hell to make a living. *But he also told me he had kids who'd been in trouble. Larry didn't know what kind, whether they'd been in the joint. He just said the parents had been 'real disappointed'.* Walsh broke the connection and swiveled toward the room. *Looks like one of the egg guy's kids is the asshole. Call the sheriff.*

Alerting the SD was standard. It provided backup. It kept patrolling deputies from wondering why men in suits were approaching a farm house with shotguns. The five agents drove in two cars toward downtown. At 16th Street they turned left and continued until 16th Street fed into SR 99. They turned right onto Gerard, crossing a bumpy railroad track, the SP line, and driving another quarter mile, slowing as they approached the intersection where Hunwardsen lived. The spring night was clear. A small one-story white house silhouetted against the black sky.

The house stood perpendicular to Gerard, both front and back yards exposed to view. The yard was unfenced and treeless. 10:30 p.m. No lights inside. The agents pulled to the shoulder. Shannon and Davis covered the rear. Hughes held ground near the radio. Walsh and Hicks approached the front door. They waited while Shannon and Davis swished through the grass to either side of the back door. A light flickered in the room facing the street. Walsh noted: *master bedroom.* Hicks clicked off the safety of his .12 gauge. Walsh felt a shiver. *Just keep behind me with that goddam thing.*

They walked silently onto the front porch. Walsh motioned for Hicks to stand to the right of the door. He rapped firmly. He heard a click. Fear said it was a shotgun pumping. Experience told him to calm down.

Steve Cassady

Who's there?
FBI, Tom Walsh.
How do I know you're FBI? The voice cracked.
Walsh thought: r*eaction normal—old people scared, waked up in the middle of their night. Farmer with shotgun, also normal.* Walsh worried about spooking him. *Call the sheriff,* he said, *Ask if there's an agent Tom Walsh, if he's investigating in your area. If you want, take down my ID number.* The old man said nothing. He cracked open the door the width of a burglar chain. A light shaft through the door brightened the porch. Walsh held his bureau ID eye level to the shaft of light. *I guess it's all right,* the voice said after a moment's hesitation. A man opened the door. He was in his 60s wearing a pajamas, robe, and slippers. His gray hair was tousled. He looked like an egg farmer rousted from bed. *What do you people want?*

Walsh stepped inside. Hicks followed, his .12 gauge cradled. Walsh spoke calmly. Hunwardsen stepped back alongside his wife. Walsh explained they were looking for a man named Hubert Hunwardsen, nickname *Huck.* Walsh scanned to the door of the front bedroom. Walsh noticed a shotgun leaning against the inside of the jam. The old man said, *We don't know any Hubert or Huck.*

Walsh said nothing. Hicks slipped into the hall and checked the two bedrooms and bathroom. Hicks returned, shrugging a signal: nothing out of line. Hicks walked toward the kitchen. Hicks stopped at the telephone table. Hicks blanched. The number below the dial was wrong. Walsh finally caught Hick's eye. Hicks shook his head. Walsh sensed what he'd seen. Walsh apologized to the Hunwardsens. He said he could see the man they were looking for didn't live there. He and Hicks retreated.

Bouncing Outside

They waved Shannon and Davis to the cars once they cleared the side of the house. Walsh was angry. His anger abated on the ride back to the office, but he was alarmed. *I never felt good about that case,* he said later. *From that night on, when we busted in on the egg farmer, I never felt good about it.*

The jailbreak had been planned for some time. In the fall of 1975, during the five weeks he and Deeta had been out of sight, Floyd Forsberg had gone to Southern California to launder some of the bank money through a hood named Frederick Hopper. Fred Hopper was once a cop, a police captain in Santa Ana. He had finished first in his class at the national academy, the FBI's law officers' training course at Quantico.

Fred Hopper had been fired for irregularities on the subject of hard narcotics. He went to law school and passed the bar. He specialized in springing scumbags on technicalities. Forsberg found Hopper through another one of the McNeil Island weight lifters, Lawrence Bernard *Giant* Graham.

Graham was versatile: a dope-dealer, assailant, suspected hit man. Graham had been paroled from McNeill in March, 1975. He returned to Southern California to work strong-arm for Fred Hopper, sidelighting as a mule running drugs and laundering money. Hopper knew Forsberg had been captured. Hopper had ideas about the rest of the bank money. He had uses for Forsberg on the outside. Hopper had Forsberg retain him as a lawyer. He assigned Giant Graham to find an accomplice to spring Forsberg. Giant Graham brought in a SoCal thug with whom he had been dealing drugs, a man named Clark Timmons.

Timmons, aka Dennis Crowly, aka Dennis Clark, was 31 years old. He baptized into crime as a teenager when he was arrested for violation of the Dyer Act—driving a stolen car across state lines. He graduated to

Steve Cassady

narcotics violations, assault with a deadly weapon, public nuisance, plus one count of second-degree murder on which he skated. Timmons had thrown a security guard off a second story motel balcony in a dispute during a party and killed him.

In prison, Timmons was a bodybuilder like Mickelson and Forsberg. He was nicknamed *Animal*. Timmons moved around. He gave his parole officer the address of an apartment in El Cajon. He rented a house in Escondido where he lived with a girlfriend, Bobette Lane. Timmons bought powder and pills from sources in Mexico and dealt them in a triangle between his home area and markets in Santa Cruz and Merced. He knew Forsberg from a stay at McNeill Island. He wasn't surprised to hear Forsberg's name come up at a meeting in Santa Ana in March of 1975.

The meeting was held at 312 Garnsey Street, the home of his buddy recently paroled from McNeill Island, Lawrence Graham. Also present was Fred Hopper. Fred Hopper set a two-item agenda. Timmons termed it *discussing some things pertaining to helping Mr. Forsberg* and working a scheme for laundering money Hopper said *came from a bank job in Reno*. Hopper offered preposterous escape alternatives in meetings held over a period of two weeks.

Plan 1: Hopper said he could get Timmons into Washoe County Jail with bogus credentials as an attorney. Hopper said attorneys are not subject to search. He said that Curtis Mickelson and Ed Malone were the only witnesses that could possibly place Floyd Forsberg in Reno the night of September 27 or who could put him inside the bank.

Hopper said he had already smuggled LSD to Hopper in Washoe County Jail. He said they could lace some LSD with poison and smuggle it to Forsberg. Forsberg could feed toxic acid to Mickelson and

Malone. With them dead, the case against him would disappear. Plan 2: Hopper would supply the firepower and pay Timmons $50,000 to snipe Mickelson and Malone as they were escorted from the Washoe County jail to the courthouse across the street.

Plan 3: Hopper would supply firepower for Timmons, who would sit on a Reno rooftop and shoot the marshals ferrying Forsberg from the jail to the courthouse. Plan 4: with bogus credentials identifying him as an attorney, Timmons would carry weapons supplied by Hopper in his briefcase and enter WCJ with Giant Graham on a Sunday night. Graham would kick the control at the bottom of the jail, while Timmons would hold the upstairs deputies at gunpoint until they released Forsberg. Timmons dismissed the first plan as flaky, the other three as too risky.

They moved to other business. Hopper had money to launder. Timmons said he could buy drugs in Mexico. He could deal them in Orange County, Santa Cruz, and Merced for clean money at a profit. Hopper handed over $10,000 in hundred-dollar bills, all in sequential serial numbers. Timmons returned in less than a week. He said he added cash to the pot and purchased 400,000 Benzedrine tabs *from some guys named Richie and Henry. I call them at an upholstery shop in Tijuana. They send over runners to get the money and deliver the stuff.* Hopper gave Timmons another 10k and said he'd hand him a batch at a time until all the money was clean.

Timmons reported to Graham's house for another load of wash on April 23, 1975. Timmons arrived with a young blonde girl. He introduced her as *Denise, from Merced.* Hopper showed up a few hours later. Timmons introduced Denise. Hopper didn't smile. Hopper wasn't receptive to the presence of Timmons' new girlfriend. He told her to wait upstairs. When she was out of sight, he took a letter from his briefcase. It was addressed to Graham, two pages long, written in Forsberg's hand on canary legal pad paper. It outlined another escape plan, this one promising. Hopper and Timmons alternated reading. They cross-checked the details and talked them through. They liked what they read. Hopper approved. Timmons read the risks as minimal. They green-lighted the plan. They set the breakout from WCJ for three days later.

Denise's last name was Catlin. She was 20 years old. Denise Catlin was as naïve as the hippies at Altamont. She couldn't register the monster was upon her. She had no instinct to discern his perfidious core. Timmons went by the name of Dennis Crowley. He carried a drivers' license and social security card in that name. A drug dealer in Escondido named *Baba* told him federal officers had approached him asking for information on someone named *Dennis*.

He figured the Dennis Crowley ID was blown. He was technically a fugitive. He had called his parole officer. The PO told him the Feds had issued warrants for parole violation and narcotics trafficking. He couldn't afford to be stopped. He explained it to Hopper. He said he had co-opted Denise to drive. Hopper seized it. Hopper suggested Denise as the wheel for the Reno jailbreak.

They called her downstairs and asked. They told her it would involve criminal activity. This was the 1970s. Denise Catlin stepped across a line she didn't know existed. She couldn't see through to the evil core. She agreed to drive on the jailbreak.

Timmons and Catlin left Santa Ana on April 24. They had packed Timmons' Mercedes with supplies purchased that morning—backpacks, ropes and knives, sleeping bags, heavy jackets, cold-weather socks, waffle-soled climbing boots, tennis shoes, backpacking cookware, freeze-dried food.

They spent the night in Merced with Timmons' friend, Hubert *Huck* Hunwardsen, an ex-con who ran a body-and-fender shop on the Yosemite Highway and who lived nearby. Denise was friends with Hunwardsen's wife, Pokey. Denise had met Timmons when Huck Hunwardsen had introduced her to Timmons at a party in Merced.

They were in Reno the next night, the 25th, a Friday. They checked into the Riverside Hotel, pre-planned choice. The Riverside Hotel stands six feet from the building next door—the Washoe County Jail. Timmons registered as Leroy Gaines. Leroy Gaines was a biker that had burned Timmons in a drug deal the previous January. Timmons had lost all trace of Gaines. Timmons figured any investigation would involve hotel cards. He figured an investigation might flush him from hiding. Timmons asked for room 633 and found it was available. The plan went into motion at midnight, Saturday, April 26th, after the graveyard shift change at WCJ.

Timmons rose from bed at 11:45. He and Denise had been watching John Wayne in *The Green Berets* on television. Timmons dressed in black pants, a thick black sweater and a black watch cap. He wore laced up black high-top tennis shoes. He slipped black socks over each of his tennis shoes. He wriggled his fingers into a dark pair of handball gloves.

Room 633 was on the southeast corner of the hotel on the side closest to the jail. Room 633 had a window view that spanned the jail's rooftop and street entrance below. Timmons looked out. He saw uniformed personnel entering and leaving—the graveyard shift change. He told Denise to grab the camera, a Kodak Instamatic 60 with an electronic flash and use it as a signal flare. *You see anybody coming,* he told Denise, *Flash that camera through the window.*

Earlier in the day, Timmons had purchased an aluminum extension ladder from a Sears and Roebuck at a shopping mall in Sparks. He had taken it up through the back stairs to the roof. It was there now, along with two pairs of coveralls, some rope, a stuff sack containing a 9 mm Browning automatic and extra ammunition, and a sack of tools. Timmons led Denise into the hallway, through the fire escape door, into the stairwell, through the door to the roof.

He opened the door into a blast from a 35 mile-per-hour wind. Timmons picked up the ladder and laid it flat across the gap between the hotel and the jail . Denise held it firm. She weighed maybe 105 pounds. She shivered in the cold. Timmons crabbed across on his hands and knees. The tool sack slung around this neck clanged on the ladder rungs.

Forsberg figured to make his break at 10 a.m. Saturday morning, two hours before the lunchtime head count. Forsberg was in *Max* housing, the segregation unit on the top floor of the jail, *very hard to get out of,* said Marlon, the federal fugitive I had interviewed at McDonalds in Pleasanton.

Marlon was in WCJ for grand larceny the same time as Forsberg, Mickelson, and Malone. *In Max housing, you're subjected to a strip search, so you can't get no tools in, 'less you balloon them up your ass. You can't cut the bars; you're on the top tier. There's no exercise yard—for exercise they let you walk up and down the tier, one at a time. Then again, sitting there 24 fucking hours a day with nothing else to think about...every now and then somebody'll pump up his nuts and make a break.*

Forsberg's plan included a trusty named Spider. Spider was a short-timer riding out his last few months.

Spider wouldn't break out—he was intelligence. Spider had trusty access to system blueprints, to construction and repair schedules. He knew the air conditioning system was being reworked. Spider told Floyd the system would be shut down on Saturday the 26th.

He knew the system included no baffles in the ductworks. Without hot or cold air rushing through, the system was, in effect, a tunnel. Forsberg was planning his break with a 21-year-old inmate name Daniel Rezin. Marlon said Rezin was probably Forsberg's bitch. Rezin was another trusty. During Forsberg's exercise period on the 26th, Rezin would open a doorway in the hallway leading to the shower room. The two of them could crawl into the ductworks through a ceiling vent that Rezin had detached from the inside. They would move on hands and knees through the ducts to the rooftop cooling unit. Timmons on the rooftop would unbolt the unit and lift it free.

Timmons took four-and-a-half hours to handle his end. Wind chill dropped the temperature to 17 degrees. Timmons worked excruciatingly slow. His fingertips went numb. He plied the bolts with liquid wrench, all of them, unsure of the connectors. He took each one a turn at a time, so as not to make noise or set off an alarm. When all the bolts were removed, he tested his work. He wedged his nearly frozen fingertips underneath the metal flashing on the perimeter of the unit and heaved. It creaked a little, but he pulled it cleanly from its gaskets.

By 4:30 a.m., he was in the shower in room 633. Denise hadn't had to flash the Instamatic. At eight a.m. Timmons was downstairs in the garage, packing the Mercedes. Denise was behind the wheel. He told her to drive across from the jail, park the car with the engine running, and *watch. When you see people come off the roof, pull up to the Island Street entrance.* He returned to the room. He went back to the roof to wait for a breakout that came off exactly as Floyd Forsberg had written on the pages of his legal pad.

Neither Forsberg nor Rezin was reported as missing until the noontime check. John Norris took the call. He bolted to the scene swearing. He backtracked the jailbreak: air vent to the roof of the Washoe County Jail. Roof of the jail to the roof of the Riverside Hotel. Roof to a room on the sixth floor rented to a man and woman, the man registered as Leroy Gaines.

Forsberg had disappeared without a trace, but witnesses made Daniel Rezin leaving the hotel dressed in coveralls and a leather jacket. Rezin caught a cab in front of the hotel. The cab company pinned the fare and destination: across the state line to Truckee 50 miles west. A bus station agent in Truckee ID'd Rezin's photo as man that bought a ticket to Sacramento. Sacramento agents combed the area near the bus depot. Forsberg had used Rezin as chum. FBI agents took him without difficulty in a hotel a block from the depot 12 hours after he escaped.

The name Leroy Gaines dead-ended. But a parking stub from the garage yielded the license number of the people staying in room 633. Norris teletyped it through. The name came clacking back: Clark Gable Timmons—a dumb-ass who took his own car on a jailbreak—currently residing in El Cajon, California. That squared with the description Daniel Rezin had given of Forsberg's accomplice: *a big guy named Clark he also called 'Animal'*.

Norris went to work on the Timmons ID. He noted that Timmons had done time at McNeill with Forsberg and Mickelson. He ran down his list of KAs and settled on one: Lawrence Field Hart, nicknamed *Tangle-Eye*. Hart was currently on parole and a member of the Gypsy Jokers motorcycle gang, a bad-ass group known for dealing hard drugs. Hart fronted as a B & F guy. He lived in the Santa Cruz Mountains in Boulder Creek, near where John Linley Frazier, Herbie Mullens and Edmond Kemper staged their killing sprees. Hart knew Timmons from a stay in the federal penitentiary at Lompoc. Hart had done a five-year stretch for narcotics at McNeill Island, the hive of assholes connecting the entire case. Norris talked to the FBI's Santa Ana office. They said they had a file on Hart.

Santa Ana believed he was dealing drugs with Timmons. They said the two were suspects in a stolen car and/or drug operation running between southern California and Santa Cruz. They said Hart was a Gypsy Joker. They also suggested two other names that might fit: Lawrence *Giant* Graham, whom they said was a mule for the other one, a former police captain from Santa Ana, now an attorney named Frederick Hopper.

They said Hopper was dirty. They thought he specialized in criminal facilitation. Norris hung up and reviewed his notes. He looked at jail records. He perked at the visitor's log. He saw Fred Hopper registered as Floyd Forsberg's attorney. He saw that Fred Hopper had visiting Forsberg every day until Wednesday the 23rd.

Floyd Forsberg had been so confident in his jailbreak scheme he took time to shower off the dust from the ventilating system, shave off his beard and change into clothes Timmons had supplied. By 10:30, Forsberg and Timmons had sent Daniel Rezin on his way toward capture. They were hustling down the fire stairs, into the Riverside's casino and lobby, then out the side entrance on Island Street. Denise Catlin was parked on Island Street pointed east. They drove out of town at normal speeds, found Interstate 80, and took the off-ramp west. They were across the state line into California 20 minutes later.

Steve Cassady

They passed Truckee where Daniel Rezin had caught the bus for Sacramento. At Auburn, 75 miles southwest, they left the freeway and went south on Highway 49. Highway 49 traverses the Sierra foothills in two lanes through gold country. They had crossed through the town of Placerville when the Mercedes coughed and cut out. Timmons told Denise to slide off to the shoulder. Denise stayed behind the wheel. Floyd scampered from the back seat and hunched in the hillside underbrush. Timmons busied himself under the hood for the better part of an hour, taking apart the spark plug wires, cleaning them, checking the distributor, wiping condensation off the points, reinstalling the distributor and spark plugs. He told Denise to crank it up. She did. The Mercedes growled to life. Forsberg jumped back in.

Two hours later at Sonora, they took Highway 120 west from the foothills and descended. After 14 miles, they turned southwest on county road J-59. They reached the valley floor in Merced in less than an hour. Denise drove into town on G Street past the west side of Merced College. She crossed the tracks at 24th and drove to 17th. She turned left on 17th and drove past the intersection of 17th and Yosemite Parkway, when 17th becomes Motel Way. She stopped at the first motel on the right, the Motel Murrieta, named after early California Bandito, Joaquin Murrieta.

Timmons registered as Dennis Crowley and paid cash for adjoining rooms, numbers 50 and 51. He and Denise left Forsberg behind after settling him in. They drove to Huck's Custom Garage on the Yosemite Parkway. They drove to 23rd and G, an ARCO station with a Hertz franchise, Walsh and Ramirez.

With his Dennis Crowley ID, Timmons rented a 1975 white Mercury Monarch. Timmons drove the Mercury back to Hunwardsen's. Denise followed in the

Mercedes. They stashed the Mercedes at Hunwardsen's shop. They returned to the Murrieta. Timmons phoned Giant Graham in Santa Ana. He briefed Graham on the escape. Giant told Timmons: pick up Deeta Forsberg in Portland and reunite her with Floyd. Timmons went that afternoon, Saturday, the 27th. He left Denise to attend to Forsberg. He called Larry Hart and asked him to ride shotgun. Hart mentioned a drug dealer in Seattle. Timmons drove the white Mercury Boulder Creek. Hart brought along a hundred jars of Benzedrine. They headed north.

Deeta Forsberg had received a coded letter from her husband in February. It said he was working on some plans for escape but gave no details. She knew nothing until April 24th, when Hopper called her at home in Portland. *Plans are made,* he said, *Get out of the house by Friday. Rent a motel for three nights, Friday, Saturday, and Sunday—where no one can find you. Make sure the room has a direct dial phone.* He gave her a 702-area code number.

She recognized it as Nevada and assumed Reno. Hopper said, *Call me here 11 o'clock Friday Night.* She registered Friday evening in the Flamingo Motel on the outskirts of Portland as Mrs. Bob Greenwood. She called Hopper on Friday as directed. He told her about the escape plans. She flitted around the room on Saturday waiting word. The phone rang at noon. It was Floyd: *Stay where you are, we're sending somebody to get you.* She received two other calls at the Flamingo. The first was a female voice calling before noon on Sunday:

This is Denise, said the voice.

Who is Denise? Deeta asked sharply.

I'm Dennis' girlfriend. He's the one coming to get you. Is Dennis there yet?

No. Who is Dennis?

Steve Cassady

Dennis is the one that's coming to get you.
No, he isn't here yet.
At one p.m. the second call came. *This is Dennis,* said the other end, *We're here, down the street, at a pay phone,* he said. She told him to come to her room. Deeta scoped Timmons and Hart. She saw no tells, no reason for suspicion. They talked briefly. She said she didn't want to leave until after dark. Dennis said they'd be back right after sundown. Timmons and Hart drove into downtown Portland.

They met the man from Seattle. They exchanged the bennies for a promise of future payment. They hung around downtown. Timmons bought a leather jacket at Charley's Menswear. They dropped in on a friend of Hart's. They drove back to the Flamingo at seven p.m. They jolted when they entered the parking lot and spotted six or seven white cars with California-exempt rear plates. Timmons looked to scamper. He told Hart to jump out and check at the front desk. Everything okay. The cars belonged to California state engineers in town for a convention.

They motored all night down Interstate 5. Timmons and Hart rotated shifts at the wheel, down the straight spine of Oregon, past Eugene, Corvallis, Roseburg, Grants Pass, and Medford. They crossed the Cascades into California and drove past Redding and Red Bluff, Sacramento and Stockton. They cut over to SR 99 at Manteca and passed Modesto, Turlock, and Atwater before exiting on 140 ramp onto Motel Way in Merced. They had driven 12 hours.

Deeta kept to herself the whole trip. She was tense with anticipation, disinclined to form new friendships. They arrived mid-morning in Merced, Monday, April 28, two days after the breakout, four days before the FBI in Merced ran a bungled raid on a frightened old egg farmer and his wife. Timmons dropped Hart at

Hunwardsen's garage. He returned to the Murrieta. Deeta was anxious to see Floyd.

Timmons unlocked the door to room 50. Floyd was not alone. He was clean-shaven—she'd last seen him in a beard. His black hair had been dyed blonde. Deeta sneered at the young girl in the room. Denise Catlin was 34 years her junior. Denise Catlin was alone in a motel room paying fond attention to her husband. Timmons introduced her as *Denise*. Deeta looked as happy to meet her as Fred Hopper had been during the jailbreak planning at Giant Graham's house on Garnsey in Santa Ana. Denise Catlin was clueless to the fact she had just been tagged to die.

By Wednesday, April 30, Larry Hart's name came up as a promising KA. That day, John Norris teletyped the Special Agent in Charge (SAC) of the San Francisco Division, Charles Bates, the SAC heading the search for Patty Hearst. Bates ordered a team of agents from the Santa Cruz field office to stake out Hart's house in Boulder Creek.

The house was in the woods on Fern Avenue where Fern dead-ended in an unpaved turnout. The agents parked in the turnout and scanned the area. They defined the shapes of dwellings through the groves of tall trees. The road had no street numbers or roadside mail boxes. Hart's place was flat-top clapboard with too many cars parked off to the side and in back of the house: a white Mercury Monarch, new, a red Mercury, about 1967, a dented black VW beetle, and an old green and cream Dodge pickup. The agents sat in their car until sitting seemed pointless.

They left their car and walked up the driveway to jot down license numbers. They looked toward the house. A shirtless man in jeans and tennis shoes bolted out the back door and disappeared into the woods. The agents couldn't chase him uphill on foot. They didn't know about the house. They walked down the driveway to their car in the turnout.

They saw the White Mercury heading down the driveway. At the bottom, it pulled out onto the Macadam coming their way, turning in front of them on Fern, moving down the hill at an even pace. The agents eyeballed the driver; he didn't fit the description of Floyd Forsberg or Larry Hart. At that point, they hadn't been looped in about Clark Timmons. The white Mercury turned right on 236, heading toward town. The agents held back. The red Mercury came bouncing down the driveway. They saw the driver clearly: bearded face drooped by scars into a permanent leer. *Tangle-Eye,* Larry Hart.

Clark Timmons had been standing at the kitchen sink of Hart's cabin when he saw the agents jotting plate numbers. *Cops,* he said, *Get rid of the drugs.* Timmons was talking to Larry Hart, Hart's common-law wife, Jackie Perry, and another woman, Kelly Stokes, girlfriend of Gypsy Joker Winston McCooney, the registered owner of the red Merc.

Timmons bolted through the kitchen door, to the top of a wooded hill, where he saw two men in suits loitering in the turnout. He returned to the house. He put on a shirt and conferred with Hart. Timmons said he was going out for a newspaper—to see if the Reno jailbreak had made the news. The agents watched from their vantage point in the turnout: Timmons left in the white Merc; Hart trailed him in the red.

The agents followed Hart down the hill, right on 236, out toward Highway 9. They stayed several lengths behind on 236. Timmons, returning, spotted Hart tailed by agents. He sped back up Fern to Hart's. He warned everyone again about *cops.* He broke back for the red Mercury. He retraced his earlier route to warn Hart. Out on Highway 9, he saw Hart headed his direction. He pulled to the shoulder and jumped from the car, engine still running.

The agents had tailed Larry Hart on a circular route. They hung back, thinking he was decoying them away from the house. They wheeled around a blind curve and spotted the red Mercury stopped alongside white Mercury parked on the shoulder facing the opposite direction. They saw a big man leaning on the driver's side. They saw his head whip around and stare in their direction. The red Mercury peeled gravel from the shoulder. The big man, the driver of the white Mercury—they could see it was the shirtless man who had fled from the back door of Larry Hart's house—dashed to the woods and disappeared.

They slid broadside next to the white Mercury. The agents jumped out and looked to the forest—a dense redwood expanse at 1000 feet elevation reaching 12 miles into Santa Cruz proper. The shirtless man was out of sight. They turned to the car. They emptied the contents of the glove box. They were careful not to smear them with their own prints.

They found gasoline receipts from stations in Northern California and Oregon. They found a Hertz rental agreement from a company in Merced, Walsh and Ramirez dated April 28 and rented to *Dennis Crowley*. One of the agents picked up a Kodak Instamatic 60 and lifted out the cartridge.

The pictures were processed later. They would show the A/C unit on the rooftop of the Washoe County Jail lifting like a trap door, the dusty faces of Floyd Forsberg and Daniel Rezin emerging from the hole in the roof where the unit had been detached.

Timmons hid in the woods. He watched FBI agents rummage his rented white Merc. He watched the sheriff's van arriving to dust for prints, the tow truck arriving to impound the car. He gathered his muscular frame and jogged 11 miles through rough redwood terrain. He stopped in Felton. He was breathing hard and sweating, pumping adrenalin. In a general store on Main Street he bought a pair of tennis shoes. He laced them on in the store and threw away his $150 dress boots. He jogged easily in his new kicks. He breezed the rest of the way to Hart's body and fender shop in Felton.

Denise was there when he arrived. She updated: The feds had shown up at Hart's house about an hour before. She said they had interviewed her, Jackie Perry, and Kelley Stokes. Denise said she showed the feds her driver's license and said she was a friend of Jackie's visiting from Atwater. She said they didn't seem too interested. She said they kept asking about *Larry and Floyd and Floyd's wife.*

Hart gave Timmons money, several thousand dollars. Timmons told Denise to round up the Forsbergs and move them fast. He gave her a few hundred dollars and told to buy a junker in her own name. Timmons left on foot. Timmons ran across town to a Mercedes garage he knew. He bagged a mechanic's shirt. The shirt had an oval name tag sewn onto the pocket. He ran from the garage to the house of a friend, Ray Bubblets, where he hid for two days.

Denise Catlin moved with fugitive fear. She bought a 1965 Chevrolet Bel Air off the nearest lot. She drove it to Jaye's Timberlane Resort. She pulled the Forsbergs out so fast she didn't bother to pack her belongings or Timmons'—even to replace the cap on an open jar of mustard. She transported them to the Hitching Post motel Soquel Avenue in downtown Santa Cruz. They hid in the Hitching Post for three days. She communicated with Timmons through Larry Hart via a pay telephone on the street.

Bouncing Outside

On Saturday, May 3, Denise, and the Forsbergs drove the Chevy to a roadside rest stop on Highway 17 in the Santa Cruz Mountains. They met Timmons and Ray Bubblets who was driving a 1969 Ford camper. Bubblets had purchased the camper for $2,200. Timmons and Bubblets had stopped at Jaye's to retrieve Timmons' and Denise's luggage. They switched cars. Ray Bubblets drove the Chevy Bel-Air back to the Hitching Post. Denise gave him a letter for mailing to her parents in Atwater with instructions to retrieve the car. Denise took driver's seat of the camper. Timmons rode shotgun. The Forsbergs were stashed in the camper shell. They wound north on 17 to 101 and up the coast to Willits. They would disappear for nearly two months that the FBI couldn't account for until later—too much later to save Denise Catlin.

Forsberg's breakout had been filed as a separate case and assigned to John Norris. Investigation followed leads into California, Oregon, and Washington. Each lead in another state made it less likely either Norris or his partner, Tom Dempsey would figure in any apprehension. Dempsey, the agent who caught the *Renrob* call pressed Curtis Mickelson in jail. Dempsey read Mickelson as obsessed with escape. He engaged Mickelson in escape talk. He elicited recall of Mickelson swimming away from McNeill Island, running into the noise of the directional beams of the sirens, picking up the stray dog.

Dempsey stirred Mickelson's ego. Mickelson narrated with flair. He smiled, a grin Dempsey said *was ingratiating bordering on madness.* Dempsey knew from the files Mickelson once had fabricated a lock pick from a paper clip. He asked about it. *Damn near had the cell door open, but the hack came back too soon. I needed maybe ten more minutes.* Dempsey heard Mickelson once lodged a slender pick up his ass.

Wrapped it in wax paper. I had to be real careful with that sucker. Mickelson smiled his ingratiating smile. Mickelson reveled in his ingenuity.

Why do you think Floyd left you behind? Dempsey broke in.

Fuck you Dempsey, Michelson hissed.

I'd get him rolling on his criminal genius, Dempsey said, *He liked to talk about it. Hell, I liked hearing it. Mike was personable for a bandit, and he told good stories. But just when he started losing himself in it, I'd snap him like a wishbone. It never failed to piss him off.* Dempsey thought Mickelson came close to dumping on Forsberg. *I could see he hated that no-good son-of-a-bitch, Forsberg. Made no secret about that. Said he was mean and vile. I thought I could work that. I always asked him how a class crook like him could tie up with a degenerate like Forsberg. This is one time he looked like he wanted to answer. But he just wouldn't take the step.*

John Norris remanded leads. Portland was looking for Deeta. Oregon agents worked KAs and relatives and came up empty. Santa Ana worked on Fred Hopper and Giant Graham. San Diego worked on Clark Timmons. Agents interviewed his wife, Rebecca. She said they weren't divorced, but she hadn't seen him in three or four years. They found Bobette Lane and Bobette's sister Robin in El Cajon.

They pushed at Timmons' border narcotics contacts. They got nowhere. San Francisco worked Larry Hart through the Santa Cruz field office. When agents flushed Clark Timmons into the woods and found escape evidence in the white Mercury rented in Merced, Sacramento was called in. The KA files of both Timmons and Hart yielded Hubert *Huck* Hunwardsen in Merced.

Hunwardsen was 33 years old. His arrest record dated back 15 years, mostly small-time stuff. It swung from teen-age burglary to possession of narcotics to failure to pay child support, to possession of a deadly weapon. His most serious conviction: bringing dangerous drugs into a jail. In 1971, he was being processed at the county farm on Belcher Road for possession of marijuana. Deputies found his shoe heels were hollowed out and filled with reds. Hunwardsen graduated from county to state. He was sentenced to Vacaville for six months to five years. Walt Weiner had run Hunwardsen's name through the system.

He relayed that Hunwardsen was on parole and running a body-and-fender shop on the outskirts of Merced. This was May 2, 1975, six days after the escape. Weiner called the Merced resident agency and told Jerry Hicks to round up Tom Walsh and hit Hunwardsen's house that night—looking for any information on the whereabouts of Hart, Forsberg, Deeta Forsberg, or Timmons.

At his office the night May 2, after his staff had bungled the raid on wrong Hunwardsen, Tom Walsh dialed Walt Weiner. Walsh reported reluctantly. He recited the sequence straight, without excuse. Walsh was conditioned to volunteer bad news early and fast—*that way it blows over fast.*

Goddamnit Tom, Weiner railed, *"You're the senior man. You should know better. I'm making this case your personal responsibility, and you better hope to hell it's not too late. Find the right goddam Hunwardsen, and find him tonight.* Weiner cooled some after his outburst. Walsh told him they had already rechecked the phone number. The number had been correct; the address had not.

The number actually matched a place out on Highway 140, the road to Yosemite, belonging to

Hunwardsen. The second raid took place at one a.m., Saturday May 3. Hubert Hunwardsen lived at the corner of Moomjean and 140. Tom Walsh knew the area—one street three blocks long a mile or two east of town on the Yosemite Highway, a cluster of cramped shanties with Pabco roofs. The shanties needed paint. Moomjean was not annexed. It had no city services, no curbs or gutters. It had weedy front yards cluttered with scrap autos. Tom Walsh pinned it as bandit neighborhood. Hunwardsen's occupation fit. *They all come out of the joint as B and F men.*

    Walsh didn't mind the late hour. Late night raids were unofficial bureau protocol. Late nights caught suspects off-guard. Both federal cars formed a vee on Hunwardsen's overgrown yard. They followed the same routine as before. Shannon and Davis in back. Hughes near the radio at one car. Walsh and Hicks to the front door. Lights blazed inside. Hunwardsen answered the door and grunted.

    Hubert Hunwardsen? Huck? We're FBI, said Walsh holding up his open leather badge folder and entering the house, Hicks and his .12-gauge trailing.

    He's tough, Walsh thought while looking him over. Hunwardsen stood 5-10, weighed 180. He had a black beard and greasy black hair. He wore no shirt. He registered ex-con menace. He had cellblock tattoos. He ventured no surprise at being rousted. He volunteered nothing. He stared at Hicks' .12 gauge and answered in monosyllables to roundabout questions.

    He knew the drill. *If they don't pull out their handcuffs and Miranda cards, they not going to arrest. Tell them nothing.* He knew Larry Hart but hadn't seen him in a while. He'd never heard of Clark Timmons. He remembered a Dennis Crowley from around town *at parties and things.* He didn't know what Crowley did for a living. He'd heard of Floyd Forsberg but never met him. Didn't know Deeta.

Hell, no he wasn't hiding anyone. *Look around if you don't believe me.* Hunwardsen's wife—Walsh thought her name was Linda at first—sat in a chair all during the visit. She offered nothing. *Huck told you how it is,* she said. Walsh asked her name again. It was Linday. Six years later, in 1981, the same year I met Tom Walsh, The *Sun-Star* reported Linday Hunwardsen calling 911 on her husband for assaulting her with a .16-gauge shotgun. The agents gave it up for the night. They backed out to the road.

In the lead car, Walsh noticed a blue Buick occupied by two women driving past them into Hunwardsen's driveway. Walsh had not yet been briefed on Santa Cruz. He saw no good reason to detain the Buick. If he had, he would have met Jackie Perry, Kelley Stokes, and their sleeping children. He would have known they had been Hunwardsen's house guests since the bureau's visit to Fern Avenue in Boulder Creek three days earlier.

Sacramento had sent in information. The feds still had it wrong. They still believed the female accomplice to the jailbreak was Deeta Schulze Forsberg. Deeta had defaulted bond and was missing since April 23, three days before the breakout. Sacramento showed no interest in the women interviewed in Santa Cruz. Tom Walsh received Catlin's name and description along with information Sacramento had relayed from Santa Cruz. Catlin's name was noted because of Atwater's proximity to Merced.

Atwater is a small air force town six miles to the northeast, home of Castle Air Base. Tom Walsh found time to think about the name Denise Catlin, *I don't know, maybe a day or two after we hit the egg farmer then finally found the right Hunwardsen.* Timmons and

Forsberg had vanished by then. Agents in Santa Cruz surveilled Larry Hart's house and job, but he was gone. Agents in Merced spotted Hart in town. Hart became the most promising lead. Tom Walsh and his staff took turns watching the Quonset hut on 140 that housed Hunwardsen's intermittent body-and-fender business. He investigated the Hertz rental lot at the Arco station on 23rd and G. Nothing shook loose.

Walsh solicited a local character named Benny Rich. *A professional fink,* Walsh said, *but selective. He'd usually rat on guys he was in competition with. I talked to him a long time. He said he didn't know these guys and hadn't heard a thing. I didn't believe him. He knew something. The town was too small not to. Maybe the price wasn't right, though I offered a good chunk of change. Or maybe these guys were too heavy for a small-timer like him.*

Walsh drove out to Atwater. The Catlins lived in a middle-income tract near Castle AFB. Walsh found their corner house on Caliente Court. He found M/Sgt Franklin Catlin fertilizing his front lawn. Catlin was visibly concerned. Walsh IDed himself and showed his badge. Catlin seemed to know the subject was Denise. He said neither he nor his wife had seen Denise for two weeks. He said that was unusual. Denise had her own place, a duplex on west 20th in Merced.

She's a good girl, you understand, he offered. *She's never been in trouble, run away, or given us any reason to distrust her.* Denise had phoned recently, apparently from out-of-town. She wouldn't say where she was. She evaded questions. Denise's mother spoke in a British accent. She said Denise hung up abruptly before answering any real questions. She said her tone was near incoherent.

She seemed to want to tell us she loved us, not for that I don't think, but like it was important for her to know we loved her—no matter what...She said a couple time: 'I'm all right, no matter what you hear.' I was asking her what she meant—but that's when she had to hang up—practically in mid-sentence. Frank Catlin said he considered calling the police—he was terribly worried—but he thought his story would sound foolish. Frank Catlin was alarmed, but Walsh believed he was relieved to confide in somebody with authority.

She's a good girl, he repeated. *But we're worried. You know she's only been on her own a little while, a couple of months now...*

It's my fault, the mother broke in, nearly in tears. *I protected her too much.*

She's very naïve, the father continued, *I just don't know...*

Walsh asked about Denise. The Catlins offered unrelated facts. Walsh kaleidoscoped a tale. Denise had graduated from high school in Virginia in June of 1973. S/Sgt. Catlin had been transferred to Castle AFB the following September. Her parents said she had broken out crying when she found they were moving to California. They said Denise was well adjusted but had trouble making friends at first. Atwater was small-town cliquish. Denise had no college ambitions. Denise took in a stray puppy and hid him in her bedroom, afraid her parents would find him and make her give him up.

Denise accompanied her mother to Bingo night at church. Denise drove her younger brother to school. Tom Walsh winced at the account. Tom Walsh profiled Denise Catlin as a lonely teenager vulnerable to a jackal's grin. He asked about friends.

Frank Catlin said she met people through jobs. She worked at a peach cannery. She worked at an earring stand on the mall. She had a friend named *Anna*. Denise was sharing her duplex on west 20th with a girl named Sandy. He didn't know the last name of either woman. He added, *There's another girl who called when Denise was still living at home. Pokey, that's her nickname. What's her real name?*

Linda, I think, the mother answered. *No...Linday.*

Walsh didn't betray the shiver he felt. *What about boy friends?*

She was going out with a guy named David last year, David Estacio, but I think that's over now. She hasn't talked about him in months. And there's this fellow from down south, San Diego, I think. She sees him when he comes to town.

What's his name?

Dennis. Dennis Crowley.

The investigation seesawed between Hunwardsen's house, his shop, and the Catlin residence. Walsh fed the Catlin interview through the system. The feds revised their view. Denise was looking more like the accomplice. Walsh vacillated. He built scorn for Hunwardsen and Hart. He empathized with Denise.

Everyone on our side was assuming now she was some street-smart hippie who knew straight up what she was doing. They penciled her in with Forsberg, Deeta, Timmons, and Hart. I wasn't so sure. The more I talked to those poor, distraught parents, the less sure I was. Maybe it was the stray puppy. Maybe it was the father in me. I got nine kids myself. I knew what those people must be going through.

On Monday, May 12, a surveilling agent noticed a fresh car among the crates in Hunwardsen's lot, a Mercedes. He ran the plates. It was registered to Clark Gable Timmons. Hot lead: The name and number on the Reno jailbreak getaway car

Tom Walsh took it as probable cause. He obtained a warrant from the local U.S. Magistrate. In Merced, the local U.S. Magistrate was a lawyer working for the government part-time out of his office. The charge was

Escape and Rescue. Walsh rounded up his crew and every deputy the sheriff could spare. They waited until Hunwardsen and Hart both were inside the shop and swarmed. They arrested Hunwardsen and Hart and impounded the Mercedes. The charges were thin, but Walsh didn't care. Walsh wanted them in custody bartering information for freedom.

Hunwardsen refused to deal. Walsh braced his wife, Pokey. She told Walsh: *He's got me and the little boy. We're afraid of what Forsberg and them would do.* Hunwardsen was peripheral and knew it. He stonewalled the federal charge. Larry Hart was directly involved but cagey. He was sure the *Escape and Rescue* charge would bounce. He wanted freedom now plus severance as an accessory to crimes committed by Forsberg and Timmons. He offered Walsh information for release. *I got enough trouble for this already,* he said. *And I don't want no more. I didn't rob no bank and didn't break nobody out of jail. I don't need the bullshit that's coming down on this*

That was Saturday, May 12. On Monday the 14th, Walsh brought Larry Hart before the magistrate for a bail reduction which amounted to an OR release. Outside, Hart delivered his first installment. He stipulated he wouldn't testify in court—*That has to be understood.* He said Forsberg was a killer: *You can't hide from a guy like that. He'd have you wasted in jail or wait till you got out.* Walsh said nothing and let Hart go on. *You know, they're going to off that little girl, Denise Catlin.*

Walsh felt gut-kicked. *How do you know?*

Because they offered me the contract, he said. *It was that guy Hopper's order. His mule, Giant, Larry Graham, asked me if I wanted $5,000 to clip Clark's girlfriend. I told him I wouldn't. I told Clark I* *wouldn't and he's in a crack over this thing. I hated to see this happen. I liked that little girl.*

Walsh noted that Larry Hart had spoken of Denise Catlin in the past tense.

Forsberg, Timmons, Deeta and Catlin had vanished. Leads dried up. Agents worked home territories. They worked friend, relatives, and KAs. Merced showed promise because of Larry Hart. *We didn't have a hell of a lot of active investigation here,* Walsh said, *except I wanted to keep the pot stirred. I was hoping to turn the wife, Mrs. Hunwardsen, Pokey, but that went from bad to worse. She was scared to death of her husband, and he was scared to death of Forsberg.* Hunwardsen stayed in jail.

Tom Walsh re-grilled Pokey Hunwardsen. She dripped concern over Denise Catlin running with hard-core felons Forsberg and Timmons. Pokey Hunwardsen said Tom Walsh was getting her in trouble with her old man even talking the feds. Pokey said, *Larry knows where they are; he calls them all the time.* Hart was in and out of town. Walsh picked him up and interrogated him. Walsh surveilled Hart.

Hart made phone daily calls from a pay booth next to a supermarket on 140. Walsh guessed Hart was in daily contact with Forsberg. He guessed Hart knew he was being watched. *I think he was telling me in his own stupid way, 'go ahead...here's how you get them.'* Walsh implored Sacramento for permission to wiretap the pay phone on Highway 140.

Under federal law at the time, wiretapping was not illegal—but dissemination of wiretapped information was. Under state law, the wiretapping was illegal, plus setting up the wire constituted trespassing. Legal wiretaps were all judicial red tape.

Even with bureau sanction, Walsh would have had to obtain a court order under Title 3 of the Omnibus

Bouncing Outside

Crime Act. The court order involved a chain of affidavits and judicial approvals. Walsh asked often. Sacramento refused every time. *They told me to take it up with the Department of Justice.*

The timing was all wrong.

It was just after Hoover died, Walsh said, *They were so worried about image. We'd carried on illegal wiretaps for years, until the late 1960s, and everyone wanted that swept under the rug. They were worried about the disclosure of the wiretaps Henry Kissinger and Alexander Haig had authorized on government employees suspected of leaking information to the press. Watergate was still a hot topic. They were worried about everything.*

Patty Heart was kidnapped by venomous fools in February of 1974. She slipped underground. Patty Hearst was caught on camera in militant costume holding up a bank while pointing an automatic rifle. Patty Hearst was missing 591 days, and the feds came across as futile in their attempts to find her.

They feared she would turn up on her own or be caught by local cops. Her saga was front page, a daily reminder that the feds swung heavy bats, but were whiffing with every swing. They spared nothing. Bureau audio analysts thought on of the SLA ransom tapes they detected background sounds of croaking frogs. At a cost of $50,000 an hour, Washington authorized Lockheed YO-3A overflights s of the Bay Area hoping to pinpoint frog ponds that might lead them to Hearst and the SLA.

Aerial spy photography of the Viet Nam era was so refined it could snap a picture of a public park and show the headlines from a newspaper lying on the face of a sleeping wino. YO-3A cameras came up dry on Patty Hearst. Patty Hearst was the granddaughter of

William Randolph Hearst, heiress to publishing empire and a San Francisco socialite-in-waiting.

She was accused of turning violently radical. *Hernap* would go down with the Lindbergh kidnapping as a crime of the century. Patty Hearst had become a political embarrassment to the bureau. Washington sanctioned Charles Bates blanket to wiretap any telephone he thought could lead to capture. Denise Catlin was a nobody from a nothing town. Sacramento wouldn't authorize a pay phone line trap on Highway 140 even it would mean saving her life.

Walsh struck out where ever he went. He drove to Atwater. The Catlin parents knew something was wrong when Denise had called them collect from Santa Cruz early in May, two days before Walsh had visited the first time. Mrs. Catlin elaborated on Denise's call. Denise had said, '*Mom, I swear I didn't do anything wrong, but there's going to be some policemen asking questions,*' *and I didn't know....* Denise wouldn't say what it was. *It was just this strange message: 'Don't tell them anything, I can lay low for a while.' I don't think she knew about—what is that, 'statute of limitations. She was telling me, 'after a couple years, it'll be all right.*

Walsh learned nothing new from the Catlins. The case went dormant in his sphere. *The action was all away from here,* Walsh said, *I was no longer getting bureau communication.* Walsh returned to mundane duties. *A few unlawful flights, a few selective service deserters. To build up my case load, I had to go out to the air base and look into missing toolboxes.*

The Merced phase of *Renrob* ended with Tom Walsh feeling completely shackled. *I thought I could do something for her if they'd only turn me loose. I wanted to get those guys Hart and Hunwardsen. I wanted to take them somewhere and kick their asses—*

to where they'd tell me something, or I'd break their goddammed fingers.

Timmons and Denise had driven the 1969 Ford camper north from Santa Cruz to Willits on Saturday, May 3. The Forsbergs stayed stashed in back. They stayed two days in a motel in Willetts on Highway 101. They cut over to the foggy Mendocino Coast, to Fort Bragg and rented a house for one month from an absentee landlord. Forsberg and Timmons tripped into Washington to pick up $45,000 in buried bank money.

Timmons and Denise left the Forsbergs in Fort Bragg. They drove to Santa Ana and cleaned the money through Timmons' Baja-to-Southern California launderette. They changed the 1969 Ford for a 1971 Travel-All. They drove back to Fort Bragg. A few days before the rent expired on the Fort Bragg house, Fred Hopper went to Giant Graham's house at 312 Garnsey and took a call from Deeta Forsberg. Deeta said Catlin wanted to split. Timmons got on an extension.

Hopper asked him if Catlin would talk if she were arrested. Timmons said he thought she might. Hopper was the alpha wolf. The order pecked down to Giant Graham, Forsberg and Clark Timmons. Hopper said he wanted Catlin taken care of. Timmons offered to take her to Mexico. The situation hung fire. They left Fort Bragg and went back down south.

Fred Hopper stashed them in Romoland, a shanty town of 1,400 southeast of Riverside. His girlfriend Joanne Jost had purchased the house with a cash down payment of laundered Renrob swag. The fugitives holed up among Mexican migrants, camouflaged by blood orange groves and desert dust.

Forsberg grew restless. He was running out of money. He wanted to rob another bank in Oregon. He wanted Timmons and Catlin to help. Moods snarled. Timmons didn't want to rob a bank with Forsberg.

Steve Cassady

Graham told him was responsible for the Forsbergs. Graham said if he couldn't take care of the Forsberg-Catlin thing Graham would take care of him.

They stayed in Romoland two weeks. Graham came to the house one day and said the FBI was close. He said they could trace the Romoland house to Hopper and Jost. Graham told Timmons to move the Forsbergs to Oregon. Timmons said he'd take Catlin to Mexico instead. He said he didn't want to ferry the Forsbergs to Oregon. Forsberg asked him whom he liked best, Catlin or Bobette Lane. Timmons caved.

They left in the third week in June, heading north in the Travel-All. They stopped one night en route. On June 26, they checked into the Riverside Hotel in Bend, Oregon. They dug in for a week. Forsberg laid out his bank scheme. He said he would hold a bank president hostage. He figured the hostage president could access funds simultaneously from two branches of the same bank. Forsberg proposed wilderness escape, backpacking into the Pacific Crest Trail. Forsberg asked Timmons and Catlin again if they wanted to participate. They said they didn't.

The FBI *was* close by then. The feds raided the house in Romoland and turned up *Renrob* proceeds with Fred Hopper's fingerprints on it. The feds turned a female in Clark Timmons' southern California stable. She gave them the Riverside Hotel in Bend. Agents from Portland swooped down and took Forsberg, Deeta, and Timmons without incident.

Denise Catlin was nowhere to be found. The Forsbergs said she had left by bus. They couldn't explain why her belongings remained in the Forsbergs' hotel room. Their story was all lies: she was one day dead. They killed her because she was the amateur. Denise Catlin couldn't be relied upon to keep quiet like a professional criminal. Like them.

Bouncing Outside

US Marshals transported Clark Timmons from Portland to the Nevada State Penitentiary on July 19. Timmons was interrogated by John Norris and Alf Stousland off and on for two-and-a-half months. Timmons was looking at escape charges, harboring charges, weapons charges. He was looking at murder charges. He was scared shitless of Forsberg.

During his trial preparation on the escape charges, Forsberg warned him: *Just remember those people are out there.* A convict named Raymond Chunn was transferred from WJC to the Nevada State pen where Timmons was held. He was put into a cell next to Timmons. He gave Timmons a message: *Just remember to keep your mouth shut.* Timmons interpreted it as threatening him and his, specifically Bobette Lane. Timmons talked anyway.

Timmons severed himself from a murder rap. On September 29, he lumped up his Adam's Apple and sang like Pavarotti. Nearing retirement from the bureau, Tom Walsh had thought ahead. He ran the arrest records of Forsberg, Timmons, Hart, and Hunwardsen. He accessed docs from the *Renrob* file, including Clark Timmons' lengthy and detailed confession. He palmed all materials.

The confession is remarkable. Timmons filled in blanks for the missing time between the May 3 flight from Santa Cruz and the June 29 capture in Bend. Timmons elided his own complicity in anything heavier than abetting escape and harboring. Timmons rolled on Graham, Hopper, and the Forsbergs.

Timmons provided specific directions to the shallow grave in which Oregon agents uncovered the body of Denise Catlin on October 1, 1975. Timmons said Forsberg buried her in a spot Forsberg was planning to hide bank money. He said it was seven or eight miles below Bend, near the Snake River turnoff from Highway 97.

Timmons was very specific. The directions convoluted into the wilderness with landmarks such as a sawed-off tree stump and a burned-out tree felled by lightning. Timmons gave the directions to John Norris and Alf Stousland during his confession at the Nevada State Penitentiary on September 29, 1975. Norris and Stousland relayed them to Portland agents.

The Portland agents found Denise Catlin's body exactly where Timmons said they would. They uncovered Denise Catlin 13 days after federal agents arrested Patty Hearst in the Bernal Heights section of San Francisco. Denise Catlin had been shot in the back of the head with a 9 .mm pistol.

Timmons claimed he knew the location because Forsberg showed him where he was planning to bury bank money. Timmons said he was out hiking at the time. Timmons said he was surprised to find Catlin gone when he returned to the Riverside Hotel. Timmons told lies. Clark Timmons led Denise Catlin to slaughter in the Deschutes wilderness. He abetted Floyd Forsberg while Forsberg executed her. It showed in jagged red flashes between the lines of Clark Timmons' dissembling confession.

Renrob, the jailbreak, the murder of Denise Catlin all were adjudicated for expedience. Floyd Forsberg faced 37 years of federal charges for parole violation, bank robbery, and escape. He faced a state charge of murder. Deeta Schulze Forsberg was draped with charges as well: bank robbery for the job she helped Curtis Mickelson pull in Phoenix; parole violation; violations of the national firearms act, perjury, escape and rescue, accessory after the fact, receiving and concealing, unlawful fight to avoid prosecution, possession of dangerous drugs, harboring…

The feds reduced Deeta to violation of Title 18, Bond Default and put her away for five years. Clark Timmons was looking at abetting a jailbreak, harboring and murder. Fred Hopper was looking at massive conspiracy charges for instigating all the above. Ed Malone and Curtis Mickelson were facing federal bank robbery indictments.

Mickelson had been right. Ed Malone could not be placed inside the Reno bank. The US Attorney had to choose, and he selected Forsberg. He severed Renrob into thirds and tried each suspect individually. Malone wouldn't testify against Mickelson, and Mickelson wouldn't testify against Malone. Forsberg was still at large—he couldn't testify against either. Malone walked. Mickelson dealt himself a reduction plus protection by returning substantial sums of bank swag, confessing to the bank robbery, and implicating Forsberg as his accomplice.

The US attorney had Forsberg for escape. Upon recapture, Forsberg was tried and convicted, sentenced to 25 years for the bank robbery and 12 more for escape. He was transported back to Bend, to stand trial for the murder of Denise Catlin. Timmons' confession nailed him. Forsberg was a stud duck in the Oregon penal system. He was 35 years old. He thought state time in Oregon for life trumped federal custody until he was 72 years old. He pleaded guilty to murder in Oregon in June of 1976.

Giant Graham wasn't charged. Timmons rolled on Hopper too. His prints were on bank notes uncovered in Romoland sealed it. He was convicted for abetting a jailbreak and money laundering. Hopper was disbarred and served a year-and-a-half before returning to Orange County to work with a lawyer. Timmons received his immunity on the murder charge for implicating Forsberg. He was witness protected. Tom Walsh found

Steve Cassady

Timmons' new identity when he ran Timmons's rap sheet. The last six charges came in 1978 under the name Terry Clark Wilson and included: robbery, conspiracy, burglary, possession of a dangerous weapon, and five counts of ADW.

    I took out at McSwain at marina boat launch at sundown. I had paddled 10 miles and released some monster endorphins. Reflection on *Renrob* revived the visceral reasons why Tom Walsh never felt good about the case. They mixed with the endorphins.

    Renrob went wide and revealed intriguing insight into criminal enterprise, but it ended all wrong. The system meted out penalties, but justice wasn't served. Denise Catlin died before she lived. Fred Hopper ordered the hit and skated. Larry Hart and Hubert Hunwardsen could have prevented the murder. They were never charged. Deeta Forsberg influenced the hit and was put away for bond default. Clark Timmons participated in the murder but was witness-protected and served short time for something else. The story ended crappy, without redemption.

    I hitched up and drove west. The setting sun presaged the rising sun of new day. Ernest Hemingway said that. It was in the title of his best novel, *The Sun Also Rises*. Hemingway lifted it from the book of Ecclesiastes. He said it to reassure himself and his post WWI lost-generation expatriates. His message: no matter the plagues of existence, life goes on according to some timeless design: the *earth abideth forever*

    That was a good enough message for tying up *Renrob*. I sped into the sunset glare thinking I might paddle next time into a story that ends better, maybe is more uplifting, and certainly more fun.

6. Back Waters—the NFL Experience

It ain't what you do, it's the way how you do it.
--Little Richard

I scoured Northern California back roads for waters to paddle. I paddled rivers, lakes, reservoirs, sloughs and estuaries for the chance to speed through NorCal back roads. I discovered and rediscovered. I found solace. I alpha-zoned. I found Zen release along two-lane asphalt running lateral to 21st century odium. I'd driven Highway 160, the delta levee highway along the Sacramento River. The Sacramento is the Mississippi of Northern California, the big river down the middle. It never disappoints.

The delta drains 2,500 miles of interconnected waterways between the Bay Area and the central valley. The Sacramento River once rose with the rains and flooded the surrounding terrain. Chinese coolies-built levees south of the city of Sacramento in the 19th century to contain the river.

The levees meander from Freeport to Rio Vista, where the Sacramento fans wide to meet the San Joaquin and head west past Pittsburg and Antioch, into the Carquinez Straits, to San Pablo Bay, into San Francisco Bay, through the Golden Gate narrows and out to the Pacific Ocean. The levees each have a two-lane highway on top. Both sides are designated Highway 160. Highway 160 follows the contours of the river. The river reflects the seasons and the weather. It is wide and permanent, always scenic. The Sacramento runs by the town of Locke.

Steve Cassady

    Locke was founded by the Chinese. The levee separates the river from arable bottom land near Locke that now yields bumper crops of pears. Locke is one street long, located at the foot of the levee east of the river. It has ramshackle wooden buildings like a ghost town movie set. Buildings in Locke lean windward. Locke threatens to blow away from the next strong gust off the river. Locke has one signature enterprise, a bar and restaurant, Al the Wops. My brother went to UC Davis in the 1960s. As a college student, he power-boated the Delta with his fraternity brothers and talked about Al the Wops. I discovered Al's in the 1970's and still anticipate every visit. Except for an electronic cash register at the bar, Al's hasn't had a new idea since the Depression, long before political correctness would have prevented the name.
    The bar is long, a drinker's bar. Dollar bills are pinned to the ceiling. The steady clientele is dominated by river people and bikers, some of them hard drinkers, but moods inside always jingle upbeat. The dining room in back features rows of old wooden tables and booths on a slanted floor. Al's serves New York steak or bigger New York steak. The menu offers what Al's chooses: one size steak or the other, green salad, French fries, pasta, sautéed mushrooms, and bread. Soup is extra, Minestrone only. Salad comes in a chintzy woven wood bowl, iceberg lettuce, kidney and garbanzo beans, with Thousand Island dressing. A jar of peanut butter used to sit on every table. Al's idea of progress: phase out the peanut butter after lunch. Al's doesn't serve prime grade-A steaks as in a Kansas City beef house, but it never serves a bad one.
    The town of Ryde, population 60, sits across from Al's, downstream on the Sacramento River. Ryde consists of a hotel, a post office/CPA business, some houses, and a water tower. I drove by Ryde from

across the river for more than three decades before I checked it out. I stopped because I was looking for someplace to drink beer after a long paddle in a deep-water slough to the east.

The Ryde Hotel was a speakeasy catering to Hollywood types in the late 1920s. It sits on the west side of 160, right on the river. Art-deco three-story peach pastel stucco with a short nine-hole golf course in back. It has a dining room and bar on the main floor that gin-drinking Hemingway characters would patronize. It is cool, dark, and anonymous. It bathes in slotted light from the sun shining through tropical plants. Ceiling fans whisk the air.

The hotel has two upper floors of rooms. The corner rooms on the second and third floor are river view suites fitted with Jacuzzi tubs and decorated in period jazz age furniture. The Ryde caters to weddings, reunions, and banquets. Transient room rent is a small part of the Ryde's clientele.

My brother treated my wife and me to a night at the Mark Hopkins on Nob Hill for my birthday in 2003. The next night, Sunday, was our anniversary. I reserved the second-floor corner room at the Ryde for $119 plus $35 for a bottle of champagne on ice. We arrived at dusk and found an envelope scotch-taped to the front door. Inside, a note for entry instructions, plus the front door key, and our room key. No one attended the desk. We were the only occupants.

California contrast: a luxury room at the top of the Nob Hill one night; sole tenancy in a reformed river bottom speakeasy the next. My wife couldn't decide if she should feel special because we had the place to ourselves—or creeped out, like we were the next victims at the Bates Motel.

In central California along US 99 post-WW II, travelers would pass as many as 50 Giant Orange roadside stands: orange colored igloos attached to hamburger shacks serving bottomless glasses of whatever juice was available from native orchards, usually orange and/or apple. Freeway travel bypassed the Giant Orange stands and killed off their business. The last to go: on Highway 99 off Avenue 22 ½ near Chowchilla in Fairmead, 25 miles from my house. It went in 2007, victim of SR 99 expansion.

Fast food chains have ruined the American hamburger. Fast food chains mass produce bad hamburgers that entire generations believe are actual hamburgers. Fast food hamburgers are overcooked to avoid E-Coli, manufactured in batches to serve in seconds. They are heat-lamped awaiting orders.

Hamburger stands serving hamburgers that taste like hamburgers are near extinct. The Mammoth Orange in Fairmead was classic, a relic of another time. But while it lasted, it was pure California roadside. It sat 25 feet off the freeway featuring an ambience of hot wind and flies, back-dropped by the non-stop whoosh of semi-truck and trailer traffic.

The hamburgers were outstanding—grilled to order and tasting like it. Before Cal Trans blocked it with median barriers, access to the Mammoth Orange from southbound 99 was death-defying. Drivers had to jam into a short turnout off the left lane with trucks and trailers climbing up their exhaust pipe. I ate at Mammoth Orange often before it closed. I'd screech across the median against two lanes of oncoming traffic and brake into the chopped-up asphalt and aggregate gravel parking lot. It was thrilling.

Lunch at Mammoth Orange: I used it to condense and revisit my vagabond life of the 1970s and 1980s. I was refitting for the new millennium. *Sartor Resartis*. These days, I am tethered to a domestic and professional existence. I stretch the tether into part-day, half-day and all-day trips. I crisscross the grid of NorCal county roads. I follow whims for yoga breaths. I live north of the Mammoth Orange.

The last time I ate at the Mammoth Orange, I took off south on Fairmead Boulevard thinking I could peel back through country roads and escape highway traffic. I turned left on Avenue 21. Avenue 21 rang a bell. The Chowchilla Bus Kidnapping took place on Avenue 21. I bounced along Avenue 21 a few miles until it dead-ended into Avenue 22. I intuited: it didn't happen here.

It must have happened on the other side of 99. I wheeled around and scorched rubber breaching four lanes of traffic across the 99 median at Avenue 22 ½. I navigated numbered rural roads and avenues until I found the extension of Avenue 21 on the south side of 99, on the back side of Chowchilla.

The crime scene was ten-minute drive from the Mammoth Orange. I backtracked to the Dairyland School on the corner of Avenue 18 ½ and Avenue 13. FBI agent Tom Walsh investigated the Chowchilla bus kidnapping from the Merced office. He told me insider stuff. It's hard to imagine a dumber crime. The perpetrators were rich kids, idlers who wanted big money independent of family handouts. They hoovered cocaine, watched 70s action flicks, and pipe-dreamed how their fortunes could flow.

Kidnapping was invented during the Depression off a simple equation. Rich people had money during the Depression. Rich people might part with their money for return of a loved one snatched for ransom. The Chowchilla kidnappers complicated the original formula. They took 26 middle-class and poor kids. They multiplied the backlash by a factor of 26. They planned on extorting five million dollars of ransom from the state of California—a bad idea.

Steve Cassady

They failed to account for all state and local law enforcement agencies brought into the picture. Backlash multiplied into insanity. The perpetrators feigned car trouble in a white cargo van without windows on Avenue 21 on the back side of Chowchilla between nut orchards and corn fields. They transferred the kids at gunpoint into that cargo van and another and drove them to a quarry in Livermore. They stashed the kids and the driver in a buried moving van.

The quarry was owned by the father of one of the kidnappers. The kidnappers had no criminal planning skills. The kids and the bus driver were indefatigable and escaped. The perpetrators were nabbed by routine detective work within days. The Dairyland School has a parking lot in back, filled with yellow buses, the kind the kids were taken from at gunpoint. The school sits in the shade from tall trees and looks like a corn belt country school right out of a Norman Rockwell painting. It belies its own notoriety.

I backtracked to the Mammoth Orange and returned to Avenue 21 on the north side of 99. Avenue 21 is chuckholes and ruts between grape vineyards and pistachio orchards. I hit the dead end at Avenue 22 and turned left—northwest. Avenue 22 runs past the gates of the Chowchilla Women's prison. Avenue 22 is freshly paved and runs fast and smooth. State prisons bring in Government money for work on roads that lead to prisons. County money leaves rural roads as chuckholes and ruts.

I knew I had to marry my wife because of an incident concerning the Chowchilla women's prison. I had taken a tour of the prison with an administration of justice class field trip in 1990. The women inside were wrapped in hard bark—incarceration hadn't softened any features. Dental work was intermittent. Tattoos were epidemic and crude. Language was coarse. The inmates called us *free world men*. They yelled it out from their cells as we toured.

I perked when the tour guide talked of community service. I got a phone number and dialed it upon return. I asked for a crew to work on the Merced College softball field— weeding, painting, and cleanup. School personnel ignored cosmetics on the athletic fields unless the fields were being used for a non-athletic event such as graduation. Coaches scramble for any free help they could get. My wife, before she was my wife, was the secretary to my predecessor as athletic director. She thought I sometimes teetered along the edge. The prison crew showed up with a guard driving a bus outfitted with an outhouse trailer.

The prison guard couldn't find the softball diamond. He went into the athletic department office. Cynthia saw the uniform and the gun belt and dummied up when he asked where I could be found. She thought I was in trouble. She wouldn't divulge my whereabouts. It took a while for her to flash on the difference between DOC and MPD or MCSD.

I sizzled a frisson when I heard the account. I had been autonomous for a long time. Nobody looked after me. Something good was happening domestically. The felons worked hard, but their presence offended college administration. The administration passed a rule prohibiting prisoners working on campus during school hours. I was hoping instead they'd pass a rule making college personnel work on athletic fields.

I took Avenue 22 until it merged with Santa Fe Road. I'd lived in the area more than 30 years and never traveled this section. The Santa Fe rail line runs through Merced. I picked up the tracks that run parallel to Santa Fe Road. I crossed the Chowchilla River on Santa Fe into LeGrand and Planada then tore down Childs Avenue to Arboleda. I was back at work in 35 minutes, the same as if I had taken 99 all choked with traffic. I broke new ground. I zoned the whole way. I don't remember passing a single vehicle.

In a period from 1978 to 1987, I did somewhat the same thing only on an epic scale. College teaching is a great dodge—provides weekends off, summers off, four weeks off between semesters in the winter. College teaching is the next-best alternative to inherited wealth. I was always available for NFL training camps, pre-season games, regular season games, post-season games, the Super Bowl, and the Pro Bowl. The Pro Bowl takes place in Honolulu. I attended the Pro Bowl three times on the NFL's dime.

I went at everything hard. I knew the experience was unique, finite, and a matter of timing. I floor-boarded the whole ride. Super Bowl XVI after the 1981 season took place in Detroit, the first time in a cold weather city. I took Amtrak across with John Madden. It grew colder as we went east: 27 degrees in Rawlins, Wyoming, 18 that evening in Denver, below freezing the next day in Chicago.

I love the trains. Trains are impervious to weather. An airplane ices over, and the thing goes Big Bopper and Richie Valens into an Iowa corn field. On the train from Chicago to Detroit, the pneumatic exit doors iced over, and wizened conductor dislodged the ice at every stop with a sledgehammer. Watching a flight engineer walking down the aisle of a DC-10 lugging a sledgehammer, I'd hear Dan Roman whistling and be fear-stabbed with images from *The High and the Mighty*. On a train, it's only funny.

I maneuvered through the week of Super Bowl XVI on a CBS ticket plus a credential from NFL Properties. I had a room on the 40th floor of the Renaissance Center. A time and temperature sign across the street registered the conditions in neon. One day, it said '1". Wind shrieking across the Detroit River from Canada chilled it down to 37 below. CBS was headquartered in the RenCen downtown.

The 49ers were headquartered in Southfield. Michael Zagaris flew in with the 49ers. Practices for both teams--the 49ers and the Cincinnati Bengals took place in the Silverdome. Streets and boulevards were rimmed with snow banks and frozen over. The whole week was colder than a well-digger's ass. We wrestled with logistics. Bad conditions meant the dilettantes would stay indoors. We planned on missing nothing. We wanted to watch practices, attend parties, tour Greek Town, cross into Canada, survey the site the *Edmund Fitzgerald* went under, and traverse the rundown glory of Michigan Boulevard.

We needed ground transportation. The NFL works a Super Bowl week trade with General Motors. They reserve a fleet of new cars, Buicks that year, stick a Super Bowl logo on the doors, and make them available to players and visiting guests. The cars are loaned out in two-hour blocks. After the Super Bowl, GM sends the Buicks to dealers and markets them at a discount as *Official Super Bowl* vehicles. I needed a car for six days, not two hours. I took a shuttle to Southfield and reconnoitered with Zagaris.

Zagaris saw DeWayne Board, the 49ers defensive tackle, exiting an NFL Buick at the carriage entrance. Board had to be near his two-hour time limit. Zagaris told him: *Hey, Peewee, we'll turn it in for you.* Board flipped him the keys. We kept the car for the week. Madden wouldn't fly. He was guest-hosting *Saturday Night Live* the weekend following the Super Bowl. *SNL* wanted him in New York Sunday night after the game. They thought he could fly in. He said no. *SNL* sent a film crew to Detroit to ride Amtrak with Madden back to New York and shoot footage.

Steve Cassady

The 49ers beat Cincinnati Sunday, 26-21. I left Zagaris in Southfield and drove back to the RenCen. I wrote my radio script on Monday morning and was done. I tried to turn in the keys in for the NFL Buick, but the check-in room was deserted. I left the keys on an empty table. Apparently, a dishonest citizen found them. I heard later the Detroit cops fished the Buick from melting snow during the spring thaw. The Buick was trashed. DeWayne Board went into coaching after finishing his playing career. He talked about that car for years. He said the NFL tried to bill him for the loss. He knew Zagaris as the 49ers' photographer. He knew me but not my name. He always told them the same thing: *I gave the car to Z-man.*

I hit for the Amtrak station with Madden and the *SNL* crew. I walked up and down train aisles at propitious moments. I logged cameo time on *Saturday Night Live*. I felt like Alfred Hitchcock. We had a stopover in Toledo. Madden noticed a thin guy in a black, baggy suit with wide wing lapels, wearing Santo Trafficante horned-rim glasses and a Popeye Doyle hat with a pushed-up brim. The guy was carrying a vinyl briefcase with a Super Bowl XVI logo on the flap: insider souvenir. Madden said, *There's one.*

He meant characters. Madden grew up poor on the streets of Daly City. He and his buddy John Robinson snuck into drive-in movies on foot and watched the movie sitting on the asphalt hump next to a speaker stand. He shagged free rides on trolley cars and gate-crashed into San Francisco Seals Triple-A baseball and 49ers football games. He frequented pool halls. He shilled for card games while in junior college in Aberdeen, Washington, at a place called, *The Mint Café*. He grew up among characters. An affinity remains. His celebrity inhibits: he can't mix like he used to; he stays vicarious. Code for *There's One:* harvest material for train talk.

The guy's name was Junior. Junior was from Philadelphia. Junior wasn't media, but he sported a media press pin on his wide lapel. I introduced myself. We talked about this and that. Junior looked about 55 and didn't laugh much. Junior said he went to all the Super Bowls, World Series, and big-ticket fights. Junior didn't like to fly—we bonded on travel preference. Junior bought me a bowl of train depot chili. Junior validated Madden's instinct. He ran the linen concession at a south Philadelphia restaurant, *Palumbo's. Palumbo's* later would burn down from a fire of suspicious origins. Figure the linen business in east coast restaurants as low-grade Mafia enterprise. Junior's last name was Cerafino.

Junior referred to the NFL's second-in-command Jim Heffernan as *Jimmy*. Jim Heffernan was from Philadelphia. Junior had press access to Super Bowl Week. Tacit guess: Junior retailed tickets, maybe ran bets, for Jim Heffernan and who knows what other 410 Park potentates. I pocketed the guess, and we re-boarded for the leg into New York. Junior stayed at the Edison on 47nd Street in New York. He gave Big Apple entertainment tips. He recommended seeing the nude spectacle, *Oh, Calcutta* at the Edison Theater near his hotel. I was thinking *Amadeus* at the Broadhurst on west 44th. I compromised, saw both on consecutive nights. *Oh, Calcutta* was an erotic romp. *Amadeus* was a two-and-a-half hour classical music downer. I am a right-brain Finn. I thrive on contrast.

Newspaper writers allude clichés about *Damon Runyon types: a shad*ow *society of grifters, gamblers, and racetrack touts*. In an undirected reading spree at San Francisco State I read all of Damon Runyon's published fiction. I travel back roads and eat blue-plate specials in downtown diners. I am conversant with the ilk. Junior and his crew were authentic Damon Runyon types, and they were sinking into the tar pits. They warranted cultivation. Their likes weren't coming around again. They all were older guys without a next-generation-in-waiting. Their house sponsors like Jim Heffernan were increasingly outnumbered as NFL followings moved from race track paddocks into corporate board rooms. We cultivated them, the characters, Michael Zagaris and I.

    Junior hung with Duke from New York. Duke worked for the Hickey ticket agency. He ran with Louie, also from New York, and Fat Alex from LA. On their fringes, the monarch of gate-crashers, Ed "Skipper" McNally. Skipper McNally was an actor by ambition, a stage electrician out of necessity, a magnificent raconteur and a dedicated drunk. McNally was from Brockton, Mass. He shared roots with the heavyweight champion Rocky Marciano.

    Skipper McNally was in his 50s, and would never become the actor of his aspirations. He claimed to have been cast somewhere in all of Elia Kazan's movies. In the movie *Charley,* Skipper was the mean baker. He wore a white T-shirt and toque and taunted the half-wit title character played by Cliff Robertson.

    The movie, *Emperor of the North Pole,* set in Oregon, surrounds a hobo-versus-train-conductor confrontation for mortal stakes. A Number One, played by Lee Marvin challenges the sadistic Shack, Ernest Borgnine; A Number One says he can ride Shack's train all the way to Portland. Shack means to kill him if he tries. The train yard comes alive with employees throwing down money betting on the outcome. A character with a green-eye shade runs up with a fistful of bills, yelling in a sharp, nasal tone, *I'll hold the money.* The green eye shade guy is Ed McNally. I have a framed poster of *Emperor of the North Pole* hanging in my family room. It reminds me of my time in Skipper McNally's outrageous company.

Skipper McNally claimed to understudy a character actor named George Mathew in the 1968 Broadway play, *The Great White Hope,* about exiled black boxer Jack Johnson. James Earl Jones played Jack Johnson in the movie version. I remember George Mathew. He was a gray-haired pug-nosed character actor. He played a bar owner guy named Shansey in *The Gunfight at the OK Corral,* with Burt Lancaster as Wyatt Earp and Kirk Douglas as Doc Holliday. In *The Great White Hope,* George Matthew played somebody named *Cap'n Dan* for the two-year run. Skipper McNally said, t*he son-of-a-bitch wasn't sick a day in two years.*

Skipper's fate on Broadway: a star wasn't born. I tagged Skipper McNally as a failed actor who decided one day to produce, direct, and cast himself in his own real-life performances. In San Francisco, he lived in a Tenderloin fleabag on Eddy Street, the Dalt. I assumed he stayed in Dalt counterparts all across America. I never saw Skipper wear the same outfit twice. I never saw him carry a suitcase.

My image: Skipper browsing through thrift shops exchanging the clothes he was wearing for a cleaner set off the rack. Skipper had a shock of white hair and a white beard. When he told stories, which he always did, his cheeks and eyes broke into laugh wrinkles. He had a penetrating voice with a Brockton, Mass accent that crossed between W.C. Fields and Walter Huston in *The Treasure of the Sierra Madre,* when Walter Huston was dancing over the gold strike and making fun of greenhorns Humphrey Bogart and Tim Holt.

Skipper was locked into gate-crasher's lore. The Kansas City Chiefs won Super Bowl IV. *Sports Illustrated* ran an interior photo of Chiefs' coach Hank

Steve Cassady

Stram being carried off the field on the shoulders of a Chiefs' player and Skipper McNally. Skipper had breached the moment. He had put on a red windbreaker and melted into post-game frenzy. He did it again when Pittsburgh won its first Super Bowl in 1974. NFL films caught head coach Chuck Noll running off the field led by Ed McNally wearing a black V-necked sweater and a rolled-up towel around his neck.

Skipper was anathema to NFL PR guys, from the 410 Park Avenue big shots down to the team guys— except for the Oakland Raiders and maybe the Pittsburgh Steelers. Old man Art Rooney had a soft spot for him. Al Davis was sentimental about him. Tommy Grimes loved him. The Raiders of that era tended to promote anything that aggravated the stuffed shirts at 410 (now 345) Park.

NFL PR guys guarded gates that McNally routinely crashed. They lumped him into a category they called *Green Flies,* named after the pests that buzz around cow shit. They couldn't penetrate their own metaphor and come off flattered. If Skipper McNally is a green fly, what are they and their events? At the top of his game, all they could accomplish was derision. They couldn't keep him out. They shut the front door, and a house sponsor would let him in the back.

We were among them. The 49ers were in the NFC championship game against Dallas in 1981, the game where Joe Montana's last-minute pass to a leaping Dwight Clark became *The Catch. The Catch* gave the 49ers a 28-27 victory, put them into Super Bowl XVI and launched their dynasty. The game took place in San Francisco at Candlestick Park. The NFC party was held the night before at a ballroom in the Fairmont Hotel. Security was simple. Dallas PR office staff sat a table next to the left of the double door entry; 49ers people to the right. NFL security chief, former FBI agent, Warren Welch, served as centurion between the two tables. Tickets weren't necessary. Personnel at either table would recognize party-goers by sight.

Recognition green-lighted them past Warren Welch. I had seen Skipper earlier in the day at a hotel bar. He asked about the party, if I were going. Translated, he'd piggyback my invitation. He was looking wrinkled and seedy. He wore a dirty billed cap, set at an angle. I said meet me in the lobby of the Fairmont at 8 pm.

The Fairmont is majestic—a stone high-rise on top of Nob Hill. It was commissioned in 1902 by the daughters of a man named Fair who hit a bonanza silver strike in Nevada. The Fairmont was finished but not furnished when the 1906-earthquake leveled San Francisco. The building withstood the quake but not the subsequent fire. The Fairmont was gutted by flames but restored for good in 1907. In terms of historical significance, the Dalt stands in derelict contrast.

The Dalt sits on Eddy near where Nob Hill bottoms out into Market Street. I didn't feature him walking downhill to the Dalt and back. I featured him finding a nearby thrift shop. I met him at eight. He was wearing a plum-colored double-knit sport coat, white shirt, patterned gray polyester slacks, and a wide silver tie. His hatless hair was pure shocking white. He looked like the bearded guy who used to advertise Schweppes tonic notched down from British colonial gentleman to skid row transient.

Skipper McNally was as inconspicuous as a street light. I shrugged. We hit for the mezzanine ballroom. I read the arrangement. I told Skipper to hang on my left hip. The PR people at the 49ers table passed me through to Warren Welch. Warren Welch had FBI eyes. He quartered rooms and took everything in. He saw me and the pariah McNally simultaneously. He stepped up to block Skipper. I angled right and stepped up the pace toward Warren Welch's right shoulder. Skipper read the block and stepped left. I engaged Warren Welch in small talk. Skipper made the door in one long stride. He hot-footed toward the free bar. I slipped Warren Welch's steel-eyed glare and followed.

Inside the ball room I was braced by Joe Browne, NFL head of public relations to the entire NFL, a tall guy with glasses and a mortician's sense of humor. Joe Browne was third in the pecking order below Pete Rozelle and Jim Heffernan. Warren Welch had submitted his report. Joe Browne administered disapprobation. *You let Skipper McNally in. He doesn't belong here,* Joe Browne said. I said, *Look around you Joe, who belongs?* The party was a monument to high-rolling freeloaders. Media members, sponsors, celebrities, coat tail riders—everyone the NFL wanted to repay for favors or from whom they intended to extract favors plus dates and wives of same.

My dad loved to quote Shakespeare. My dad liked the line, *basking in reflected glory.* NFL parties are all reflected glory. Nobody attends who plays between the lines on Sunday. I pointed toward the middle of the revelry, at the free shrimp and open bar. I asked Joe Browne, *Who out there actually gives a shit about football? Who belongs, Joe?* Joe Browne wasn't getting anywhere. He faded with something like, *Well, don't do it again.*

Dick Maxwell was next. Dick Maxwell was NFC head of public relations. He wore tortoise shell glasses. He was shorter and younger than Joe Browne and not as funny. Dick Maxwell had tried to tell Michael Zagaris, 49ers team photographer, that the league would restrict his NFC championship game access to one corner of the field. Michael railed. He was shooting 49ers history for the home team. He demanded total access. He launched epithets against 410 Park.

He included the word *cocksucker*, directed if not at Dick Maxwell at least near enough to him that Dick Maxwell blanched. Michael Zagaris rethought his rage. He yielded to discretion. He said, *I left, before I burned any bridges.* Dick Maxwell started in on me: *I heard a strange thing, Steve. I heard you let Skipper McNally into the party.* I snapped: *If you're going to tell me the same thing Joe Browne said, forget it—I've already heard it from him, and he outranks you.* Dick Maxwell looked shocked. I rolled: *But tell me, Dick, exactly what's the problem with him being here?* Dick Maxwell sputtered. He was straining to object on solid grounds: *He's a...a ticket scalper.* I said, *Look around. These are high-rollers. They already have tickets.* Skipper was oblivious. Skipper drank in copious haste. He was working the big room, downing double vodkas, spieling prodigious thespian lies.

The 49ers kicked into dynasty status with that 1981 season: *The Catch* and a victory in Super Bowl XVI. The 49ers under Bill Walsh came from nowhere. They exploded into history with a no-name roster. Their success changed the picture, made them attractive enough to warrant serious security protocols. Their dynasty stifled fluid access and made them take things and themselves seriously. Prior to *The Catch*, they were desperate for attention.

We exploited their pre-dynasty desperation. Michael Zagaris dove into character. He laced up football cleats in the locker room two hours before the game and clattered down the tunnel. He commanded unlimited access. He had photographed 49er games since he was a teenager with a Brownie Hawkeye and gate-crashed with credentials, he made himself out of colored card stock. In 1980, pre-dynasty, we took a trip to New York for a game with the Jets.

I was used to the Raiders. The Raiders would fly in two days early and acclimate to a new time zone. The 49ers went in the day before. We lost three hours going east and were a full day behind in road-trip hi-jinx. We didn't reach the team hotel in New Jersey until 5:30 p.m. on Saturday night. We had to hustle to salvage what was left of the weekend. George Heddleston advanced the Jets game—he was PR director. The advance man begins set-up in the host city the Tuesday before the game. He secures all arrangements. He's available for the home town press. His last duty on Saturday is to settle the team and traveling party into their accommodations.

George Heddleston met us at the hotel. NFL PR guys in that era ran toward the convivial. George Heddleston was more convivial than most—he liked his road trip Saturday nights.

We were gassing with George Heddleston. Looking past his left shoulder, I spotted someone standing next to a lobby couch. I nudged Zagaris. Zagaris told Heddleston: *Look, George, there's a friend of yours.* Heddleston looked. He saw Skipper McNally. He said, *Oh, shit.* He knew: with Skipper in the building, it would all go bad.

He didn't know when or how, just that it would. We helped. We told Skipper we were heading to Manhattan—meet us at P.J. Clarke's on 2nd Avenue at midnight. Skipper asked, where's the hospitality room? NFL teams set up a suite on the road and stock it with booze, chips, dips, and nuts. They leave it open for the traveling party. Skipper regarded the room number of the hospitality suite as a hotel comp: free booze all night, possibly a flop on a couch. We told him the hospo suite number and left.

Skipper went all the way. It went way worse than George Heddleston had imagined. We bopped into midtown Manhattan on a city bus. New York City on a Saturday night is always entertaining, but nothing major occurred that night. We hit P.J. Clarke's at Midnight. We didn't expect Skipper, and he didn't show. About 12:30 a customer offended one of P.J. Clarke's bartenders. The bartender's girlfriend was sitting on a barstool, and the customer hit on her.

The bartender was from central casting out of *The Sopranos,* tall, thick, and black haired. He sprinted from around the bar wearing a white apron. He dropped the customer with a short right hook. Nobody in the crowd reacted. The customer isn't always right in New York City. We bussed back to New Jersey after one a.m. We hit the hotel lobby at two and decided on one pass at the hospitality room.

Hospo was on the 17th floor, about midpoint down the hallway. The elevator doors opened to loud clamor from mid-point down the hall. We guessed at the source. The 49ers traveling party included beat writers, car dealers, sponsors, some front office people, some alumni. A retinue hit us at the threshold.

Hospo was chaos—drunk and vocal, arguments flaring all over the room. The spokesman, a beat writer from the *San Mateo Times* who since has died, Garry Niver, pointed to Skipper in the middle of a verbal dispute by the bar. Niver said: *That guy says he knows you.* We admitted he did. Niver wouldn't stop: *He won't tell us his name. He said you guys invited him up here. He's got no business here.* I loved that one: freeloaders packed the room like anchovies in a tin. *And...*Niver sputtered*...He's a liar.*

I liked that one even better. It was true. Skipper McNally was a monumental liar. Skipper would ramble in endless monologue dropping names with

Steve Cassady

indiscriminate variety. He helped the Secret Service arrange seating for Henry Kissinger at a Red Sox game. He helped Al Davis work reads for strong safety coverage after the NFL moved in the hash marks.

He was the subject of envy because of his relationship with Sandy Koufax. (*I had a nice professional relationship with him. I always knew where I stood, and I never wore out my welcome. I would always talk to him when I had something constructive and pertinent to say.*)

He bandied words with Walter Winchell on boxing. (*Winchell didn't know the first fucking thing about the boxing racket*).

He pontificated on Adlai Stevenson (*I think Adlai taught us all a great lesson when it comes to press conferences, and students today in the sciences and humanities should go back and study Stevenson.*)

He revealed his bond with Vince Lombardi. (*He was always around the city. He used to eat in the restaurants I hung around when I was on Broadway. Vince Lombardi was always a great theater fan; he loved the theater. You build up a rapport with the guy.*)

Our tacit agreement with Skipper: Keep the lies outlandish for maximum amusement, and we won't dispute a thing. Skipper held up his end always. Skipper was biblical—he didn't hide his light under a bushel. Mickey Mantle consulted Skipper during the 1963 World Series after Sandy Koufax had struck out Mantle with a 3-2 overhand curve.

I saw the game in my Uncle Ralph and Aunt Dorothy's den in Westwood when I was supposed to be attending classes at UCLA. Even with primitive camerawork of the era, I knew it was an all-time great pitch. It dropped 12-6 over the middle of the plate. It sizzled in hard, bit air at Mickey Mantle's letters and

Bouncing Outside

shot down toward his ankles. It was unhittable, maybe the best pitch ever.

Skipper: *Mantle said to me, 'that's got to be one of the greatest pitches I've ever seen in baseball. I'm kind of curious what Ted thinks.' I called Williams a day or two later. He asked, 'what happened to that ball, was it loaded?' I said, 'No, just pure strength'. He said, 'Jesus, what a pitch.'.*

Skipper thought of Reggie Jackson as a protégé. Skipper was a confidante to his Brockton, Massachusetts home boy, Rocky Marciano. (*We always trained him to go 30 rounds.*) Skipper acted as an advisor to Eddie DeBartolo as DeBartolo was scaling the vertical slopes of NFL ownership. Skipper McNally cast himself as the Leonard Zelig of professional athletics. Who wouldn't believe his stories?

Garry Niver also was bothered by Skipper's response to his group's skepticism. Somebody called him on some fanciful tale Skipper told with himself as protagonist. His replied in his ear-piercing nasal Brockton, Mass voice: *Fuck you, you cocksucker.* Shit was spraying from the fan blades by the time we arrived. We wouldn't tell anyone Skipper's name, and Skipper wouldn't back off an inch.

The group was demanding an accounting, and none was forthcoming. The free booze flowed. The night got drunker. I'm a one or two-drink guy. I had hit my quota six hours earlier at P.J. Clarke's. The situation in the hospitality was beyond repair. I went to bed.

I woke to Zagaris' knock about nine in the morning. He had been to the hospo for coffee. He was lost in laughter describing the wreckage. He saw Skipper flopped on a lobby couch. He talked about furniture tipped over, drink glasses on their sides, bottles strewn on table tops, chips, dips, peanut shells spilled on the rugs. Zagaris said, *But...It's not all bad...look:* He was holding up a navy blue cashmere V-neck: *I got myself a new sweater.*

The story should have ended there. We went down to the lobby. George Heddleston saw us. He looked bad—like he hadn't slept well. He said he had been fielding complaints about *the gatecrasher* at different times since 2 a.m., and our names had come up. Heddleston said: *I don't want to see either of you two guys for a very long time.* We avoided him during the bus trip to Shea Stadium, the game—a loss to the Jets—and the bus trip to the airport.

Somewhere over the Rockies at 37,000 feet on the way west, I was hanging out in the galley. I fly calmest standing in the galley. From several aisles starboard, three members of the envoy bandied outrage. One said, *You know that gatecrasher?* The others nodded. *You know what he did?* The others didn't know. The first one said, *You know Ed Alvarez, Eddie D.'s attorney?* They did. *Well, Ed Alvarez left his favorite sweater in the hospitality room last night, and that son-of-a-bitch took it. He stole Ed's favorite sweater.*

All the way west, I tried to tell Zagaris about Ed Alvarez's favorite sweater. For one reason or another—he was sleeping, people in earshot, we were eating, I was elsewhere—I never did. We deplaned at SFO and rode the escalator to baggage. The whole way, we were within earshot of the wrong ears.

Zagaris traveled like a bindle stiff. His luggage was barely a notch better than a handkerchief tied to the end of a walking stick. Zagaris pulled his ratty suitcase off the carousel. Zagaris yielded to an impulse unique to the beat of his own drum. He dropped his suitcase, unzipped it and started to rearrange the contents for a tighter pack. I nudged him with my knee and hissed out the side of my mouth. He wouldn't listen—he was fishing the sweater from his bag.

Bouncing Outside

The traveling party was all around. I hissed: *Close the fucking suitcase—I'll tell you why later.* He relented. The upshot of the whole thing: Skipper McNally was branded as a gatecrasher, liar and thief. George Heddleston exiled him from Candlestick Park—like exile could keep him out—and told him why.

Skipper denied with customary tact: *I didn't steal any fucking sweater.* Zagaris felt bad. Zagaris' didn't feel bad enough to restitute or confess. He gave the sweater to his wife, who wore it for years. They all missed the exculpatory truth about Skipper McNally and the sweater. It was 80 degrees and humid that day in New York. He wouldn't have taken the sweater because he wasn't at that moment cold.

Traveling with Michael Zagaris on NFL football trips was a total gas. Michael Zagaris seldom stifled his id. The results were pure entertainment. We were in Atlanta one weekend. Michael went to the hospitality suite. No one else had shown. Except a fawning room attendant. He wrote it off as a southern thing. The attention embarrassed him.

He didn't want a cold towel for his forehead or his Beatle boots polished. He could find his own bananas or pour his own drinks. It didn't hit him right away he was in the wrong room. He didn't find out he was lounging in Eddie D's personal suite until after the excess attention had driven him out.

Michael Zagaris is superior mimic. He apes speech patterns from Elvis Presley to Lyndon Johnson to British rock stars to southern black football players. In Cincinnati one weekend, he called early on Sunday morning and harangued in some south Alabama black patois: *Get your lazy ass out of bed.* The voice on the other end wasn't mine: *Who is this?* the voice demanded. Zagaris stayed in his patois: *Well, who's this?* The other end of the call was backup running

Steve Cassady

back Lenville Elliot. He said, *This is Lenville.* Zagaris, still in character, said, *And you don't know who this is?* Lenville said he didn't. Zagaris hung up.

We blurred the line between work and play. We navigated the blur through from August to February for ten years. We were credentialed by competence. Unrelenting good work breeds tolerance for eccentricity. Eccentricity shot us full throttle into the fast lane of the entire experience. The need to stay eccentric motivated the good work. It all fit.

The year I rode the trains with Madden, I met Zagaris in LA for Super Bowl XVII between Miami and Washington. Zagaris had an assignment from NFL Properties to shoot Super Bowl color for the week. They rented him a car, a subcompact. We ran it around the LA Basin for two days looking for photo ops and deemed the rental car all wrong on two grounds. It was too small to carry all our stuff, mostly his photo gear, plus it already was out of gas.

We made it to Hertz in Westwood on fumes and upgraded on the same account for a bigger car with a full tank. We worked off the cover of NFL Films. The name was magic. We discovered it midweek at the Rose Bowl when we had to cross barricades to shoot pictures of George Toma and his crew of painters and groundskeepers prepping the field for the game. The yellow jackets responded to the title NFL films; they didn't seem aware that the real NFL Films didn't shoot stills. We found it a common misconception.

We crashed impenetrable gates, Zagaris carrying his .35 mm Nikons, me his accessory bag. Pre-game, we entered the officials' room and hung with the zebras. We went to the CBS booth. Madden was broadcasting his first Super Bowl. He saw us: *What're you guys doing here?* I winked, he laughed, we stayed a while. All week, we went through verboten doors by

Bouncing Outside

saying *NFL Films*. It worked invariably. We viewed Super Bowl XVII through microscopic proximity.

We flew to SFO from LAX on the last flight Sunday. Michael Zagaris' dilapidated luggage always returned heavier than it began. NFL Properties had picked up the room tab. Zagaris had dialed up in room service most meals during the week. We slung our bags onto the security checkpoint conveyer. I glanced at the screen as Zagaris' bags passed through: X-ray images highlighting a tidy arrangement of Marriot flatware and dishes, including cruets for vinegar and oil. The cruets had been an issue. He was at first worried about slopping and vinegar and oil over his belongings. I suggested he drain the contents and wrap the cruets into one or two of many crested towels he was appropriating. *Good idea,* he said.

Super Bowl XVIII was in Tampa between the Los Angeles Raiders and the Washington Redskins. I was in New York over winter break from Merced College. Mid-January, second semester was looming. I told Madden I was heading west. He said, what about the Super Bowl—he was thinking radio show logistics when he would be jammed by a broadcast schedule.

I said I was broke, and school was starting. He said he'd pay me an extra grand to stay the week in Tampa. I perked. A precocious baboon could teach the first week of a community college English class—it's all assessments and procedures. I called school and extracted a week's leave contingent on paying my own subs. I arranged for subs by telephone.

I called Zagaris. He dialed Al LoCasale. LoCasale offered a seat on the Raiders charter from Oakland for best rolls of Zagaris' Super Bowl pictures. Zagaris called John Wiebusch and double-booked the same deal with NFL Properties for a significant fee. I called Wiebusch. I said I would be in Tampa without a place to stay. He said if he secured me a room, he'd want a story. I agreed. He said he'd pay me $750 for a flashback sidebar on game strategy to run in the spring. I said, reserve the room. NFL policy: they reimburse, they do not front expenses.

I had no operating credit card—no way to cover the room once I hit Tampa. I'd worry about that later. I called Zagaris, usually more impoverished than I, and told him we had a place to stay. Madden and I took Amtrak from Penn Station to Tampa. We arrived Sunday night. I was staying at a Hilton, in a room block-reserved for the NFL. I told the clerk the NFL would arrange payment with a company credit card when the traveling secretary arrived later in the week.

I spent Sunday afternoon strolling concentric paths from the hotel scouting for a headquarters beanery. Near the University of Tampa, I spotted a Cuban diner serving full meals for $4.99: thin steak asada, salad, yellow rice, and black beans. The clientele was first-string: UT students, male and female, hard-eyed Cubans looking like they barely had made the boat lift from Mariel; orderlies and nurses in green scrubs from a psycho ward at a hospital across the street; whacked out street people flush from selling plasma at a blood bank near the nuthouse. The place rocked.

The setup was scattered all over west Florida: the media hotel in Tampa, team hotels in St. Petersburg, and Orlando. I needed a car. Early on Tuesday, I ran into Frank Cooney, then working the Raiders' beat for the *San Francisco Examiner*. Frank Cooney was a rounder with a personnel problem. He had invited two women in for Super Bowl week. He had them stashed in separate hotels and had two tickets for the game in adjoining seats. Frank Cooney wasn't necessarily interested in these two women meeting each other and comparing notes. He was looking for a single game

Bouncing Outside

ticket in another part of the stadium. He wanted to pay face value for another ticket and scalp one of the two he held for a profit. He told his tale.

I said I needed a car. He said, *If your reputation wasn't so bad, you could check out an NFL car.* The Detroit story was still current in the minds of some. I said, *Frank, I want a car for the week, not two hours.* I found a lobby phone and called Tommy Grimes at the Raiders' hotel in St. Pete. He said I could buy a face value ticket from the Raiders—to see Sandy Gardiner in the office. I found Frank Cooney. I said: *I can get you a single ticket, face value.* I read him as desperate. I said, *I need a car.* I had read right. He took me downtown to Hertz and used his *Examiner* credit card to rent me a Pontiac Fiero.

I drove to the Raiders' hotel in my sleek new Pontiac. I jawed with Sandy Gardiner waiting for the game ticket. I saw a box filled with unlined silver pullover windbreakers featuring Raiders logos. I admired them. Sandy Gardiner told me they were for the coaches. We talked about other things. She said she wanted to take her mother to Bern's Steakhouse, but the place was booked solid all week. I asked to use the phone. At a bar the night before I had met a woman very much inebriated who said she worked in the Mayor's office. She said city government in Tampa wanted to be exemplary hosts.

She had no idea who I was. She said if she could do anything to improve our stay in Tampa, call her. She gave me her card. I called her about a reservation at Bern's for Sandy Gardiner and her mother. She didn't remember me, making the offer, or giving me her card. I shamed her hard under threat to the reputation of Tampa as a Super Bowl host. She relented. She took the number and called back twenty minutes later. She said she'd called in favors, and we had a

Steve Cassady

reservation for two at Bern's in Sandy Gardiner's name that night at eight p.m. Sandy Gardiner was thrilled and appreciative. She said, if she could do anything.... I continued to admire the coaches' windbreakers.

I walked to my new car ten minutes later with a windbreaker in my size and a game ticket for one of Frank Cooney's female imports. Back at the Hilton late that night, I ran into Junior, Duke, and Louie. They had fleshed out their crew with a few compatriots whose names I didn't catch. They were loitering on the rug in the hallway next to my room shooting craps. They asked if I wanted to play. I said no. They asked if I minded if they played on. No, again. The scene was too rich; it would be unthinkable to interrupt. The next day, Junior tracked me down and gave me tickets for the Commissioner's party on Friday night. Another Super Bowl week wired.

The Commissioner's party was invented as a bribe to solicit good media relations. Over the years, the Commissioner's party has devolved with snobbish exclusion. In 1983, it cost a half-million bucks. It is a closed function, as pompous and security conscious as a party for 3,500 guests can become. Junior said some years the party tickets are harder to find than game tickets. The party is held in a conspicuous location and given an overblown theme that no one but the party organizer pays the slightest attention to. In Tampa, the party was held in a tent the size of a Zeppelin hangar and given a circus theme because Clyde Beatty used to winter his show in Florida.

The floor was covered with straw, high wire acts were running overhead. Tranquilized jungle cats— lions, tigers, jaguars, leopards—lumbered the periphery in cages, sloe-eyed and sluggish. The whole thing was bizarre, like something out of Hieronymus Bosch and his of *Garden Earthly Delights*. The sinners roved the

Bouncing Outside

party unaware of their excess and gluttony because they are too busy eating and drinking. *We pay for 1/28th this goddam thing,* Tommy Grimes told me in Tampa, *and I have no idea what it's for.* That's point.

It isn't about anything except eating food rich enough to sponsor gout and drinking quality liquor until facial capillaries explode. Players never attend, neither do coaches. No one attends from participating teams preparing for Sunday's game. The owners do; their section is roped off. Zagaris walked into the owners' section. He showed his camera to the yellow jackets guarding the red velvet ropes. He said, *NFL Films.* I went in later, flashing a roll of .35 mm film. I said, *I've got to bring this to the NFL Films guy.* I went through the velvet ropes only to see if I could. Nothing occurred inside that I gave a rat's ass about—nothing beyond rich people indulging.

The week went well. I spent much of it evading the front desk. I had to be back in Merced for classes Monday morning. Flights out on Sunday night were overbooked, unless I left before the game was over. I had caught the essence of the week. I already had the story. On media day, Tuesday, players are assigned tables in a ballroom for interviews.

They are identified by small centerpiece pennants showing their uniform numbers. Al Locasale invented the system for Super Bowl XI—it prevented writers asking dumb questions to the wrong people and players having to identify themselves to media members about to ask them dumb questions. Jim Plunkett's table, number 16, was mobbed. Marcus Allen's table, number 32, was mobbed. David Humm, number 11, had his table to himself. David Humm was a third-team quarterback from Nebraska. He was left-handed and didn't throw hard. He was Kenny Stabler without the big-play instincts, social indiscretions, and Alabama swagger. David Humm was a student of offensive football. He filled a cassette with usable insight deconstructing the offense from both teams. I was done. I didn't need to attend the entire game to write a story due two months later.

I killed two birds. I still had no money. Kickoff was 3:25 EST. I called a travel agency in Merced. The agency was owned by a Merced College board member. I coaxed the agent to advance a ticket on a 6 p.m. flight to SFO to from Tampa International. On Sunday morning, our room looked unique but not tidy. We had grease-penciled pithy Little Richard song lyrics on the mirror. We scattered the place with newspapers and souvenirs. We used lamp shades as hat racks. Room service trays and dinnerware found homes on horizontal surfaces unoccupied by dirty laundry.

Peter Read Miller was hanging with us on Sunday morning. Peter Read Miller is from LA and takes pictures for *Sports Illustrated.* He was lounging on one of the beds nearest the phone. The phone rang. Peter Miller answered. His instinct was perfect. He said, in order: *Yes, it is...no, he's not...yes, I'll be sure to tell him.* He hung up. He said, *that was the front desk—they want the room paid for this morning. I told him you weren't here.* I caught the cues. I packed up and took the elevator down to the garage.

I walked from the garage basement up the ramp and outside. I found a shuttle to the stadium. I left the game seconds before the end of the first half, right after Jack Squirek intercepted a *rocket* screen that Joe Theisman threw from his own 12-yard line. Jack Squirek was an anonymous reserve linebacker who had made a play for the ages. He ran in the interception to give the Raiders a 21-3 lead in a game they would win 38-9. Tampa was dead to traffic during the game. Cabs were plentiful. We sailed to the airport.

Bouncing Outside

I was westbound at 37,000 feet by the time Chris Bahr kicked the final field goal in the fourth quarter. I had completed one chore before I left. From the airport I called the hotel and demanded to speak with the front desk manager. I worked up indignation. I said I was duly annoyed from being pestered about the bill. I was planning to return to the room post-game to write a deadline story and would consider any interruption a professional affront. I said an executive from NFL Properties would come by before checkout on Monday and handle the whole thing.

The manager was placated. I had shielded Zagaris for the last night in the hotel without front-desk hassle. I flew home. I never did find what happened with that bill…or one a year later at the Hyatt Regency in San Francisco I handled somewhat the same way.

In the movie *Red River,* Matthew Garth, played by Montgomery Clift, finishes impossible cattle drive begun by his father figure, Tom Dunson, played by John Wayne. At trail's end in a Kansas cow town, the cattle buyer, played by Harry Carey, Sr. tells Matthew Garth: *Three times in man's life he's entitled to bark at the moon. When he marries, when his children are born, and when he finishes a job he was crazy to begin.* Zagaris and I went *Red River* in June of 1983. We pitched it to NFL Properties: drive around America to interview pro football heroes from our youth. Properties read it as profiles in nostalgia.

Our idea was more vague and didn't necessarily translate. We viewed it more spiritually. We tagged players whose careers didn't make them rich, regular guys from the era of the single bar face masks and Riddell football shoes that epitomized the toughness of the game before its broad-base ascent. The toughness made the game worth playing. It separated the sheep from the goats and accounted for passion.

Steve Cassady

    We collected names and phone numbers and stopped all planning with that. We meant to wing it: drive to America until we found the story, or it found us. We would drive in period authenticity. I had bought a 1966 copper-colored Ford Galaxy convertible, a gas hog—it burned a gallon every eight miles. It had power steering but not power brakes. It had a heater, irrelevant in summer, but no air, irrelevant because we figured top down the whole way. The Galaxy drove like a semi and leaked vital fluids. It was two decades past its prime, the same as the players we listed.

    They came from an era we knew only from mythic recall. In the 1950s my family was the last on the block to have a television set. We lived in the Salinas Valley. TV signals from the Bay Area couldn't penetrate the Santa Lucia Mountains. We received one local channel clear and a few others in snow. We were family of five. My family was all chiefs, no Indians. Everybody had separate tastes that did not coincide. I hogged the set for two things nobody else could stand: *Roller Derby* and *Pro Football Highlights*.

    Pro Football wasn't yet invaded and contaminated by television. Networks didn't televise national weekly games; affiliates weren't broadcasting regional games. Pro Football Highlights was my only visual connection to an arresting myth. The highlights came through only one camera angle, high overhead. They elided all slop.

    We saw 30 minutes a week of long runs, completed passes, crushing tackles, acrobatic interceptions, and dramatic touchdowns. We saw no orchestrated showboating or hey-look-at-me theatrical dance routines. The announcers were hokey; they alliterated without shame. They were perfect for an audience of ten-year olds. Teams that stunk looked good on the highlights. Tobin Rote and the lowly Green Bay

Bouncing Outside

Packers played as prominent in the highlights as Otto Graham and the world champion Cleveland Browns.

Pro Football Highlights was the genesis of our cross-country trip. John Wiebusch commissioned the idea on faith and spec for $1,200 front money. John Wiebusch was nervous. The tight-asses at Properties pressed him on the wisdom of front money—especially to us. He wanted details. We evaded—we had no details except the one we were reluctant to share: we were nuts to embark. We went in character in an unstable car on an 8,000-mile road trip without budget, itinerary, or plan. We dropped the top and left Merced smoking Palma Fina cigars.

We had a Three-A map. We were headed to America in search of pro football's gritty forefathers. We drove to Westwood to pick up our $1,200. Over lunch John Wiebusch asked again if we'd scheduled all our interviews. We changed the subject. In fact, we wouldn't make our first phone call until Amarillo, Texas, two days out. We back tracked the route the Joads would have taken if Route 66 had not been subsumed by Highway 40 subsequent to the Okie exodus from the Dust Bowl.

We took off east from LA and picked up the Mojave Desert on Highway 58 through Barstow and Needles. We crossed the Colorado River into Arizona, and the trip was on. The car stalled in Kingman, and we had to replace a timing chain gasket. We stayed in an 18-dollar a night auto court, and were back on the road at first light. We drove through the Painted Desert of Arizona and the high plains of New Mexico. We reached Amarillo late at night. The Ford was wide and had bench seats. Highway 40 offered abundant shoulder room outside Amarillo. We pulled over into the sagebrush and slept in the car. We showered at a truck stop in Groom.

Steve Cassady

In McClean, some base rock was bouncing off an empty flatbed. A pebble caromed off the road toward our car and spider-cracked the windshield, next to where we had wedged a totem for the trip, an empty box of super hero cookies.

We baked all day through the Texas Panhandle and Oklahoma farm country. Zagaris wanted to stop at the federal prison in El Reno, Oklahoma. Zagaris' friend Jack Miller was serving time—he had been detained at the Canadian Border near Montreal and couldn't account for the multiple hundreds of thousand dollars in his Halliburton briefcase. The feds weren't buying that he *forgot* where it came from. They offered a plea in exchange for incriminating information on bigger criminal fish. Jack Miller said the bigger fish were man-eating sharks—cooperation would get him killed. He rode out the charge. Highway signs warned of escaping prisoners posing as hitchhikers.

The signs on the road to the prison parking compound warned of possessing drugs, alcohol and firearms. I was sure we were two out of three. I had bought a .380 Beretta when I was excavating the *Renrob* thing. *Renrob* left behind too many unindicted co-conspirators. Murder has no statute. I felt better having some way to shoot back. The Beretta and two full clips were lodged in the spare tire well in the Galaxy's trunk. I could only imagine what Zagaris was carrying. Zagaris' drug use had abated from its Altamont peak. He was as hipped as anyone about cocaine in the seventies and early eighties. He was as obtuse as anyone over its pitfalls.

Enlightenment had come with a jolt. He was recently given to small seizures called, *cerebral episodes*. Zagaris had a long-hair doctor from the Haight who said cocaine ingestion was the problem and forecast continued use as Russian roulette. He told

Zagaris he could snort the contents of a small suitcase and survive. Or he could take in one wrong line and drop instantly dead. I wasn't willing to ignore the warnings about guns and drugs. I dropped him at the gates and picked him up a few hours later.

We passed the Arkansas border and stayed at a bad motel with a leaky toilet near Little Rock. We crossed the Mississippi into Memphis the next day and hit the PR office at Graceland before the gates opened at ten. Zagaris worked up a suitable accent. He sounded like Red West, Elvis' crony. He told the PR lady we were driving cross country writing about pro football in the 50s and 60s. He said, *and no story about football in the 50's and 60s would be complete without mentioning E.*

She agreed whole-heartedly, on what grounds I couldn't say. The premise was preposterous. She asked what we needed. Michael said a tour of the estate and souvenirs. We saw the room *Elvis decorated himself.* It was hideous, with wallpaper in jungle cat patterns and a bar top scarred with razor cuts. Elvis and his crew had some bad habits. We saw the pink Cadillac Elvis bought for *Mamma.* We saw Mamma's and Vernon's and Elvis's graves.

We took pictures of ourselves in front of the wrought iron entry gates. We scooped up embossed matchbook souvenirs covers and bought a couple of shot glasses in the gift shop. It was my 40th birthday. I phoned in a radio script to Madden and had a birthday dinner chili dog at a truck stop on I-40 near Jackson. We sat near a talkative trucker. He was carrying load of Nikes from Portland to Knoxville. He was animated—read hopped on Benzedrine. I paced his meal. I wanted to finish before or after—I wanted no part of the road he was driving. We were letting the story come to us; we were in no hurry.

Steve Cassady

We rolled across Tennessee into Knoxville. From Amarillo, the second day out, we had called Doug Atkins who lived in Knoxville. Doug Atkins was a hall-of-fame defensive end. He played in his prime for the Chicago Bears; he ended up with the expansion New Orleans' Saints. Doug said call him when we hit town. We found a downtrodden motel in East Knoxville. A guy lounging under the alcove noticed our California plates. He had chin stubble. He wore wrinkled green fatigue pants. His belly protruded past missing buttons on a red aloha shirt. We chatted. He said, *Hell, we got an old boy around here you ought to talk to.* We said, *Who's that?* He said, *Doug Atkins— played for the Chicago Bears and New Orleans Saints. One of the best that ever was I'd say.*

He nodded over his shoulder to the bar adjoining the motel. *I own it. It's big Doug's hangout. He's here 'bout every night. I'll call him you want. Make sure he comes straight here after he gets off work.* In the room, we phoned Monty Stickles in San Francisco. Stickles had played for the 49ers out of Notre Dame and like Doug Atkins ended with the rag-tag expansion Saints. I wanted confirmation of a tale.

Pro Football Highlights didn't reveal it, but the game wasn't overly decorous, pre-television. Now everything is exposed and sanitized. Langston Walker, a 6-8 offensive tackle for the Oakland Raiders a few years ago, played D-line on PAT defense and regularly elevated to block kicks. Art Donovan, the old Baltimore Colts' defensive tackle, talks about his technique for discouraging 6-8 Ben Davidson from blocking kicks when Ben Davidson played for the Green Bay Packers in the late 1950s. *We get in the huddle one day when we're playing the Packers,* Donovan said, *and somebody says, wherever that big Davidson lines up, the guy in front of him punch him. He lines up in front of me, and, bam, I hit him in the stomach as he's starting to jump up for the block. He's doubling over sucking in air. The next time he jumps, he jumps up holding his stomach.*

Monty Stickles fit into the era. He was an old school tight end, when tight ends were more outside tackles than inside wide receivers. Stickles played within the rules when the rules suited him. He strayed when they didn't. Stickles loved talking about Doug Atkins. Stickles said Atkins was a legend in New Orleans: *The Big Man—He was the enforcer. With his bottle of scotch, his .45, and his pit bull, 'Rebel', he ruled the French Quarter.*

I prodded Stickles. *That's right,* he said, *It was in training camp when the Saints were training in San Diego. It was about the time the rookies started carrying those big portable stereos and playing loud rock music. Doug and Dave Whitsell came in one night about curfew time—while some rookies were playing their music louder than Doug liked it. He told them the shut it off. One of them said, 'what's the matter, old man, you need your rest?' Doug got that crazy look in his eyes like he'd have when he was getting ready to tee off on a blocker. He pushed into the rookies' room, pulled his .45 from his waistband under his shirt and pumped a round into their stereo.*

Doug Atkins, 6 foot 8, showed in the bar after six. He walked bow-legged and limped. He was a working stiff. He said he was just like everyone else; he didn't know he would afford to fix a leaking roof before winter. He was in movie once, *Breakhart Pass,* with Charles Bronson. Doug is a character named Jabbo, a bad guy who rides with Levi Calhoun, played by the bald-headed character actor, Robert Tessier. The movie takes place in cold country. Jabbo has two speaking lines, both uttered in a train car while holding a shotgun on Richard Crenna, Charles Durning, and Ben Johnson: *You Sonofabitches, what the hell's going in here.* And: *You dumb pilgrims, ain't nobody in that engine.*

In the flick, Jabbo wears a long fur coat, a wide-brimmed black hat. He mostly sits on a horse in the snow, glaring with menace before doing Levi Calhoun's dirty work. Doug Atkins had been typecast. He asked us: *Why'd you boys pick this place?* We pointed to the fat guy with the green fatigues and aloha shirt with two buttons missing over his boiler. *He said he's your buddy, and this is your hangout.* Doug Atkins said, *I hate this place. Let's get the hell out of here.* He took us to a roadhouse up the street. He ushered us in. He greeted bartenders and drinkers as if they all belonged to the same rogue fraternity.

Doug pointed to a table full of chicken wings and cheese cubes. He said, *That's dinner, boys. Least the start of it anyhow.* When the chicken wings and cheese cubes ran out, Doug pressed the owner for a few plates of oysters. We talked old-time football until the bar closed. Doug Atkins played 17 year in the NFL. In the tradition of defensive ends from Len Ford to Deacon Jones, he stalked the quarterback with abandon.

He had legendary size and strength. He was as tough as a bare-knuckle boxer. Doug Atkins' last play in professional football, his signature move: he hurdled a tackle crouched to block him. *At 39, coming off a broken leg, I jumped a tackle in my last game and got the quarterback.* He waited 13 years for induction into the Hall-of-Fame. He thought the wait was unjust.

Somebody said it was 'cause I had bad moral character. That's so much 'zaggeration. I'm a streak drinker, so they say I got a drinking problem. I carry one gun; they say I got three. I got one pit bull; they say I breed them. Listen, I'll put my character up against any of them, preachers and all...I don't lie, cheat, or steal. I've never tried dope. I don't mess with nothing that don't belong to me. But I'm outspoken, and I guess that kills everything.

We rolled over to Doug's house. Doug's wife Reba is an understanding woman. She fed us stew at three a.m., as though she were happy to do so. We came back for breakfast at 10. Doug had bought sausage sandwiches from Hardee's. We left around noon. Doug and Reba were standing near the Galaxy on the driveway. Doug said, *wait a minute, Boys, I got something...Reba! I got it, Doug,* she said.

Reba disappeared into the kitchen and returned screwing lids on two six-ounce canning jars sloshing with lucid amber liquid. *I know about this stuff,* Atkins explained. *Checked it out nineteen ways. It's good, the stuff the boys theyselves drink. They wouldn't give me nothing bad. They do, they know it's their ass.*

Doug Atkins set the tone for the story: a fast-lane roadie without itinerary, immersing into grainy recall from the NFL's colorful past. We saw it then: we were time-traveling to Pro Football Highlights of the 1950s, working off a double seam: capturing the essence of a bygone era; capturing our own *by the way how we do it.*

Clouds bunched over. I hit the button for the top. The top leaked. Warm summer rain dripped on my forearms and pants legs. We drove all that day, Saturday. We forked northeast at Bristol, Tennessee, cross the state line into Virginia and steamed through the broad green dales of the Shenandoah Valley. At Middleburg, we turned east and moved through the dusk toward Washington, D.C. We spent Saturday night and Sunday with Zagaris' brother Bruce, a Washington lawyer. Sunday night, we called Art Donovan in Towson, Maryland. We had an HBO feature filmed in a country club bar and assumed he

Steve Cassady

was a bartender like Coach in *Cheers*. Turns out, Art Donovan did okay. He owns the country club.

He was a WW II vet who bought liquor stores with the championship money he received from the Colts after the 1958 and 1959 seasons. He served us Heineken Beer and talked for two hours. *Hey, I'm from the Bronx. What else does a New York kid do? I grew up hanging around the candy store shooting the bull.* Art Donovan's father, Arthur Donovan worked for the New York Athletic Club as a boxing instructor for 55 years. Arthur Donovan, Sr. was the third man in the ring for 18 heavyweight championship bouts. Art Donovan tells great stories; Skipper McNally sober whose stories actually are true.

Donovan played maybe the worst team in pro football history, the 1952 Dallas Texans, and the best—the Baltimore Colts after Weeb Ewbank was named coach of the Colts in 1954. *I'll tell you about him. Weeb Ewbank is the frugalist sob I ever saw. Weeb Ewbank still has his recess pennies. They're in a tin can buried in Oxford, Ohio. I'll tell you what, though. Weeb Ewbank assembled the greatest football team in history, the 1957, 58, and 59 Baltimore Colts.*

Art Donovan shot the bull about famous and no-name teammates, and we hung with him rapt until late afternoon. He wanted to know our next destination and interview. We told him, Pittsburgh, and John Henry Johnson. Art Donovan hadn't forgotten old rivals. John Henry Johnson played running back at 230 pounds for the 49ers, Detroit Lions, and Pittsburgh Steelers.

Johnson had frequent run-ins with opponents. Art Donovan reset his monologue: *You know, he hit (Carl) Taseff, when he was with Detroit, about killed him. It was on an extra point. Taseff was blocking, and John Henry hit him with his elbow and broke his nose. Taseff damn near bled to death on the trip home. We said, sooner or later, we're going to get him. He was on the kickoff team, John Henry, he returned kicks. We said he comes near our bench, everyone keeps the capes on, and whoever gets a shot at him...well it was me. BA-BOOM...I hit him a shot then dropped my cape and ran out to play defense. Ray Krouse, who played for Detroit, told me, watch out for him. He's an alley cat, he'll fight you...*

We headed for the car. Donovan yelled from the top step of his wide country club porch. He said, *"Hey, you see John Henry Johnson, give him a message from me.* We said, *Sure, what is it?* Art Donovan said, *Tell him to go shit in his hat.*

We detoured into New York City. I dropped Zagaris with friends of his in the east village, rock and roll types that worked in a music store. I crossed the Triborough Bridge and ramped onto the Bruckner Expressway toward Connecticut. We'd been traveling like hobos. I had friends in Old Greenwich that offered a night's respite from the fleabag accommodations we'd frequented since leaving California.

I drove back to the village the next day and picked up Zagaris, and we headed west through the Holland Tunnel into Newark, New Jersey and west through Harrisburg, Pennsylvania en route to Pittsburgh. Zagaris said he'd had a nice visit with his music friends. They were sympathetic to his abstinence from cocaine. They offered some vitamins instead— prescribed them as beneficial. They were wrong.

We passed the inverted thimble haystacks in Amish Country at 85 miles an hour with Zagaris twitching out with a cerebral episode. He was going completely weird on me. I was furious. I castigated him for ODing on vitamins upon advice from drug users. We were 3,000 miles from home, him without medical insurance, us without money. We speculated on ludicrous worst-

Steve Cassady

case options. I told him if he died on me, I'd stuff him in an Amish haystack, and the plain people would find him come reaping time. He recovered; I calmed down; and the thing became funny before we hit the triangle where the Susquehanna and the Monongahela join to form the Ohio, the three rivers of Pittsburgh.

    We dialed John Henry Johnson. We met him near the fountain in the park by the river—across the Monongahela from Three Rivers Stadium. We hung with John Henry Johnson all day. He said he had an apartment *on the shady side of town.* He said he was mostly single. He repossessed converter boxes for Warner Cable. He was disappointed he wasn't working somewhere in football. John Henry Johnson wasn't then enshrined in the hall-of-fame and should have been. He played 15 years and retired number three all-time in rushing yards.

    He was the complete package—he ran, caught passes, blocked. He was a ferocious tough guy. An undersized linebacker named Hardy Brown played for the 49ers the same time as John Henry. At 6-0, 180 Hardy Brown was pathological. He had a slightly deformed shoulder he converted into a weapon he called his *hump.* Hardy Brown wasn't cerebral. He didn't work well within the scheme of a defense, and it shortened his career.

    He free-lanced for the purpose of inflicting pain. He set himself on the balls of his feet, crouched, and sprang like a puma—all his psychotic energy flowing through his deformed shoulder into his prey. Hardy Brown threw his hump into ball carriers and receivers with wicked intent. In 1951, he kayoed the entire starting backfield of the Washington Redskins. He claimed to have knocked out 21 that 1951 season.

    I located Hardy Brown some months later. He lived in Manteca 60 miles north of Merced on SR 99. I phoned, and his wife answered. She said Hardy was a wet brain and couldn't talk. His wife could—she kept me on the phone for a half-hour yakking about Hardy Brown's dark demons. Hardy had been sent to live in a Fort Worth orphanage as a youth. Hardy Brown's wife once saw highlight clips of him throwing his hump. She asked him how he could be so cruel. She retailed Hardy's answer: *I see the ball carrier and I picture my mother's face.*

Johnson could be measured by the bar of toughness set high by Hardy Brown. *When we was with the 49er's, he never tackled me all year in practice. He'd try putting that hump on me, he knew I'd put mine on him.* John Henry Johnson told tough-guy anecdotes that brought Pro Football Highlights alive in the dark bar where we spent most of the afternoon.

He mentioned the next guy on our list Dick *Night Train* Lane. He mentioned Larry Wilson, the St. Louis Cardinals defensive back who invented the safety blitz. *I ran over him, rolled him up, stepped on him. He played ball with one arm in a cast. He had more guts than anyone I ever played against. I'd hit, boom, and knock him down. I'd hit him with my fist. He'd still get up. Ain't too many guys I know could do that. I tried everything to intimidate him. Rolled him, rolled him back. Twist his head. He'd have his helmet 'cross his face when he got up. Couldn't ever see. But he'd get up and come back at you every time.*

John Henry told us not bother trying to find Night Train Lane at home, call him at the Police Athletic League where he works. We did and were in Detroit by noon the next day for an appointment.

Dick Lane launched a Hall of Fame career from a sign he saw out the window of a city bus in West Los Angeles. He played only one year of college, 1947 at Scottsbluff JC in Nebraska. He left school mid-year

Steve Cassady

and joined the Army. He played on service teams at Fort Ord and was offered a scholarship at Loyola in Los Angeles just before Loyola dropped football.

Lane found a job at North American aircraft. He was hired as a *filer*. He thought it was a desk job. Turns out he filed big sheets of oil-coated metal with a hand rasp. He didn't know the procedure for quitting, but he heard the word *terminate*. He told the boss he was *terminated*. He saw the logo of the Los Angeles Rams painted on the side of their headquarters on Pico Boulevard. He ventured in and sold himself from a scrapbook of clips from Juco and service ball.

Lane told us his story while driving around Detroit. He was appointed by Mayor Coleman Young to head the Police Athletic League. He didn't like the car he was given—the trunk wasn't big enough to hold his golf clubs—he was driving from one bureaucratic stop to another looking to replace the car.

Lane played for the Rams, the Lions, and the Cardinals. He invented the necktie tackle and on-field fights started because of it. He thrived in an era where cornerbacks lined up almost exclusively man-to-man. He was a born gambler betting the interception against the big catch. He won more than he lost. *My whole career they called me unorthodox. But that was more or less by design. What they called unorthodox, I called setting them up for the kill.*

We toured Detroit with Night Train Lane. Late afternoon, he dropped us at the Galaxy parked at the PAL building. At the car, we spread the US map on the hood. We drew a route with a felt-tip pen. We decided to head south through Michigan, cross into Indiana, then pick up Highway 70 at Indianapolis and swing southwest toward the Mississippi. We both knew the next stop: St. Louis to find Larry Wilson.

Bouncing Outside

We stopped that night at a crappy motel in Terre Haute. The air outside smelled of processed rubber tires. I woke at 2 am to a lighted room. Zagaris, another cerebral episode—his next to the last of the trip. He was reading the Gideon Bible and jotting funeral directions on a motel scratch pad. He wanted to talk. It was freaky, but he made it a little better by insisting I deliver the eulogy.

I imagined Orson Welles playing Father Mapple in *Moby Dick*. The thought was reassuring enough to fall back asleep. The last CE occurred two nights later at night on Highway 25 between Colorado and New Mexico. We were cresting a peak, elevation 7,500 feet. The Galaxy was cruising top down. The black sky was alive with starlight. The thin night air intoxicated. Zagaris had punched in an Elvis tape. Zagaris was rocking, miming wild ass guitar moves to *Heartbreak Hotel*. Mid-riff he was sucking in deep drafts of Rocky Mountain air. He sucked in too deep once too often and sparked a brain frazzle. Michael Zagaris overdid everything: the only man on earth could OD on vitamins and fresh air. One of a kind.

In St. Louis, we drove to Busch Stadium. In the parking lot we thought to check our finances. I had kept my share in the front pocket of my pants. Zagaris had the same system. Zagaris fished out a wrinkled dollar bill. Mine were folded, but I only had three of them. 2,000 miles from California; we had four dollars left. One of us, maybe both, hit on our next move: pictures of ourselves at Stan Musial's statue.

We found *Wildcat* Larry Wilson in his office inside the stadium. He remembered me from the draft-day stories. He was happy to recall the old days. Larry Wilson once played a game with both arms in casts. He once had a cut over his eyebrow stitched without pain deadeners because the dumb-ass Cardinals' team doctor forgot to pack Novocain.

Wilson played one game with a collapsed lung. He was like 5-10 and 160 and stood up to John Henry Johnson, which means he backed down from nobody. Larry Wilson treated us to lunch and told more stories. The free lunch preserved all four of our dollars for the rest of the trip. Back at the Cardinals' compound, we saw Bill Bidwell. Bill Bidwell shook hands and asked how we were doing. The iron was hot.

As an NFL team, the Cardinals owned 1/28 of NFL Properties. I said, *Bill your magazine sent on a story but forgot to fund our trip home.* He asked, *how much you need?* I had money due home in a few days—I calculated how much I could carve out and still make a house payment. I figured I could beat a hot check to the bank in Merced. I asked him to cash a check for $200. He nodded. I wrote it, he took it to the front and returned with the 200. I caught Larry Wilson's reaction. Incredulity. It said Bill Bidwell didn't throw money around as a habit.

200 bucks wasn't enough. It was cash only. We still had three nights lodging and 10 tanks of gas to consider. We were speeding out of Missouri on I-40. A pickup approached on the right lane. The pickup was rural, battered with a gun rack and corroding red paint. The driver and passenger looked like Sonny and Duane from *The Last Picture Show* on their way home from the border. They gestured thumbs-up to our car. They held up blue cans of Busch Bavarian beer. We gestured thumbs up. They tossed us a couple.

We finger-popped the beer and drank a freeway toast with our new friends. We knew the trip was going our way. I seized the solution. I had one tapped-out MasterCard. Technology hadn't yet introduced instantaneous credit information. Credit Card charges were phoned in. I paid scant attention to credit card procedure, but I knew merchants didn't call in a charge below a certain amount. I thought the amount was 50 bucks. I thought safe—half less a dollar.

I told Zagaris, *We'll 24-buck ourselves all the way across.* The Galaxy burned 200 miles to the tank. We checked the system at the next fill-up. It worked. We made it fool-proof. As long as we had at least 24 bucks' cash, we didn't even sweat the credit card charges—if one bounced, we could pay cash.

Bouncing was remote anyway. Extrapolating: it would take days for MasterCard to register an overdrawn card. The merchants would never know if they never called in. We hoarded the 200 for fast food and incidentals. We 24-bucked dinners, gas, and motels, seedy even by our hobo standards.

I drove the whole way, 7,000 miles in 11 days with a no planning in an unreliable car, and somehow it all worked. I wrote the story headlined *American Classics,* in two parts, illustrated by Michael Zagaris's photos. Properties paid us both a double wage. *American Classics* proved more than a brace of magazine stories. It was a personal anthem for a 12-year escapade through professional football, the last great trip.

Within three years, the string had run out. The NFL had lost its tolerance for characters. Skipper McNally had died. Duke had died. Big money took over. Corporate geeks with the sense of humor of Saddam Hussein's twin sons dominated pro football operations. Sellouts were the order of business—in every sense of the term. Spirits sagged. I had done everything I wanted to do. It was turning repetitious.

I took my last super bowl run in 1988, two years past the point I was still in the loop. I had moved on. At Merced College, I switched emphasis from English to Athletics. I was in my rookie season coaching women's softball. Six years later I would be athletic director. I wasn't planning on attending.

Zagaris talked me into it. The game was in LA, at the Rose Bowl, between John Elway's Denver Broncos and the New York Giant coached by Bill Parcells, with Phil Simms at quarterback. I didn't care about either team. John Wiebusch floated me a credential. I told him I'd see him for lunch on Tuesday. I took one last push, for sentimental reasons and to see if I still could. I could and did, but it was just more of the same.

I had moved on. The past was rich with stories, but it needed to stay in the past.

7. Highway 12—the Aviator

Hollywood is a place where a man can get stabbed in the back while climbing a ladder.
--William Faulkner

In the late 1960s, my parents bought small house in the northern Sierra, 3,500-foot elevation, in Dutch Flat, population 200, give or take the vagaries of employment statistics and the inevitability of actuarial tables. Dutch Flat features a Hollywood set of Gold Rush period architecture: a 100-year-old hotel closed for 50, a Methodist church at least that old, a general store, a post office, an Odd Fellows Lodge, and an ice cream parlor/video rental shop.

Dutch Flat is scenic, but inert. It sits among evergreens, red dirt, and undulant granite hills 3,800 feet below Donner Summit, 2 ½ miles off Highway 80, halfway between Sacramento and Reno. 3,500 feet elevation is perfect for a getaway mountain house, far enough above the snowline to be picturesque, not so far as to induce hard winter travail.

The Donner Party found out about hard Sierra winters when their cross-county journey ended in frozen death and cannibalism at 7,300 feet. The author George Stewart lived in Dutch Flat in the 1940s while he wrote the novel *Storm,* about the unfortunate Donner Party. My Uncle Ed bought George Stewart's house; we invaded Uncle Ed's Dutch Flat house for a week most summers during my grammar school years.

My Uncle Paul retired from government work in 1965. He bought a ramshackle house around the corner from Uncle Ed's. Uncle Paul's house could have understudied the West Virginia shanty where the Clampetts struck bubbling crude. Uncle Paul was clever. He had been fired from government work with the Department of Labor during the McCarthy red scare witch hunts of the 1950s. He had been accused of pinko leanings by a colleague older and less senior than he. In government work during the McCarthy era, that was a formula for instant promotion. The feds weighed the evidence against Uncle Paul. Mostly he was guilty by association for knowing some other GS guy also thought to be pink. The evidence against the other guy was his association with Uncle Paul. Awaiting eventual reinstatement with back pay, Uncle Paul worked construction in Vallejo. Uncle Paul developed skills he used to restore the Dutch Flat property.

My folks bought their place in 1967—a clapboard house, single-wall construction with an unstable foundation and a rusty tin roof. The house needed work which appealed to my father, who was possessed by a Calvinistic need for enterprise even during time off. The Dutch Flat property was irresistible because it was cheap—he paid 8.5k for the house, a large lot, a small barn, and an outbuilding in back he converted to cottage status, replete with a small kitchen and its own bathroom. I occupied the little house while writing my master's thesis for SF State in the early 1970s.

Reaching Dutch Flat from Merced is a matter of navigating 165 miles of intersecting freeways for 2 ½ hours: Highway 99 out of Merced to Sacramento, merging with I-80 in Sacramento, elevating on I-80 into the Sierra past Rocklin and Auburn, past the timber line near Colfax and ten miles later to the Dutch Flat off-ramp. One day in the early 80s I varied the routine.

I intended to reach Dutch Flat via motorcycle without consulting a map or driving a freeway. I made it except for a 14-mile stretch along I-80 between

Auburn and Colfax. In those days, I was riding a 750 Yamaha V-twin Virago. The Virago torqued in the low end; it was great for beating traffic off the light on boulevard runs. It was damaging to the spinal column for long-haul road work. I took it anyway: out G Street which becomes Snelling road. Snelling to J-59. Left on J-59 27 miles past LaGrange to the 108 junction, right on 108 toward Sonora. Left on 49 at Sonora for 76 miles to Placerville. Across highway 50 in downtown Placerville through the gold fields of Coloma to the last six miles of Highway 49 just past the hamlet of Cool—Highway 49's most picturesque section.

The final lap before the freeway leg: three miles of hairpin descent toward a canyon carved over eons by the north fork of the American River; across the canyon over a tall stone bridge with arched pilings; up a three-mile hairpin ascent into Auburn and I-80.

From there: Auburn to Colfax on I-80, dip into Colfax, pick up old US 40 for the final two-lane run of 10 miles past Rollins Lake and Gold Run. I rated the bike ride to Dutch Flat as offbeat excursion, a scenic diversion that ended with back spasms—me bent over like Mr. Barnaby in *Babes in Toyland*. Since then, upon reflection, I have registered it as coalescent.

It fueled the impulse for roads less traveled by. It provoked an innate affinity for rivers—I crossed the Merced on Snelling Road just before the town of Snelling. I crossed the Tuolumne just past LaGrange on J-59; the Stanislaus on Highway 49 at the Calaveras County line at New Melones Lake; the Mokelumne at Jackson. Along the 27 miles of Highway 49 between Placerville and Auburn, the south fork of the American parallels the road past Gold Hill and Coloma where John Marshall struck pay dirt at Sutter's Mill in 1848.

The rivers held the scenery rapt the whole way. The rivers made the trip intuitive. They connected to

Steve Cassady

things still in the future, sometimes decades into the future. At Angels Camp, where Mark Twain wrote about the *Celebrated Jumping Frog of Calaveras County*, highway 49 meets the junction of Highway 4 as Highway 4 rises towards Ebbetts Pass.

Highway 4 runs past Murphys and Arnold and 22 miles later, Spicer Meadows, with its unparalleled view of the Dardanelles. The American is whitewater heaven along Highway 49 before it turns due west below Auburn and flows past Folsom. It settles into the calm backwater of Lake Natomas and courses through the spillways of Natomas Dam then meanders flat except for occasional class II rapids for 22 ½ miles through the back yards of Sacramento. It ends in Discovery Park under I-5 in junction with the Sacramento River. Highway 49 tees up with I-80 in Auburn, the freeway between Sacramento and Reno.

Denise Catlin left I-80 for Highway 49 when she was driving Floyd Forsberg on his breakout from the Washoe County Jail. My epiphany much later: the roads were jailbreaks of my own, obscure from scrutiny and traffic. My jail was temporal oppression—mainstream crowds, thought, action, and expectation. Over time the escape routes became anodyne and balm. They transcended themselves.

In San Andreas, Highway 49 bears right, northeast as it heads toward Placerville. Highway 12 originates as the left fork of the junction with 49 at San Andreas. Highway 12 heads due west and ends up 157 miles later—maybe three hours travel time—at the Pacific Ocean. Highway 12 leaves San Andreas in the Sierra Nevada foothills with the high Sierra rising in snow-capped majesty in the background to the east. It drops into the great Central Valley through vineyards and horse country of Lockeford and Clements, fertile rolling

Bouncing Outside

terrain, the kind Barbara Stanwyk and Lee Majors ruled as the Barkleys in *The Big Valley.*

Highway 12 dead ends at Freeway 99 in Lodi but resumes west one off-ramp to the north. It crosses through Lodi on Kettleman Lane and passes under I-5. It takes the form of a long arching drawbridge at Terminous. Visible from the apogee of the Terminous drawbridge, Mt. Diablo looms dark green in the far horizon to the southwest, peaking at 3,849 feet in Contra Costa County. Rice paddies, sod farms, and asparagus fields fan out on the flanks.

A network of Delta sloughs, islands, and deep-water channels spreads low in the near horizon. Highway 12 crosses the Sacramento into Rio Vista over the half-mile long Helen Madhere drawbridge. Highway 12 dips and rises 27 miles to Fairfield at I-80 midway between Sacramento and San Francisco. It joins I-80 for three miles southwest before exiting due west into Napa, the Napa Valley wine country, and into the Valley of the Moon through Sonoma and Glen Ellen, where Jack London built Wolf House.

Highway 12 crosses the coastal range and drops onto Highway 1 at Bodega Bay, where the former 49ers coach George Siefert fishes the Pacific, and Alfred Hitchcock filmed *The Birds*. From the Sierra foothills across the valley floor to the Pacific shoreline, Highway 12 cuts two blacktop lanes 157 miles: among the most interesting roads in the universe.

Highway 12 centers in the Delta. Just across the Helen Madhere bridge over the Sacramento River at Rio Vista. A right exit splits one way south to downtown Rio Vista, the other north along a levee road toward Ryer Island. The north option ends in a car ferry boat ramp crossing Cache Slough to Ryer Island. The ferry ride is free and available 24/7/365. The Real McCoy, powered by twin diesel engines, is the oldest running piece of equipment still in use by Caltrans. It holds six to eight cars and crosses the slough in three to four minutes. From Ryer Island, the cable-driven J-Mac holds maximum four cars and takes two minutes to cross Steamboat Slough to Grand Island.

On Grand Island, a left turn from the levee road onto highway 220 runs into Ryde. The levee road itself continues to Hogback Island where an Iron Ranger collects four dollars for launching a boat on its accessible ramp. The Delta is a maze of interconnected waterways. The slough around Hogback Island is calm on weekdays, free of power boats and jet skis. I paddled around Hogback Island for a tranquil three hours early in the morning one day in the spring of 2005. Hogback Island is 75 minutes from my house. I saw bird formations in the sky in the morning while paddling around Hogback Island. Something clicked. I drove home tumbling the click through my skull.

The next night, I saw *The Aviator* at the multiplex theater in downtown Merced. *The Aviator* is Hollywood's most recent spin of Howard Hughes legend. It shows more fidelity to truth than the 1964 *roman a clef*, Harold Robbins *The Carpetbaggers*.

It opens circa 1917 with Howard Hughes as a boy in Texas while his doting mother sponge germs from his body and warns him on the imminence of cholera. It ends circa 1947 with Howard Hughes led away by his corporate handlers while babbling without coherence, the *Future is Now*. In between it retails the standard smack of the Howard Hughes legend.

Howard Hughes lived the Hollywood high life. He was a prodigal movie maker and aviator. He was a mega-scale corporate conniver. Underlying all: Howard Hughes was among American cultural history's all-time whacko. I claim access to another side, maybe a better side. That was the click I felt the

Bouncing Outside

day before. The bird formation and a man named Ed Lund. The movie sent me to the attic, where I retrieved boxes of stuff I had stored 25 years earlier.

I reacquainted myself with the legend. Short form: HRH was born with a silver spoon in the center of the "black gold" Spindletop region in Houston on Christmas Eve in 1905. His mother was high-tone Houston society. His father was an Iowa lawyer who hit for Texas to strike it rich in the oil fields. Hughes senior was stymied by rocky resistance and with a man named Sharp invented and patented a conical boring bit with 166 cutting edges that could excavate hard rock faster than any drill in use.

He leased rather than sold his bits. His bits penetrated rocky oil fields that previously couldn't be drilled. Oil was bubbling under the rocky pan, but wildcatters couldn't access it. Wildcatters broke boring for fortunes. The demand for breaching drill bits never abated. Business boomed. Howard Robards Hughes, Sr. secured epic wealth on lease royalties. Howard Hughes' parents both were dead by his 18th birthday. A Houston judge granted HRH legal adulthood when he was 19, allowing him full control of Hughes Tool. HRH was filthy rich before he could vote.

With inherited money diverted from Hughes Tool he financed forays into two incipient LA industries: movies and aviation. Like Hemingway, Fitzgerald and other 20th century legends, Howard Hughes was within five years of being the same age as the century, and he kept pace with its unprecedented technology. With his dual passions, in fact, he inaugurated much of it.

Headlines followed. HRH made innovative and budget-busting films. He bedded down starlets. He pioneered aviation development. He dodged taxes, suborned government officials, influenced elections, and bloated his carpetbagger empire. He went into business with the CIA and Richard Nixon. He went into business with the mafia and the Mormons and bought Las Vegas. He was an intensely shy and private man who found himself subject to incessant tabloid rumor, scandal, and suspicion. He died in 1976 at age 71 a mental and physical wreck.

The stuff in my attic boxes counters with his aviation episodes. On January 6, 1906, in Kalispell, Montana, 13 days after Howard Hughes was born in Houston, a hard scrabble Norwegian farm couple named Lund had a baby boy, Edward. Ed Lund's parents worked the Montana earth like their parents had farmed in Norway. Ed Lund grew up in overalls. He woke with the roosters, milked cows, chopped and stacked wood, tended stables, and forked hay. He skied two miles to school in the winter. In the summer, on dreamy occasions, he would lie on soft grass and look at birds in formation and flight.

He imagined more. Orville and Wilbur Wright inaugurated possibilities two decades earlier at Kitty Hawk, North Carolina, in 1903. Ed Lund saw the birds in the high blue Montana sky and dreaming of piloting flying machines. His parents assumed he would follow his common clave ancestry, tilling the soil until he died and was buried on the family farm.

Ed had other ideas. In 1923, at age 17, he dismayed his parents by hopping a freight train to Spokane. He worked repairing roads and tired fast of the heft of a pick and the smell of tar. He hitchhiked to Seattle and spent a season picking apples. At the end of apple season, Ed Lund and four buddies from the orchards piled into the only car among them and drove to California to pick oranges.

Two from the group were from Los Angeles. They disappeared upon arrival in Long Beach. The owner of the car left next—none of them had gas money. Ed

Lund and the other guy hitch-hiked into LA with 35 cents between them. They landed a foundry job and celebrated by investing their 35 cents in coffee and hot dogs at a stand across the street.

They loitered at the hot dog stand looking for a place to flop until work began the next day. The owner of the stand, a man named Roy, eyed them as vagrants and braced them. Ed Lund came emanated from stolid Scandinavian farm stock. He hadn't learned deception or lies. He told Roy their plight and traced it back to the road work and apple orchards of Washington.

Roy had a house in Venice with an extra room. He brought the boys home, and his wife fed them. The foundry now was too far away. Roy introduced Ed Lund to a friend who owned a garage in the neighborhood, and the friend hired him as a mechanic. Roy was expert welder—with a small shop in his garage. Ed Lund worked turned wrenches all and spent evenings learning to weld. Roy taught him well.

Ed Lund didn't leave the Montana farm to become a grease monkey. He grew restless for the reason he left home in the first place. He talked with Roy. Roy called a fellow named Harmon at Douglas Aircraft. Aviation was an infant industry in 1924, and LA was its cradle. LA is a desert leading to the Pacific. It depended for fresh water from the LA River which was depleted early in the 20th century. LA couldn't sustain growth, let alone proliferate to its present congestion without fresh sources of hydration.

William Mulholland engineered an aqueduct which diverted water 250 miles from the Owens Valley in the eastern Sierra. The aqueduct was completed in 1913. LA's future was ordained as sprawling, unregulated growth. While it was finding its eventual form, most of it after WW II, LA was perfect for the two industries captivating Howard Hughes, movies and aviation. LA in the 1920s had inexpensive and wide-open acreage plus 329 days a year of sunshine—ideal for movie sets, paradise for test flights. Movie lots proliferated. Dirt expanses with Quonset huts sprung up as airfields. Entrepreneurs envisioned limitless growth for aviation, commercial and private. LA was to flying machines what Detroit was to motor cars.

    The fledging industry was moving faster than it was training labor. Aviation in 1924 was desperate for competent welders. Ed Lund hired on at Douglas. He was inside the door of the ground floor of the aviation industry. Three years later, Charles Lindbergh would fly *The Spirit of St. Louis* non-stop and solo from Roosevelt Field in Long Island to Bourget Aerodrome in Paris, and the boom was on.

    War aces, playboys, adventurers, self-taught pilots all were building and testing aircraft in Southern California. Ted Woosley was president of Thunderbird Aircraft. Woosley had engineered a bi-plane with a rebuilt OX5 engine. Air shows were as frequent in those days as NASCAR races are today. Ted Woolsey's bi-plane won every race in its class in every air show he could find. Woolsey went into production and brought in Ed Lund as a partner. They had no corporate backing, no financial cushion at all—just the optimistic zeal of youthful dreamers.

    They built 15 planes in nine months. They sold them each for 10 to 15 thousand dollars each and used proceeds to fund construction of the next one. Thunderbird was an adventure and a training ground more than it was a sound business proposition. Thunderbird eventually went bankrupt.

    Ed Lund had climbed fast. In an emerging industry, he was now as experienced as anyone. He met Otto and Wally Timm, owners of Timm Aircraft. The Timms hired him as assistant superintendent, overseeing repair, rebuilding, and modification of various kinds of aircraft. Among other projects, Timm Aircraft redesigned and built two-seater trainer monoplanes for Roscoe Turner, maybe the most famous World War I flying ace for which aviation now was a way of life. Tire and oil companies brought advertising on the sides of the flashiest aircraft with the most renowned pilots.

Timm Aircraft redesigned a Stearman bi-plane for playboy-pilot Ross Hadley whom companies had solicited for product association. They rebuilt a Stearman for Richard Haliburton, who was planning to ship a plane by boat to various international ports then fly it into exotic lands acquiring material for a book he would call *The Magic Carpet*. Haliburton was last heard from in China where he had sold or exchanged his Stearman for a Chinese junk with the intention of sailing to the United States. No trace of d Haliburton or his junk ever surfaced again.

The Timm brothers had built a solid business. They sold it to Pacific Automotive. Wally Timm stayed on to run the business. He put Ed Lund in charge of the aircraft division. Wally Timm didn't last as part of someone else's company. In 1927, he left Pacific Automotive. He secured a new location at Grand Central Air Terminal in Glendale and once again opened his own aircraft development business.

He invited Ed Lund to join. Ed Lund went along for the wonder it promised. Ed Lund was welding an airplane part one day and noticed a thin shadow crossing his bench. He traced the shadow to spot behind his back. He saw a tall man standing there. Ed Lund had no idea how long the man had been standing there. The man spoke with a slow high-pitched Texas drawl. He introduced himself. He said he owned the shop next door. He said his name was Howard Hughes.

Ed Lund had never heard of him. He only noticed it was like looking in a mirror: same age and lanky frame, both men 6-4; same facial features and coloring. Howard Hughes said, *you're doing a fine job; I see your reputation has not been exaggerated.*

Howard Hughes said he was making a war movie that featured flight sequences. He said the movie was called *Hell's Angels*. He started talking about some of the planes he was using in the movie. He said, *Frankly, I'm having a little trouble keeping some of my French Newport planes in the air. I'd like you to come out and see what you can do.* That evening Ed Lund and Wally Timm loaded a plane with bottles of oxygen and acetylene. They flew to the Van Nuys airport where a *Hells Angels* air sequence was being shot.

Howard Hughes greeted them wearing rough knickers and an open-necked shirt. Ed Lund and Wally Timm worked two hours revitalizing some planes that had seen their best days in World War I. Ed Lund was launched. He was 21 years old and in the company of greatness. Howard Hughes would become historically iconic. Ed Lund would work backstage in Howard Hughes' aviation pursuits for the next 12 years. Ed Lund had left the farm. He had seen something in those birds in the Montana sky.

I met Lund in 1978. I had just finished writing *Spanning the Gate*, the construction history of the Golden Gate Bridge. Baron Wolman at Squarebooks had published it. Baron Wolman had taken flying lessons and bought a Cessna. Baron Wolman had a wide range of contacts in a range of eclectic endeavors. Somebody from his new circle of private pilots talked to him about Ed Lund—said Lund had written a book about his association with Howard Hughes and was looking for a writer to polish it.

Bouncing Outside

I was in San Francisco one day, talking to Baron Wolman from a pay phone in Union Square. He gave me the Lund information. I called Ed Lund in LA and flew the next day to meet him. Lund picked me up at LAX. He lived on the west side, off Sepulveda Boulevard in Culver City, but he drove to an opulent mansion in the Wilshire District, 100 Fremont Place—a gated community formed to protect old LA money from sordid urban truth beyond the gates.

The house belonged to socialite journalist Patricia Barham. Patty Barham's father had been the publisher of the old Los Angeles Herald in the Hearst chain. Her mother was an eastern European princess. Patty Barham was LA blueblood. She grew up in the same social circle as the Hearst family. She had attempted a biography of Howard Hughes collaborating with a former Hughes Aircraft executive named Marvin Burtnett. Marvin Burtnett worked for Hughes as a senior aeronautical engineer from 1939-1943, when Hughes Aircraft still was headquartered in Burbank, before it moved to Culver City and went into post-war production of spy satellite stuff.

Marvin Burtnett described his pedigree as *some working association with Howard Hughes.* In fact, he possessed little insider knowledge as much as he knew people who worked with HRH projects. Marvin Burtnett thought he could mix material from his insider contacts and with the standard HRH iconography and co-author a readable book with Patty Barham. They crapped out about the time they crossed course with Ed Lund who was attempting the same thing based on his true insider status limited to aviation episodes. They gave Ed Lund their outline and notes.

His venture and theirs was destined to go nowhere. Howard Hughes had never authorized a biography and wouldn't. Six years earlier in 1972, a writer named

Steve Cassady

Clifford Irving had staged an elaborate hoax. He claimed HRH endorsement and actually produced a manuscript. Howard Hughes had disappeared into exile in 1958. Clifford Irving's effort was sophisticated with some excellent if fabricated source material. It didn't work. Clifford Irving's biography was exposed as fake and landed him, his collaborator, and his wife in jail. Howard Hughes emerged from exile only long enough to indict Clifford Irving.

HRH's legend was complicated and abstruse. A true biography would require the subject's authorization, in addition to a ravenous staff of professional researchists with copious access to corporate, government, and public records. Ed Lund had only his first person recall concentrated mostly in the span of 12 years. Patricia Barham and Marvin Burtnett didn't even have that. Their stuff was derivative and as deep as a gossip column in a socialite monthly. Ed Lund was asking the impossible. He had a story to tell, but the intrigue of Howard Hughes had already gone ghoulish.

The public was fascinated with Howard Hughes' meretricious myth, not the aspect that purified the myth and included Ed Lund. Howard Hughes was a recluse the last 18 years of his life. He operated under the protection of a Mormon palace guard living in Bahamian hotel when he died in 1976.

He had been stalked by cooperate interests in businesses he controlled but was mismanaging. He had been sued by TWA shareholders and spent years dodging subpoenas. He had been gripped by a deteriorating mental disorder. For most of his post-WWII life, HRH was a tabloid headline waiting to renew almost daily.

Ed Lund had a story to tell, but a market for *The Other Side of Howard Hughe*s was non-existent. Lund's account was as wholesome as his Montana farm boy roots. *The Other Side of Howard Hughes* was excerpted in the March,1974, edition of *Millionaire* magazine, the same issue that ran a feature story on socialite-journalist Patricia Barham. Ed Lund's account had no comprehensive book length substance for a subject as layered such as HRH. It had neither density nor dirt. Pun intended: it wouldn't fly.

A year later in 1979, two writers named Donald Bartlett and James Steele published an extensive biography of HRH called *Empire,* subtitled, *The Life, Legend, and Madness of Howard Hughes.* It ran 652 pages of small-print text, with another 59 fine print pages of dense documentation dedicated to chronology, appendices of corporate earnings charts, sources, notes, and indices. It told the whole story.

The part that Ed Lund knew better than Bartlett and Steele comprised about 6 percent of the total Howard Hughes' story. Bartlett and Steele nailed the other 94, beginning with Hughes' foray into Hollywood and moving through the events that followed.

Howard Hughes had challenged Hollywood convention making *Hells Angels,* released in 1930, for 3.8 million dollars, the most expensive film of its time.

Hughes made *Scarface* in 1932 about organized crime. *Scarface* featured unprecedented violence, and HRH had to sue the Hollywood censors to secure its release. He made an unwatchable western in 1941, *The Outlaw,* putatively about Billy the Kid that became famous mostly for its salacious exposure to Jane Russell's heaving tits. *The Outlaw* was denied approval by the Will Hays office—Hollywood's official bluenose censors, but HRH generated profitable publicity beating back their disapprobation and securing release. Howard Hughes owned RKO Studios from 1948 to 1955 and ran it into the ground.

Steve Cassady

Howard Hughes was romantically linked to Hollywood stars from Jean Harlow to Ava Gardner to Katherine Hepburn. He married Jean Peters in 1957 but never lived with her, and the couple divorced in 1971.

Hughes formed Hughes Aircraft and funded it with ToolCo profits. In anticipation of World War II, he built experimental military aircraft that netted millions in government contracts but manufactured no planes ever used in the war effort. HRH was the subject of senate investigations for failure to fulfill his wartime contracts. HRH assumed majority control of TWA.

Hughes Aircraft segued into the 1950s building spy satellites, and HRH was linked to the CIA's attempts to assassinate Fidel Castro. Hughes *loaned* Richard Nixon's witless brother Donald $205,000; the amount was never repaid; the story leaked time to help John F. Kennedy beat Nixon by a the barest margin in the 1960 presidential election.

HRH laundered campaign contributions of 50 thousand a pop to the Nixon camp for the 1968 election through Nixon crony Bebe Rebozo. Hughes dodged taxes obsessively. He formed the Hughes Medical Institute and turned over all the Hughes Aircraft stock to the institute. His billion dollars a year weapons factory became a tax-exempt medical charity. The medical institute was never more than a shell.

Hughes' name, and the names of his henchmen, appeared consistently in conjunction with the Kennedy assassinations and the high crimes of Richard Nixon, including Watergate. HRH moved to Las Vegas, where organized crime figures began transferring casino ownership to Hughes front men. Hughes owned 65 percent of TWA but was sued by stockholders for 145 million dollars for anti-trust violations. He was forced to divest and sold his shares in 1966 for 546 million dollars. He was indicted (charges eventually dismissed) in the takeover of Air West.

Hughes lieutenant Robert Maheu had CIA affiliations linked to the Fidel Castro assassination attempts. HRH sold ToolCo stock in 1972 and renamed his empire The Summa Corporation. His health was shot by then, mental and physical. He was a full-blown hypochondriac. Phobic dementia controlled him. He was totally reclusive. Reports had him watching movies in his penthouse suite in the Bahamas 16 hours a day and receiving intermittent injections of codeine from mountebank medical practitioners.

Post-mortem X-rays showed syringe tips broken off in his arm veins. Reports had him ungroomed with stringy hair down to his shoulders, a beard as long as Methuselah's, and overgrown finger and toenails unclipped for months at a time. HRH died in 1976 aboard a private jet en route to a Houston hospital from the Bahamas. He was 6-4 and weighed 93 pounds. His appearance was so distorted, the Treasury Department used fingerprints to ID his corpse.

He left behind an estate estimated at two billion dollars. Four hundred prospective heirs claimed a share; 22 cousins emerged as the finalists. Three states—Texas, Nevada, and California—slammed the estate for inheritance taxes in disputes heard three times by the Supreme Court. Hughes Aircraft was subsumed by Hughes Medical Institute, which sold it to General Motors for five billion dollars. Four Las Vegas and six Nevada casinos fell under Summa Corporation control. HRH bio, short form: one king-hell life packed into 71 years above the ground.

Ed Lund's account was brief by comparison and homespun, but 25 years later, it plays. The story line is simple: Ed Lund was nearby when HRH made aviation history—he side kicked the purest chapters of Howard

Steve Cassady

Hughes' bizarre life story. Ed Lund considered him a friend, and a thoroughly inventive, creative, and far-thinking man. Ed Lund was caretaker to an account of HRH's genius and passion for aviation distilled of its soap-opera impurities.

HRH had migrated to LA from Houston after buying out his grandfather's and uncles' shares in ToolCo. He co-opted one of his father's business advisors, R.C. Kulldell, to run it. HRH had been corresponding with his uncle in LA, Rupert Hughes, a Hollywood screen writer. Uncle Rupert told him Hollywood wasn't as glamorous as its image. HRH went west anyway. He was 20 years old. In LA, he tagged along with Uncle Rupert.

Movies hooked him. The business side eluded him, at least at first. Major studios monopolized the industry. Flesh-eating sharks ran the majors, movie czars such as Louis B. Mayer. The czars controlled content, production, and distribution. Upstart tyros were swallowed whole.

With 40k of ToolCo proceeds, HRH bankrolled a movie about a Bowery bum who adopts a baby. The movie was written by Ralph Graves, a friend of HRH, Sr. HRH anted the 40 grand in exchange for a front row seat in production. He wanted to learn the business first hand. He amended the ToolCo charter and changed the name of a corporation within ToolCo from Caddo Rock Drill Company to Caddo Productions. HRH lost his ass on the movie about the big-hearted bum.

He worked with an amateur's grasp of cinematic complexity. He viewed the film upon completion—by then named *Swell Hogan*—and realized it stunk. He had perfectionist standards—he refused ever to release the movie. Uncle Rupert gave him hell for wasting his money on movies and advised him in avuncular fashion to return to Texas—said he was in over his head.

Bouncing Outside

HRH interpreted the advice as condescending and recast it as a challenge: make movies more extravagant than Rupert Hughes with all his Hollywood experience could even imagine. He hired an experienced director, Marshall Nielan. He watched with attention while Marshall Nielan secured experts to counter mistakes he made from inexperience in *Swell Hogan.*

He invested 150k in a Nielan movie called *Everybody's Acting* and turned a profit of 100k. He signed director Lewis Milestone to a three-year contract; their first film, a comedy, *Two Arabian Knights,* won an academy award. HRH gave himself two years to learn the business then he went full epic with *Hell's Angels.* Movie magnates ostracized him. He outfought them. He hired renegade directors, filmed risky scripts, flung Toolco money at all problems and guaranteed distribution by purchasing 125 theaters across the country.

This was 1927, the year Charles Lindbergh crossed the Atlantic solo. At the time, Ed Lund was spending weekends at the Clover Air Field in Santa Monica, exchanging repair work for flying lessons. Ed Lund learned to solo fast and spent every free hour airborne.

Howard Hughes likewise was intrigued. He conscripted Charles LeGotte to teach him. LeGotte was a WWI French ace. LeGotte said HRH learned to fly in 15 hours and could have soloed in 10. HRH was a natural. LeGotte taught him in a WACO-9, an unstable crate unsuitable for stunt flying. HRH was relentless. He purchased his own WACO-10 and retained LeGotte to train him. He conceived *Hells Angels* while stunt flying in his WACO-10.

Ed Lund and Wally Timm listened in 1928 as Howard Hughes explained the technical details of simulating WWI aerial battle scenes, filming the original planes in conjunction with miniatures. Ed Lund saw it then: Howard Hughes had fused his passions. He was teaching himself big-ticket cinematics by crash-coursing his way into aeronautics—sometimes literally.

One day early in the *Hell's Angels* production, stunt pilots encountered difficulty keeping squadron of old planes in formation upon takeoff. After take and retake, all the planes lined up except one. HRH judged it a pilot incompetence. He took the stick himself. At 100 feet altitude, the WWI relic reeled out of control, and he crashed. HRH returned to the set-in bandages.

He was obsessed with the picture to the exclusion of all else. HRH had married at 19—to Houston heiress Ella Botts Rice, grandniece to the founder of Rice Institute. Ella resisted his agenda from the start. They were young and rich. She loved the Sybaritic life of black gold Texas society. Ella's social vision bored HRH. He had other ideas. He had already diversified ToolCo. He organized the Gulf Brewing Company in anticipation of legalized beer in Texas, and beer sales in Texas doubled his inheritance. Ella came west with reluctance. After *Swell Hogan,* she seconded Uncle Rupert's advice to return to Texas. Howard would not budge. His first marriage went remote and estranged while he obsessed over dog-fight realism.

He dug into WW I research. He hired a staff of 100 aeronautics experts. He hired America's foremost airplane salesman, J.B. Alexander, and together they went worldwide to buy up outright the largest fleet of aircraft ever assembled except by a government.

From Anthony H.G. Fokker he acquired every available German plane that had seen action in WWI, Fokker D-V 11s, Gothas, massive bombers. From England, he purchased all available British S.E. 5 Sopwith Camels, Snipes, and Avros. He retained the services of 30 WWI fighter pilots and called them technical advisors. He hired 78 stunt pilots. He hired a crew of 150 mechanics for maintaining, servicing, and repairing ships damaged in the air battles that lifted off daily from three separate locations.

He acquired tracts of LA acreage, which were converted into hangars, movie sets, flying stations, and battle fields. He sectioned off one area and built an exact replica of *The Jolly Baron's Nest*—a British term the RAF used to ID the Aerodrome of Baron von Richtofen. HRH went aloft in his WACO-10, directing mimic battles, signaling airborne instructions to the ten cameramen-pilots and the 78 fighter pilots.

Hells Angels simulated reality, and reality intruded repeatedly with forced landings, accidental crackups, and mid-air collisions. Stunt pilot Al Wilson was flying a German Fokker and with 20 other pilots was returning to the *Jolly Baron's Nest*. Above a thick bank of clouds, Al Wilson's Fokker propeller flew off. Wilson bailed thinking he was over the Hollywood hills. The plane crashed into a hibiscus bush near the Beverly Hills pool of producer Joseph Schenck, who was hosting a patio cocktail party. The propeller hit a boulevard sidewalk. Al Wilson parachuted onto a neighboring roof. He jumped to ground in a leather flying jacket, a German AF helmet, goggles, and scarf.

HRH based every incident in *Hells Angels* on WW I actual occurrence. He retained Dr. K. Arnstein of the Zeppelin Company as technical advisor for replicating of the part the Zeppelin played in the air war. As the filming bore on, the technical problems grew. The old planes were made out of wood. Wood glue degraded and caked. Their fabric covering rotted.

Hughes was a perfectionist presaging later obsessions. He was maybe a half-century ahead of his time in his insistence upon the importance and accuracy of special effects. Through takes and retakes, the pilots punished the planes with trick gymnastics. Hughes' solution: replacing wood with metal and welding seamless joints. Ed Lund moonlighted on *Hells Angels* for two years helping fabricate solutions to aircraft damage made inevitable by HRH's obsessive insistence on verisimilitude.

In pure secrecy, Ed Lund also worked with a man named Barney Korn to construct miniatures to mix in with the actual planes during filming. HRH realized it was impossible to shoot everything he wanted with large planes. He authorized the miniatures. Barney Korn apprenticed Ed Lund, and they turned out miniature bombers out of wood with sheet copper covering on the wings and fuselage.

The miniature bombers had an 11-foot wing span and stood 18 inches from the ground. Miniature bombers were flown over the set of a miniature ammunition dump constructed in small scale detail on the Sunshine Ranch in the San Fernando Valley near Chatsworth. Roscoe Turner flew the actual bomber from near the San Fernando Water Reservoir, up over the hill to the miniature ammunition dump and back again. Cameras shot the Roscoe Turner's flights from every angle and altitude for three days.

Barney Korn flew in the miniature bomber on a piece of piano wire 1,100 feet long. Inside the miniature, running from the nose section to the tail, a piece of copper tubing attached to a ball bearing sheath which the piano wire slid through. With the piano wire passing through the airplane and attached to a pole, the plane would slide down from the reservoir side of the miniature ammunition dump.

At the far end of the ammo dump, Barney Korn and Ed Lund placed a large pole equipped with a fulcrum off which they could accelerate and decelerate the bomber. They filmed these runs repeatedly at different speeds and angles before actually detonating the dump. The editors cut in montage effects with the full-scale dogfight footage HRH was directing airborne from his WACO-10.

Zeppelin scenes were plot integral, but no dirigibles extant. Barney Korn and Ed Lund constructed three miniatures, 27 feet long and 30 inches in diameter, from riveted truss stamped dura aluminum alloy. Helium-filled balloons floated the miniatures. They fashioned propellers from celluloid discs. They covered fuselages with dyed Irish handkerchief linen with painted German insignias.

For the miniature dirigible shots, they used the hangars out of the Old-World Balloon School. The scene called for dirigibles dropping over the city of London after being hit broadside by a German plane. They used up different miniatures to simulate different parts of a dirigible breaking up and falling to the ground. The original they saved for the final shot when it would be set on fire and dropped over the set.

The movie was all but finished when talkies emerged. HRH had taken this film too far; he would not be left behind. An Indy filmmaker before his time, HRH could not sustain the indignity of a mega-scale flop. *Hell's Angels'* previews showed audiences had registered as incongruous the pantomime of the silent era. Planes roared. They blazed and crashed. People talked. They screamed under stress.

The silent screen rendered all of HRH's futuristic special effects incredible. HRH wouldn't settle. Advisors suggested dubbing in sound for the dogfight sequences. *Hells Angels* was two years in progress, gobbling budget, running toward three million dollars in production costs, an unprecedented number.

HRH stunned his financial consultants with a solution: rewrite the script, re-do the whole picture. The female lead in *Hell's Angels* is an English girl, played by Greta Nissan. Greta Nissan's speaking voice was Norwegian guttural. HRH scrapped it all. He had shot three million feet of film at a multi-million-dollar cost and discarded 95 percent of it.

He tested female leads to replace Greta Nissan—June Collyer, Ann Harding, Carole Lombard—and liked none of them for the part. By chance he attended a Chamber of Commerce air show at Mines Field in Inglewood, the early incarnation of LAX. The air show was a Chamber attempt to drum interest for upcoming air races. Cliff Henderson directed the show. Entry cost 50 cents. Howard Hughes drove a jalopy Model-T, dressed like a barnstormer, and never carried money—he didn't have the half-buck.

Cliff Henderson knew him. He admitted him, hoping to lure him into financing the air races. HRH couldn't care less about the air races—he was interested in the planes on display, especially the new DC-1 from Douglas. At the Douglas display he saw Jean Harlow whose husband was an airplane salesman. She was drop dead gorgeous with long blond hair. HRH was thunderstruck. He saw his female lead and visualized her blonde hair platinum. He had himself introduced. He signed her for a screen test. She aced it and was contracted for *Hell's Angels* at $125 a week.

Hells Angels resumed production. The work consumed HRH 18 to 20 hours a day. Ella Botts Rice Hughes rightfully felt neglected. She packed and left for Texas. She won a divorce decree in 1929 charging that Howard Hughes was *irritable, critical, fault-finding and inconsiderate, steadily neglecting her.* Her charges all were true—symptomatic of genius gripped by obsession. She received an uncontested settlement of one-and-a-quarter million dollars, payable in four installments. HRH bore on. He worked day and night oblivious to calendar, clock, or cost.

He spent weeks perfecting camera angles and explaining to pilots what he wanted. He flew the camera plane, directing with hand signals. He wanted to capture action, depth and suspense. He stayed up all night often to watch dawn break. He kept crews on standby for days and weeks waiting for the right combination of conditions. He watched the rushes and thought the aerial footage looked real time slow. He realized he needed a backdrop of clouds to capture the relativity of real time speed.

Southern California skies are 47 weeks a year blue. He hired a meteorologist who eventually located appropriate cloud activity in Oakland. He transposed the entire set to the skies over San Francisco Bay. No stones were left unturned in a Howard Hughes production. Film colony skeptics watched him while on the verge of ridicule. They saw no way HRH could make costs, which had risen to the neighborhood of four million dollars.

The film finally was finished in 1930. It premiered at Grauman's Chinese Theater in Hollywood, a true Hollywood event. 600 police deployed for crowd control. The film received a standing ovation upon its conclusion. The miniatures held real. Charlie Chaplin wired HRH: *After being present at your premiere, I have concluded the Zeppelin sequence is the most dramatic episode I have ever seen.*

Newspapers raved over its FX reality, calling it *a front seat at a war*. *Hell's Angels* played to capacity crowds for 19 weeks at Grauman's. Howard Hughes recouped his cost on the most expensive film ever produced. He turned a profit—or so his people spun the story. Bartlett and Steele report that he lost a 1.5 million. Either way it was only money, and ToolCo's at that. He had made his point to Uncle Rupert and the

Steve Cassady

film colony skeptics. He was 24 years old, and he had just knocked Hollywood flat on its ass.

Flash forward five years: early 1935. HRH was planning something big. Ed Lund was still employed by Timm Aircraft in Glendale. Howard Hughes still retained his shop across the street. Ed Lund was working one day with Glenn Odekirk. Howard Hughes walked in. He said, *Ed, I've just flown in from New York with a Sikorsky S-38. I've having a few problems with the plane itself, and my on-board mechanic has given up and quit. Look, Ed, how would like to go to work for me?* Ed Lund had a good job during the Depression with Timms. Howard Hughes provided the adventurous unknown. Ed Lund wasn't disposed to blind risk. He stayed with Timms. He told Howard Hughes he would work for him nights and weekends. He recommended Glen Odekirk for Howard Hughes' vacant mechanic's position.

Ed Lund and Glen Odekirk solved the immediate problem on the Sikorsky. The plane was running hot. They installed additional oil radiators. Lund stayed on call for nights and weekends. Hughes and Odekirk took the Sikorsky east and for several months. Hughes eventually caught up with Ed Lund at Timm Aircraft and told him what was percolating through his genius brain: *Ed, we are going to build a racing plane that will break every existing speed record.*

HRH flipped obsessions from filmmaking to air speed records. He assembled a staff. Glen Odekirk would manage his aviation shop. Hughes hired Dick Palmer as aviation specialist, with Stanley Bell as his assistant. He hired W.C. Rockefeller as an aerodynamics scientist and meteorologist. He hired Charlie Perrine as radio and electronics engineer and Gus Seidel to run the pattern shop. He hired Nadine Hensley, the first of his Mormon employees, as a secretary. Counting Howard and Ed Lund, a team of 15 worked for two years on a racing plane.

The team came to be known as *Howard Hughes' Hush-Hush Boys*. Ed Lund stayed with Timm except for nights and weekends while the rest of the team blueprinted the project. When they were ready for construction, Ed Lund went for the ring. He quit Timm Aircraft and became Howard Hughes's assistant superintendent in charge of production.

Movies had become secondary. Hughes had left Lewis Milestone in charge of Caddo Productions. Caddo was making Scarface and *The Front Page*. Both would be high-profile money makers. *Scarface* was a roman a clef for the rise and fall of Al Capone. It featured unprecedented violence. HRH beat the censors by claiming the film was a protest against criminal proliferation of Prohibition crime.

The *Front Page* had pedigree; it was written by Ben Hecht, adapted from his successful Broadway play co-written with Charles McArthur, husband to Helen Hayes, parents of the guy who played Dan Williams in *Hawaii Five-0:* The *Book him, Danno* guy. Howard Hughes never visited the sets while shooting was in progress. He would watch the rushes at night and leave production notes for Milestone, most of which would enrage Milestone who thought HRH was meddling. Meanwhile the *Hush-Hush Boys* were building the racer plane as compact as possible.

The intent: carry a maximum amount of supplies in the minimum of space. The fuselage design was brand new: flush riveting to eliminate any air drag from protuberant rivet heads. The design called for an 1100 horsepower engine reaching a top speed of 360 miles per hour. *The Hush-Hush Boys* were working for perfection unheard of in the aircraft industry.

Steve Cassady

The team worked double-shifts, and Ed Lund supervised both. He was often on duty 16 to 20 hours a day, seven days a week. They made a model, tested it at Caltech in Pasadena but found innumerable problems. They had to build a different cowling because the speed lagged. They had to modify the wings. Air turbulence over the fuselage wasn't correct, or the tail surface was buffeting a little in the wind tunnels. The problems continued to mount.

HRH believed if the blueprint was precise the model should work. He wasn't satisfied until the model would do 360 miles per hour. They pushed through trial and error. Secrecy created obstacles.

The team worked in the confined space of a secure hangar. That gas tanks had to be as large as possible to carry a max load of fuel. Manufacturing them and fitting them into place inside the hangar proved a monumental task. The team designed and installed the first ever retractable landing gear which folded flush with the belly of the fuselage. With airplane sitting in the hangar, its gear down, team had to simulate the air pressure against the gear to see the effect upon retraction. To simulate air pressure, the team placed rubber shocks on the gear then tried to retract it through the resistance of the shocks.

Howard Hughes would sit in the cockpit and repeat the process tens of times until he was satisfied it worked. HRH stood 6-4; the confined space made for awkward conditions. Climbing out of the cockpit one time he tore his pants. HRH climbed in and out to test and retest mechanisms. He was oblivious to his bare ass. He was concerned with airspeed. The cockpit seat was designed so Howard could adjust it upward to see when he was taxiing; downward, after takeoff.

For proper vision during landing he would land the hatch back and raise the seat, wearing a helmet and goggles, because the raised seat elevated half his face above the height of the windshield.

Howard Hughes had this feature designed for wide range flying; the height adjustment mechanism alone had been developed at a cost of six thousand dollars. Every test short of actual flight was conducted inside the hangar. Actual flight would breach secrecy but had to occur. In the middle of the night, a van company with motorcycle escorts transported the plane to Mines Field in Inglewood. The racer stayed on the ground for final checks. The team tested it by taxiing down a runway back and forth for two days. Dick Palmer suggested someone else make the first trial flight.

HRH said, *I test my own planes.* The team watched him taxi, lift off, elevate, and disappear. Time passed. No word, no sign of plane or pilot. They made phone calls trying not to sound frantic. They discovered that he had landed at Burbank Airport. He had in-flight trouble with the landing gear. He didn't have enough oil pressure to put the gear completely down. The team had worried about the problem during the hangar tests and had developed a contingency.

They connected the gear by hose to the engine and installed a gate valve. Should the plane develop insufficient oil pressure, the pilot had only to turn the valve, and engine oil would flow into the hydraulic system of the landing gear, forcing it down. HRH had to employ the safety valve and chose to land at Burbank, the closest strip. The team returned the racer to the hangar shop for modifications.

Top secrecy was blown. When carrying out tests at Caltech, the *Hush-Hush Boys* had to provide design specs to the US military. The test flight revealed the specs had morphed into a product. Top ranking USAF generals swept into the hangar. HRH wanted to deny entry but relented. The next test would make it all public anyway. The next test took place one month later. HRH arranged for officials from the Aeronautical Society to clock the flight.

Howard Hughes took off from Burbank. He flew south to Santa Ana, where a three-kilometer course had been set up over Orange County farm land. On hand to observe: Lawrence Therkleson of the National Aeronautical Association, pilot Paul Mantz, and aviatrix Amelia Earhart. Along with Charles Lindbergh and Wiley Post, Amelia Earhart was part of the three-headed face of American Aviation.

In 1932, five years after Lindbergh, Amelia Earhart became the first women to fly solo across the Atlantic. She would die at 40 while attempting to become the first woman to fly around the world. Her Lockheed Electra was lost in the Mid-Pacific near the Howland Islands. Neither she nor the plane ever was found.

Howard Hughes was in immortal company making his speed runs in 1935. Amelia Earhart and the other two observers agreed that Howard should fly both directions twice, taking off twice each against the wind and with the wind. The observers would watch and clock from an observation plane and average the speed of the four flights.

HRH maxxed the drama. At the time the speed record was held by French ace Raymond Delmotte in a plane that had cost the French government one million dollars. He had set the record on December 26, 1934 with a flight speed of 314.419 mph. HRH began his first run at 302 mph. He took his second on a dive from the sky at clocked in at 346, but the run was disqualified because of the dive. He banked in for his third run and hit 352. He did another at 339. He averaged 339, but the DQ in the second run tainted the test. For a record to stand as official all four runs had to be consecutive. Daylight was sinking into dusk. Everyone agreed to try again in the morning.

Howard Hughes took off with ease the next a.m. The first three runs surpassed anything he had done the day before. Nearing the end of his fourth run, his engine died just after crossing the clocking line. The observers and the team watched in horror as the plane disappeared on the ground in the horizon into a cloud of dust. They sped to the scene expecting a bloody mess.

They saw HRH dripping purple but unscathed. He was leaning against the plane with a pen in his hand scratching notes. He had crash-landed into a beet field. The beets were high and ripe. The produce had cushioned the belly slide of HRH's landing. He wasn't bleeding. He was drenched in beet juice.

Howard Hughes looked up: *Did I make it?* Ed Lund told him: *You not only made it, you are the luckiest guy in the world.* In spite of a clogged fuel line which forced the crash landing, Howard Hughes had set a new air speed record of 351.79 mph. HRH was most concerned over the cockpit cover which had blown off during the first run and slowed the plane 15 mph.

He was concerned that he had used only 900 of his available 1100 horsepower. The team inspected the plane and found only minor damages: a bent propeller, a torn fuselage, and a broken landing gear. Howard Hughes said, *I was trying to put the plane down, and it hit the ground when the landing gear was only about half-retracted. My supply of gasoline had apparently been exhausted, and when I tried to cut in the other tank, the motor refused to take it.* The team discovered later the H-1 racer still had 35 gallons left, but an obstruction of sediment in the feed line had cut off the fuel as though a valve had been snapped.

Howard Hughes wasn't finished with speed. He directed his ambitions toward the transcontinental record held by Roscoe Turner. During the Bendix Air Race in September, 1934 Roscoe Turner had flown from Los Angeles to New York to 10 hours, 2 minutes, and 51 seconds. HRH let on he was rebuilding his racer. He didn't let on that he had purchased a Northrup Gamma from his friend, aviatrix Jacqueline Cochran. Jackie Cochran had needed money, and Howard Hughes coveted her plane. He leased the Gamma with an option to buy.

Working with greater secrecy than with the H-1 racer, he didn't treat the plane as though it belonged to somebody else. Using the racer as a cover, *The Hush-Hush Boys* streamlined the Northrup. They changed out the engines and modified performance levels. They worked on the H-1 and the Gamma simultaneously.

HRH was dating Katherine Hepburn. He told her goodbye in LA on January 13, 1936 without divulging plans to anyone except Larry Therkleson, his official timer. HRH didn't use the whole runway on takeoff despite a 3,000-pound fuel overload. He banked before reaching the edge of the field. At 15,000 feet, he tried the radio and discovered the antenna had broken away. An hour later in thick weather, he was flying blind without radio contract. He was burning fuel too fast. He climbed another 3,000 feet.

At Santa Fe, New Mexico, the air cleared a little, but a little further on, it turned so turbulent the disc of his magnetic compass jarred itself off its pin. At this altitude he was sucking down oxygen from a mask. *It's the damnedest experience,* he said, *First you feel kind of sleepy and start to yawn. Then the heartbeats change and your head begins to buzz.*

You grab for some oxygen, draw it in quickly, and suddenly the motor seems to make more noise. Color all around changes from white to reddish yellow. It's uncanny. He flew without a radio, or even an accurate

Bouncing Outside

compass setting. At Columbus, Ohio it turned dark and he could reckon by moonlight over the Alleghenies.

Approaching Newark, he was concerned about landing without tower permission. He had no radio. He prayed he was the only aircraft on approach. He already knew he was the fastest. He roared over Newark Airport in the modified Northrup Gamma at 12.42 a.m. Elapsed time: 9 hours 27 minutes, 10 seconds. He wore a gray double-breasted suit, yellow flying jacket, helmet and goggles. He jumped from the plane and telegrammed Katherine Hepburn with this message: *Safe and down at Newark.* The following day, when the import of his achievement was revealed, He met with aviation officials and newsmen.

He said, *I wanted to go New York, so I tried to see how fast I could do it.* He added, *I have wanted to beat Roscoe Turner's record for two years. Primarily, that is why I made the hop. But I was also interested in checking fuel consumption and speed at high altitudes.* Upon return to California, HRH found that Jackie Cochran wanted to repo her Northrup Gamma.

The Hush-Hush Boys dismantled the conversions and restored the Gamma to its original condition, replete with the original engine. HRH sold the plane back. Jackie Cochran announced she would attempt to break Howard Hughes' speed record in the same plane in which he set the record. She did not account for the conversions. She never knew about them. She made the attempt in original equipment but was forced down by malfunction over Indianapolis

HRH aimed to retrofit the H-1 racer. He wanted to stay ahead of Jackie Cochran and everyone else. He sought a record which would not be surpassed. The *Hush-Hush Boys* dedicated the next six months to H-1 conversions. They designed a completely new wing out of spruce plywood, molding it in the shape of an airfoil, increasing the wind spread from 25 to 32 feet. They enlarged the fuel tanks to an increased capacity of 280 gallons. They fabricated a Durlium fuselage with flush-out welding. They replaced the engine with a Pratt and Whitney Twin Wasp, rated at 825 hp, which they supercharged to deliver 1,100 hp at sea level. They installed a new type of oxygen tank.

It had tubes leading from an oxygen tank to a rubber mask. It was designed to leave the mouth clear—for inhalation through the nose, and exhalation through the mouth. Two valves adjusted the mixture of oxygen with outside air. They test flew the newly modified H-1 along a hundred mile straightaway of railroad tracks north of LA in the deserted regions of Saugus. HRH flew the strip dozens of times, against and with the wind.

He flew each time with the engine operation at pre-calculated rpm using a predetermined rush of horsepower. After each test, the team would drain the tanks and measure gasoline and oil consumption to the last drop. They were leaving nothing to chance.

HRH was experimenting with a notion: the efficiency of high altitude flying. He sensed that instruments calibrated at sea level would register false readings at high altitude. He flew experimental runs at 15,000 feet over a 70-mile course between Mt. Wilson observatory and San Jacinto Peak over the southern Sierra. He discovered he was traveling 15 mph faster than his instruments showed.

He wanted dead on instrument readings for his record-breaking attempt to New York. The team charted fuel consumption at various speeds and different thrusts of horsepower and compared the results with the gauges. When HRH and his team had cross-referred the charts with the gauges and compiled a true measure, and calibrated the instruments, he knew: *Boy, we can make it, we can make it.*

HRH and his *Hush-Hush Boys* had built virtually from scratch the first-ever precision constructed aircraft. Not one rivet had been left to guess work; no mechanical details were left to speculation. At 11:00 pm, Monday, January 18, 1937, on the runway of Burbank Airport, HRH opened the throttle of his H-1 racer and lifted off into the deep pitch of a moonless night. The plane appeared to stagger briefly before accelerating and vaulting airborne.

He swung eastward toward the San Bernardino Mountains, over Tejon Pass. After disappearing into low clouds, he climbed steadily to 20,000 feet at 200 mph. HRH had anticipated refueling in Chicago, but he saw it wasn't necessary. The super-charged Pratt and Whitney was consuming only 27 gallons per hour, while ground speed remained hot.

He would shoot the works: non-stop from LA to Newark in the greatest sustained flight speed ever. 60 mph tailwinds between LA and Albuquerque, New Mexico, pushed the H-1 to 380 mph. Over Winslow, Arizona at 20,000-foot altitude, HRH experienced difficulty with the oxygen apparatus. He had to stay at high altitude. The mountains near Winslow rise as high as 15,000 feet. An overcast sky restricted visibility. For oxygen, the new apparatus had him breathing through a cup attached by hose to an ordinary hospital tank. The system works fine in hospitals. It had never been tried in air. It didn't regulate.

HRH was either sucking in too much or not enough. He could have done better by taking deep breaths. The cabin heater malfunctioned too; he was freezing. The first of his six gas tanks nearly was dry. He reached over to cut in the next tank and knew he was in trouble. His hands and feet felt leaden. He couldn't reach his hand from the stick to the valve, let alone flex his fingers to switch the tanks.

He couldn't get his hand to his face to pull over the oxygen cup that wasn't working. He knew he'd be asleep in minutes. He couldn't work his limbs. He couldn't bail if he had to. He had no choice: he nosed down to 15,000 feet and immediately felt better. He was fully conscious. He managed to pull the oxygen cup from his nose.

He'd heard that yelling courses oxygen into the lungs. He let out a primal scream and felt better. He moved his arms and legs until they felt right. He ripped the cup off the tube leading to the oxygen tank and stuck the tube itself into his mouth. His breathing stabilized, but with the tube in his mouth he couldn't eat. He had brought two bars of chocolate but couldn't use the oxygen tube and eat too. It was a question of eating or breathing. He chose breathing. HRH lost maybe ten minutes during the oxygen crisis.

The H-1 was equipped with an airline-type radio receiver, but HRH already decided not to fly relying upon radio range beacons used by commercial airline pilots. He was flying above all air traffic anyway. By design, he was shortening the distance by cutting across all established airways. The only purpose for the radio now was weather reports. He checked in over Wichita and St. Louis. Near Indianapolis he found the wind was causing him to drift to the south.

He angled into a crabbing position to stay on course. Over Pennsylvania, he began the long descent into Newark, still eating up the distance at five and one-half miles per minute. He pointed the racer's nose straight down and picked up speed as gravity spurred the winds and the engine. HRH had been unreported from the ground during the entire flight.

Bouncing Outside

Approaching the Newark Airfield, he throttled back his engines for the first time since lifting off at Burbank. His landing gear was down; his flaps were lowered. He was ready to scorch the runway when a United Airlines transport plane was taxiing on. The tower gave the take-off signal to the transport. HRH reacted fast. He gunned his engine and screeched up. He circled the airport ten minutes before landing. Howard Hughes had flown above the weather for 2,490 miles at an average speed of 332 miles per hour, making his official elapsed flight time 7 hours, 28 minutes, and 25 seconds. He broke his own record by nearly two hours and 67 miles per hour.

HRH always thought beyond his immediate goal: he was looking far ahead—to flying above the weather and its future for commercial aviation.

He said, *I was genuinely interested in showing the public what can be done with high altitude flying. Flying at 380 miles per hour, at 15,000 feet, felt no different than riding in an air transport plane at 150 miles per hour. The flight merely proved that technical developments in flying have been very great in recent years. Transport pilots are already aware that greater speeds can be made with modern aircraft by flying high, and also greater economy is achieved. At present, there are many minor, but difficult problems which must be solved before passenger operations can be successfully carried out at these greater heights.*

Word traveled fast. Photographers converged onto the airfield. The H-1 was highly photogenic—sleek with an unusually long landing gear and newly designed propellers. Noticeable among the throng: a claque of Japanese snapping pictures. Nobody thought about it at the time, but many did later. HRH could not have anticipated Pearl Harbor, but the photographers did. The H-1 became the virtual prototype for Mitsubishi's Japanese Zero.

Two months after his record-breaking flight, in March of 1937, HRH received the Harmon Trophy for his contributions to aviation in 1936. The trophy was established by pioneer aviator Clifford B. Harmon, in memory of departed comrades in the *Lafayette Escadrille*. Howard Hughes accepted the trophy in Washington, D.C. from President Franklin D. Roosevelt. FDR reminded HRH he was among elite company. The only other Americans to receive the award: Charles Lindbergh and Wiley Post.

HRH had made aviation history. Lindbergh was immortal for his solo flight across the Atlantic in 1927. Wiley Post was a one-eyed stunt flyer with big ideas. He wore an eye-patch and compensated for poor depth perception by relying on the rudimentary instruments of his day. In 1930, he had set the speed record for flying between Chicago and Los Angeles, nine hours, nine minutes, four seconds.

Wiley Post had died in a plane crash in 1935. He was surveying mail and passenger routes between the west coast of the United States and Russia. He was traveling with Oklahoma humorist Will Rogers. He landed in a lagoon near Point Barrow, Alaska. He lost a wing on takeoff and crashed into the lagoon.

While he lived, Wiley Post, among others, resented the fact that a dirigible, not an airplane piloted by an American, set the record for round-the-world speed.

The Graf Zeppelin commanded by Hugo Eckener in 1929 circumnavigated the globe in 21 days. In 1931, Wiley Post and his navigator, Harold Gatty, left Roosevelt field in Long Island in his Lockheed Vega named the Winnie *Mae*. They had a flight plan that included fourteen stops—among them, Newfoundland, England, Germany, the Soviet Union, Alaska, Alberta,

Canada, and Cleveland, Ohio. They shattered the Zeppelin's mark. They traveled 15,474 miles in eight days, 15 hours and 51 minutes.

They were received as triumphantly as Lindbergh had been in 1927—white house luncheon, ticker tape parade, world-wide acclaim. Howard Hughes belonged in their company—and Amelia Earhart's—with his record-breaking H-1 flight in 1936. He was 31 years old and an aviator for the ages. Ed Lund had reclined in the prairie grass as a boy on his father's Montana farm. He saw birds in formation and imagined flying. He left home at age 17 in 1923 to push his dream.

14 years later he was integrated with HRH into aviation history. He couldn't have conceived of it turning out this way. Or what was yet to come.

Steve Cassady

8. The American—Around the World

...Individuality is freedom lived.

--John Dos Passos

I grew up in Salinas off the central coast in a family of five. Salinas lies northeast of Monterey, 15 miles off the Pacific. The 15 miles deny Salinas any scenic proximity to the ocean, but they permit an alien climate that chills its inmates to the marrow. Marine winds swing coastal summer fog into Salinas in the late afternoon during the late spring and through the summer. It didn't register when I was a kid, but I hate cold weather in the spring and summer.

My mother didn't work a job. My dad raised us on a junior college teacher's salary when junior college teachers earned a reductive wage. I started teaching in the junior college the same year my father retired after 33 years in the system. I hit the lotto by comparison, just when salaries for teachers were inching toward respectability. My entry wage was higher than my father's retirement.

We grew up poor but never knew it. My father was frugal and opportunistic. My dad was an arch provider; my mother, a college graduate herself, a supreme home economist. They banked money, saw to it we ate well, lived in comfort, had big Christmases, and wore basic clothes. My father saw it as simple. He said, *you want more, work for it.* We did. It was a good way to grow. We all built esteem by carrying our own water.

We went places in the summers, free-loaded, actually. We'd spent a full week most summers at the Russian River near Guerneville with my parents' German friends, the Hellwigs, and another week at my

Bouncing Outside

Uncle Ed's house in Dutch Flat. Uncle Ed didn't care—he'd married well. My aunt Gen was a babe with family coin. Uncle Ed didn't mind sharing his summer getaway with his brother. Dutch Flat in the summer: endless exploration into mountain terrain, all red dirt, granite rocks, and evergreen trees—dawn to dusk freedom; fishing in the Bear River; swimming in the gravel pit; majestic sunsets glowing over the treetops; deep starry nights, pine smell permeating.

Reaching Dutch Flat from Salinas pre-freeway was a bitch. We piled all five into a two-door sedan in, a succession of Ford V-8's, a '37, a '49, a '54, and a '57, and drove two-lane roads that still passed through downtown, U.S.A—through Gilroy, Morgan Hill, San Jose, Fremont, Irvington, through Oakland, Berkeley, Hercules, Pinole, Crockett, across the Carquinez Straits to Benicia, Vallejo, past Cordelia Junction, Fairfield, Vacaville, and Davis. It was a long-ass trip.

We were cramped into the Ford like straphangers at rush hour without room to wiggle. My dad would transport as many comforts from home as the car would hold. We brought food. My dad couldn't see spending money in restaurants when we could pack our own, meaning my mother could. My dad had a fussy palate; he liked only my mother's cooking. If forced into attending a pot-luck he ate only what my mother brought. He ate in restaurants only under duress. He said half the time while eating out, he felt like slapping a citizen's arrest on the chef. My dad was witty.

The trip to Dutch Flat seemed like it took days. I remember Sacramento as the climax point. We rolled down the windows in Sacramento, and the summer heat rushed in. I inhaled the heat. I didn't realize at the time, but Salinas was dead to me as a place to settle with the intake of Sacramento summer heat. Sacramento intrigued me. Highway 160 took us right through town

Steve Cassady

as 15th and 16th streets. Sacramento had a capital building and Sutter's Fort. It had 100-year-old trees hanging a canopy of shade over city streets lined with two and three-story Victorian houses. It had bridges over rivers, and rivers themselves, the rush into the confluence of the American and the Sacramento. My dad ruled we couldn't ask, *are we there yet?* We were supposed to figure it ourselves and did. Sacramento meant almost: 63 miles up highway 40 through Roseville, Auburn, Colfax, Lake Rollins, and Gold Run and down dale into Dutch Flat.

    Decades later while securing spots to paddle my kayaks, I gravitated to Sacramento, especially the American River, for reasons doubtless connected to my boyhood family trips to Dutch Flat. Sacramento had a kayak shop proximate to the American.

    It had free access that actually was fee access, but the fee was trifling. Once in gear, I tested some things on the American. I sustained a routine of three-hour paddles on the American and other water ways, but I was thinking bigger. I generated a long-range someday dream: paddle the Sacramento down the spine of Northern California, the Sacramento Valley from Redding at the base of the Siskiyou to the Ryde Hotel in the Delta, a distance of 220 miles.

    I scoped the American. I pushed to find my one-day limits. Just below Natomas Dam at Hazel Avenue off Highway 50, starting at Sailor Bar on the north side, the river flows 22 ½ miles to Discovery Park and its junction with the Sacramento. It flows through exurban, suburban, and urban Sacramento, past Fair Oaks, Rancho Cordova, past Sacramento State University. It flows under I-80 near Cal Expo and under I-5 near the State Capital and Old Town.

    It crosses under bridges at Sunrise, Watt, Howe, and 65th Avenues. Mike Gallagher and I tried the

Bouncing Outside

distance on my birthday in 2004, but we started late. It was already cooking at 104 degrees when we reached Howe Avenue at the ten-mile mark. Our wives were planning a party that evening. We would miss the party if we went all the way. We took out at Howe and shagged home. I went after it solo on Labor Day weekend. The summer heat hadn't abated; still 100 plus in the afternoon, but I went at it smarter.

I checked into a hotel the night before. I had the Santa Cruze—the wooden boat couldn't navigate the few rapids, rocky shallows and errant tree limbs along the way. I put in at Sailor Bar just below Natomas Dam at 7:30 a.m. I encountered the only class II obstacle, San Juan Rapids, 45 minutes later, where the river bends left below Sunrise. Playboat paddlers come to San Juan Rapids to practice. San Juan rapids involve a left turn into fast shallows and gravel bars. The rapids are land-marked by a Tudor mansion back-dropped by trees set on a rise above the river.

A string of mansions follow west for miles. Their expansive green lawns slope toward the river from *Great Gatsby* East Egg back yard opulence. I'd shot the San Juan rapids maybe a half-dozen times. The Santa Cruze is barely suitable for the task. Playboats are better. But playboats have the long-range capability of galvanized beer tubs. I knew the drill: turn the corner at the Tudor Mansion, paddle hard to the left edge of the white water, crab low into the eddy and carve out high on the turn when it straightens out.

It wasn't intimidating. I have balance; kayaking isn't possible without it. People have asked if I ever took lessons for water exits from a rolled kayak. I said. I didn't need lessons; I don't plan on rolling. I took the San Juan Rapids without a hiccup, swilling maybe a pint of foaming water into the cockpit. Arrogance validated. Ten minutes later, I veered right around a gravel bar just as I had in June.

In June, veering right was a good decision, but. conditions had changed since June. The water was lower and faster; tree limbs more invasive. In September, right is a bad decision. The bow of the Santa Cruze hit a tree limb barely submerged between the rocks and the shore and rolled me over into an aggressive Class II current.

I kept hold of the paddle. The boat overturned and stayed stuck in the tree branch. My float bag shot into the current, along with my water bottles and food pack. I didn't have much in the float bag: wallet, cell phone, car keys, and loose change. No reason panic: the room key to the hotel room was in my shirt pocket. If nothing else, I could hike back and take a nap.

A husband-wife bird watcher team ambled by. They looked on with sympathy. I felt weak and stupid like Fredo Corleone. They helped muscle the boat through the current onto shore, where I flipped it to drain. Ten minutes later, I was back in the boat.

Five minutes after that, I came upon another gravel bar. I hung the right again when left was still the answer and flipped again. I held the paddle again, but this time the current grabbed the boat. I saw it bottom up, disappearing around the next bend.

I scrabbled up the woody shore to a walking path beyond the trees and followed the river line downstream. I couldn't see the river itself through the willows until I had passed the bend to a flat stretch where the current eddied into a still backwater pond. I walked down to the water.

I saw an old man wearing a golf hat and wrap-around ultra-dark sunglasses, the kind with wide triangular earpieces worn by octogenarians, bass fishermen, and albinos. The man wasn't fishing for bass and was not albino. He was viewing the pond. A middle-aged woman, ankle deep in the water, palm to her forehead, peered downstream.

I guessed she was his daughter. I saw what he had seen and figured they had seen my overturned boat standing where the current had taken it, the errant float bag bobbing nearby. She was looking downstream for a drowned guy bubbling to the surface like the mercury-weighted bread loaves in *Huckleberry Finn*. They saw me walk up with a paddle. The old guy looked disappointed. If I had drowned, his day was made—a big story to break the monotony around the game room at the senior center. A drowned paddler: beats the shit out of Scrabble.

I dewatered the boat, re-geared, and put in only a half-hour behind schedule. The rest of the paddle was scenic but uneventful. Sacramento Parks and Rec has done a superior job arranging its riverfronts.

The public has noticed and availed itself. Asphalt bike paths run most of the way on both sides. River access beaches like Willow Creek crop up at every thoroughfare access along the river, Sunrise, Watt, Howe, 65th. I passed swimmers, rafters, wading fishermen. I saw kids swinging from ropes connected to shoreline tree limbs. I saw hikers, joggers, and bikers. I paddled under freeways and railroad bridges.

I paddled for hours until my arms and shoulders pushed past fatigue into aching metronome rhythm. I counted strokes from bridge to bridge. I went alpha deep into the edge of hallucination. I loved it. I knew I would make it. It was Labor Day weekend. The last leg to Discovery Park the river was rimmed on both sides with recreation boats moored to the shore. People sat aboard drinking wine and beer listening to party music staring at the river. I flashed a gestalt.

Steve Cassady

The boaters are trapped by their getaway. They're moored in gas-guzzling water hogs idling their vacation as if they were stuck in a traffic jam on an urban freeway, which in a way, discounting the scene of the river, they were. I didn't feel weak and stupid any more. I was exhausted, dehydrated, and hungry, but I had paddled maybe 20,000 strokes in 5 hours 20 minutes in 100-degree temperatures along 22 ½ miles of urban waterway. I was pumped. Nothing gratifies like breaking through conventional limits. Nothing is more Emersonian or possibly American.

Howard Hughes pushed his limits beyond convention as a way of life and always wanted more. He nailed the record for speed and was intrigued by how it ramified. Howard Hughes thought bigger than most. While prodding the H-1 project to unprecedented performance, he harbored simultaneous long-haul ambitions. He was not the first to fly at stratospheric altitudes, nor the first to recognize the efficiency of flying above the weather. But he was the American pioneer in imagining its relativity to commercial aviation and the first to prove his imagination was within practical range.

His big idea was forming as early as 1933, when Wiley Post flew around the world in seven days plus and beat the mark of the Graf Zeppelin. HRH's planning occurred before, during, and after the air speed records, he set in 1936. Ed Lund recalled his first clue. He was in LA, asleep as normal people would be at 4 a.m. when the telephone woke him. Howard Hughes wasn't especially sensitive to the convenience of others. He didn't apologize for the 4 a.m. call.

Ed Lund rubbed his eyes and realized it was Thanksgiving Day. Howard Hughes was oblivious. He said, *Ed, I would like you to leave immediately for Kansas City.* Ed Lund asked, *Right now?* Howard

Bouncing Outside

Hughes explained he had decided to purchase a DC-1 from TWA. He said, *Don't crowd yourself Ed. It's just that I don't want Jack Frye* [president of TWA] *to strip the plane of its equipment before we get possession.*

Howard Hughes and Ed Lund talked for an hour. Hughes hedged on the real reason for obtaining the DC-1. He only mentioned the plane's obvious features. TWA had been using the DC-1 for surveying messenger routes. It was equipped for endurance with extra gas tanks and special riggings HRH wanted to examine. He thought it might be adaptable to experimental flying. Ed Lund hung up figuring the boss would say more when he felt like it.

In 1935, TWA flew from Mines Field—now LAX—to Kansas City once a day. Ed Lund called the counter in Inglewood and booked passage. He threw a few necessities into an overnight bag. Nasty clouds and snowfall grounded him in Albuquerque. HRH was at ensconced at 7000 Romaine in Hollywood, the retooled Lockheed factory that served as headquarters for all his west coast business. Ed Lund called him from New Mexico. HRH said, take a train to Missouri.

He filled him on the urgency. Aviation was on the move. Wiley Post's record-breaking flight spurred things. In the public mind, aviation was the province of stunt-flyers, barnstormers, and wing walkers. HRH feared commercial aviation would be stillborn as an industry unless proved reliable for the masses. He wanted to outfit the DC-1 for a record-breaking global flight that would provide said proof.

He said, *Ed, I want you along as co-pilot and flight engineer.* Ed Lund jolted with a thrill. He reached Kansas City two days after Thanksgiving. For two weeks he worked with TWA's chief test pilot Harlan Hull, giving the DC-1 a complete inspection and overhaul. He talked daily to HRH. HRH flew to

Steve Cassady

Kansas City on Christmas Eve. It was bitter cold in Missouri; the airport was all but frozen in.

HRH's response: *let's take her up for a run, then.* Ed Lund asked, *Do you have any idea what day it is?* Howard Hughes said, *sure, it's my birthday.* Ed Lund said, *It's also Christmas Eve.* HRH said, *You're right. Let's get going and get it over with.*

They trudged across the desolate airstrip in sub-zero Midwestern winter weather. Planes in those days were equipped with steam heaters; ice cannot produce steam. The heater failed while taxiing. They returned to the hangar and worked all night in meat locker temperatures managing to make the heater function. They dragged Harlan Hull from his Christmas hearth and lifted off. The heater malfunctioned again, and Howard Hughes aborted the flight. Harlan Hull threw a tantrum and left. Ed Lund worked through Christmas and days beyond baby-sitting and reworking the DC-1. HRH had gone east to conscript a crew.

By February of 1936, Ed Lund had the DC-1 equipped as specified. Howard Hughes met him in Kansas City, and they flew non-stop to New York. Several nights later, HRH told him they'd be leaving for LA at 3 a.m.—have the plane ready but leave it in the hangar. At 3 a.m., HRH arrived by taxi with Katherine Hepburn. The DC-1 was outfitted like a cargo plane—no passenger seating.

Katherine Hepburn was high-society Connecticut elegance and one-of-the-boys wrapped in a single eccentric package. Howard Hughes had taught her to fly. Katherine Hepburn sat on an overturned carton in the cargo hull and didn't complain. They flew into Burbank and began work on the DC-1. They outfitted it with special radio equipment, additional new tanks and new engines. They tested and retested the plane making all modifications in their machine shop.

They took a test run to Santa Barbara. On touchdown, HRH said, *Ed, I've decided to dump the DC-1—it'll never attain the record I want, so why waste time. Come on, we're leaving for New York.*

They lifted off and flew east. HRH stashed Ed Lund in a Manhattan hotel suite while he went shopping for planes. Luxury living wore thin. Ed Lund was on the verge of returning to Glendale when Howard called and told him they were flying to Miami. They flew south. Ed Lund stayed in a posh hotel in Miami Beach and heard second hand that HRH had test flown a Sikorsky Amphibian to Bermuda. HRH ditched Ed Lund for weeks. Ed Lund fumed at idleness. He ditched back. He flew back to New York, then to Kalispell, Montana for a vacation to visit family and fly fish for native trout.

Two weeks later, he felt a tug from destiny. He returned to New York. HRH ran him down and told him to fly to Bridgeport, Connecticut to inspect a Sikorsky Amphibian S-42 he just had purchased. Howard Hughes didn't seem to notice that Ed Lund had been AWOL for two weeks.

Ed Lund, Glen Odekirk, and a couple other *Hush-Hush* boys worked six months rigging the Sikorsky for a round-the-world flight anticipated to lift off in July. The Sikorsky skewed the schedule; it presented nothing but problems. The manufacturer wouldn't deliver parts; the plane wouldn't modify to match the blueprint.

Ed Lund was fed up with the whole thing and quit. He returned to New York and found employment with Charlie Babb, at the time one of America's leading aircraft dealers. Babb hired him to head up the New York operations at Floyd Bennett Field. He headquartered at 230 Park Avenue. In September of 1937, Howard Hughes called him at Babb. He said, *well, Ed, the plane is finally finished.* It had run more than two months behind schedule, throwing off the timing for the around-the-world flight that year. HRH didn't seem to register that Ed Lund had quit his Sikorsky project. HRH flew the Sikorsky to the west coast. Upon arrival, he learned that Lockheed had developed a new plane much faster than the Sikorsky, though it was reputed to be fragile in the tail. HRH was insecure about his records. He didn't intend to set a record in the Sikorsky just so someone else could top it in a Lockheed. HRH cut his losses.

He mothballed the Sikorsky alongside the DC-1, bought a Lockheed-14, and put his team to work. The team installed two 1,100 horsepower Wright Cyclone engines, additional fuel tanks, and gauges. They flight tested the Lockheed for extra load with 24 thousand pounds on board. The Lockheed passed all tests—it headed east by June, 1938, for final outfitting.

Ed Lund still was working for Babb at 230 Park Avenue. The aviation industry ran counter to Depression business trends. Aviation was hot in 1938. Paperwork for Babb was piling up. Plane sales were increasing, sales people and customers were mad-rushing back and forth, repair work was building up, and the Babb Company was expanding into foreign countries. HRH interrupted Ed Lund's busy schedule.

From Burbank, he called and said, *Ed, we are on our way to New York. I still want you to go with me on the round-the-world flight I want to look over the plane and tell me when it's ready after we get there.*

Ed Lund was a responsible executive with allegiance to Babb. 1938: America still was sunk in the Depression. Ed Lund was paid well in a growth industry. He'd be a fool to give up his job, but he was also hooked on HRH's manic vision. He split the difference. He angled a leave from Charlie Babb and returned work for Howard Hughes. HRH, anxious to reach New York, flew the Lockheed-14 east at 17,000 feet in 10 hours, 32 minutes, and twenty seconds. It was a new record for commercial flights. HRH had hired a publicity man named Al Lodwick.

Al Lodwick's job as PR man was to ensure the round-the-world plans received no publicity. He zinged an idea. The World's Fair was scheduled for New York in 1939. Al Lodwick convinced Grover Whelan—director-president of the World's Fair—to persuade HRH to serve as "aeronautical director". The plan ramified. HRH would name his Lockheed-14 *The World's Fair 1939,* and use it to publicize the event world-wide. HRH could bring the Lockheed into New York under cover of his new assignment.

Grover Whelan place five rooms at Floyd Bennett field at HRH's disposal. The rooms were divided into press and radio sections. The press surrounded the project with near total ignorance of its destination. Howard Hughes announced a non-stop New York-to-Paris good will flight. He said he would be delivering VIP invitations to the World's Fair. The team worked undercover in plain sight.

HRH had gone hard on emergency innovation. He wasn't ending up like Amelia Earhart or Wiley Post. He built contingency for an ocean landing. He couldn't find the lifeboat he envisioned, so he designed and built a collapsible one. Charlie Perrine and Dick Stoddart made the lifeboat radio-equipped. They designed a 15-watt battery transmitter with a failsafe. Should the battery give out, the transmitter could be operated by a hand-driven waterproof generator.

He added a bottle of hydrogen and a balloon to lift an antenna into the sky to begin transmission. He had more: 250 balloons for inflation and dispersal out the raft every half-hour to form a trail; breath condensers for straining salt water for emergency hydration; a flare pistol with red and white flares contained in waterproof tins with a can opener attached; shotguns, fighting spear, fishing rods—all this for the life raft.

HRH was in his element innovating against the prospect of doom. He insisted on an extra generator to handle overload. He anticipated forced landing in the Siberian wilds; he designed two million candlepower plexiglass lights for the nose of the aircraft. Their purpose: on close landing, one light could focus down to see a runway; the other to focus out toward infinity along the landing field.

HRH spent weeks adjusting and shielding the lights for max ground illumination with the minimum glare from fog or mist. He filled an empty space beneath the floor of the ship with thousands of ping pong balls. Ping pong balls are pure buoyancy—total vacuum inside filament thin plastic. In event of a water landing, HRH said, *it'll be like floating on a fishing line. It will help us stay afloat longer, especially if we empty the gas tanks for additional buoyancy.*

The press caught on to the commercial order for ping pong balls and interpreted it as a publicity stunt for the World's Fair—Howard Hughes distributing ping pong balls to Euros to advertise the event.

HRH was hell-bent on breaking the record. He intended on stopping in each point on the itinerary long enough only gas up, fulfill immigration requirements, and log registrations. He planned to eat on board. He tanked in fresh water and stocked the plane with food. He investigated digestive and nutritional properties of foods easy to preserve and methods of preservation.

He researched more than 20 kinds of breads and decided on Black Russian Rye because it stayed fresh for weeks. He added cheese, lettuce, tomato, ham, boned turkey, and sweet butter and milk all sealed under pressure. All the food was wrapped in waterproof bags.

He thought ergonomics before the word existed. The team built and revised mock-ups of radio and navigation compartments and installed special chairs that tested easiest on the spinal column. Parachutes were placed on racks near the door. The crew drilled with the parachutes until they were ready to jump in seconds. Each parachute was equipped with an emergency kit containing four days' supply of food, water, and hunting and fishing gear.

His staff in New York worked on navigation contingencies. W.C. Rockefeller was HRH's chief meteorologist. Charles Perrine was chief of radio. Each man had four experts assigned to him working on weather maps until they had collected data on more than one thousand observation stations.

Dick Stoddart was part of the crew on loan from NBC. Dick Stoddart suggested using an experimental compass developed by Fairchild. Normal navigational compasses could not beam in at night, except from shooting to the stars for a bearing. In overcast skies, the system failed; stars were invisible; no bearings were possible. The navigators could tune it in Fairchild's compass and point the needle on any station.

They could take two bearings on two stations and plot their position exactly—the method is called *cross bearing*. HRH adapted all modern technology. He installed a newly perfected *Sperry Gyro Pilot*, both an auto-pilot and a steering device for over water flying. HRH anticipated landing somewhere foreign without an interpreter. He composed a black book that cross-indexed simple phrases and questions into multiple languages. He condensed and classified and translated data for each leg of trip.

Steve Cassady

His black book digested information pertinent to each crew member, not only on board but upon landing. The information included distances between all points, anticipated winds, gross load, flying time, re-fueling time, proposed ground speed, air speed, and weather reports. Al Lodwick worked with the Pentagon in Washington to secure flight clearance over Canada, Germany, United Kingdom, France, Belgium, Lithuania, Poland, Latvia, and the Soviet Union. He acquired commissions plus intelligence from each government regarding fortified zones, ports of entry, and immigration and customs requirements.

Every feature of the modified Lockheed-14 was calculated, designed and built to balance the ship's center of gravity. HRH and his chief mechanic Glen Odekirk checked and rechecked the two hundred plus pieces of equipment on board.

Weight was an issue. The plane figured to carry 3,000 pounds of equipment and crew. Among the bulky innovations: 700 pounds of radio equipment installed by Dick Stoddart. Radio broadcast capability had arrived. HRH wanted radio control adapted to the Lockheed-14 for navigation and flight information.

Dick Stoddart wanted broadcast potential; the type employed by live sporting events. It was July, 1938. Europe was escalating hostility. Time for liftoff was approaching. The German Embassy sent in a telegram rescinding Germany's over-flight authorization. The Germans were preparing to invade Eastern Europe en route to conquering the world for the Third Reich. They were sensitive to the prospect of spies. They dictated alternative detour routes.

The flight was still being advertised as a good will mission to Paris promoting the 1939 New York World's Fair. Grover Whelan wanted to fly along—to make the presentation to the French himself. HRH aced him out with tact, pointing to the weight problem of an already overloaded aircraft. Crowds formed.

NBC described the scene: *Howard Hughes, the young sportsman...Howard Hughes, the aviator and his non-stop flight to Paris, France.* For two years, Dick Stoddart had fabricated a 700-pound bulk of broadcast equipment for a round-the-world flight under the noses of his employer, NBC, without divulging a hint of the actual destination. The Lockheed-14 bore the registration number, NX18973.

HRH fired up the engines and drowned out the noise of a cheering crowd, the largest at Roosevelt Field since Lindbergh took off in *The Spirit of St. Louis* in 1927. The crowd was cheering a flight they believed was destined to Paris to hand our VIP invitations and souvenir ping pong balls. HRH taxied beyond the runway onto the grass before straightening out for liftoff. With a 3,000-pound load he wanted to utilize every inch of the 3500-foot runway.

HRH cranked the engines to a crescendo. The Lockheed straddled the runway lights, and the crew felt what Ed Lund called a *tremendous impact.* HRH cut the engines. Ed Lund jumped from the plane and looked for damage. He saw none and concluded the lighting struts had struck the plane's bottom. HRH cranked the engines, and they caught. He swung around for takeoff. The overloaded ship hit the runway at barely 20 mph then picked it up. The boundary markers flashed by. The belly of the plane brushed the tops of the red clover blanketing the field at the south end of the runway. It was 7:19 p.m., Sunday, July 10, 1938. The plane lifted sluggishly as though on the edge of a stall. The crew was tense.

HRH took it into a straight climb and made a very slow turn. The Lockheed passed over Jamaica Bay at 15- or 20-feet altitude, ascending barely. It cleared house tops and power lines over the Rockaways, pointing to the Great Circle Route over the east coast of the United States, heading toward Newfoundland.

Liftoff was dicey, but HRH piloted it eventually to cruising altitude, and the crew could exhale. At 8:26, the crew could see the lights of Boston; at 9:20, Rockland, Maine; at 9:55, Novia Scotia. At 10:30 p.m., Dick Stoddart reported to headquarters at the World's Fair grounds in Flushing Meadows, Long Island.

Headquarters was connected to CBS for a national broadcast. Dick Stoddart riffed a time and temperature, our-flight-is-going-smoothly, report for the national radio audience. In the cockpit, HRH and Ed Lund glued their eyes to the instrument panel and talked about mountain ranges and checkpoints.

They reviewed scheduling. The navigators Tommy Thurlow and Harry Connors figured to alternate four hours on, four hours off. Dick Stoddart could rest between prearranged radio broadcasts. HRH would fly most of the time, relieved occasionally by Ed Lund. Tommy Thurlow was the third pilot; he could sit in between navigation stints for an hour's relief. They roared across the Atlantic toward Paris at 180 mph, their ultimate destination still secret.

Dawn broke. Dick Stoddart established radio contact with France. HRH spoke in the mike: *2,250 miles from New York, latitude 27 degrees North, longitude 50 degrees west.* He said, *we are on schedule and expect to make the Irish Coast by 10:00 a.m. With any luck, we hope to make Paris by noon, New York time, making our crossing in approximately 17 hours as opposed to Lindbergh's 33 hours.*

Visibility was poor all through the crossing. Harry Connors and Tommy Thurlow navigated by instruments without so much as a dull glow breaking through the clouds. When the overcast thinned, and the sun rose, the crew discovered they were way ahead of schedule. They had picked up some luck, a 50-mph tail wind seldom encountered over the Atlantic in July. They computed their ground speed at 250 mph.

Dick Stoddart had contacted six surface craft ranging from three hundred to five hundred miles and obtained radio bearings from each. HRH wanted Tommy Thurlow to plot radio cross-bearings. Tommy Thurlow had no faith in radio bearings from signals farther away than 150 miles. He was right.

Three of the bearings fixed the Lockheed to the south of its course; three to the north. The rising sun in the clear morning sky toward the south provided a base for recalculation. Direct measurement indicated the Lockheed was an hour out of Ireland, ahead of schedule with ample fuel to reach Paris.

HRH opened the throttles across the Irish Coast over England and into France. HRH and Ed Lund spotted the Eiffel Tower dead ahead. Descending into LeBourget, Harry Connors, Dick Stoddart, and Tommy Thurlow shifted as much weight to the tail as they could. They wanted to compensate for the lightened load of empty gas tanks. They moved themselves back as far as possible and took the emergency water cans with them. HRH circled the field and glided the Lockheed onto the runway.

The New York World's Fair 1939 completed the flight from New York in 16 ½ hours non-stop, 3 ½ hours ahead of flight plan projection. The crew was relieved to touch down after an arduous first leg. HRH exited first to flash bulbs, microphones, and ecstatic Frenchmen yelling, *Vivent les Americains.* Official marks: 3,640 miles in 16 hours, 38 minutes. HRH broke off a scoop to the gathering of press: *We are allowed two hours here, then we are off to Moscow.*

HRH: going all the way—the news was broadcast internationally. He summed up the first leg: *The flight was really uneventful despite trouble shortly after the start. The engines were rough, and the compass did not function. We radioed ahead for a new compass here in Paris, but in mid-ocean the compass began to function correctly, and we are not changing it.*

Some radio difficulties are being smoothed out, and we are installing a new antenna to replace ours which broke. The flight over the ocean was perfect. We hit the small corner of Ireland exactly on the dot we had picked. We saw a bit of land near Cherbourg on the French coast and then nothing until we came below the clouds outside of Paris.

We flew here at an average of 6,000 feet, generally at 180 to 190 miles per hour. Mechanic Lund found the elevator control slightly bent, but it was not serious enough for repairs here. The crew took no food—only water and cigarettes. We flew blind for eight hours while waiting for daylight and then flew by instruments. We saw little land until we reached Paris. We had 300 gallons of fuel left.

The American ambassador William Bullitt arranged a banquet catered in the airport administration building. The locals were celebrating. The crew was disinterested—withdrawn into preparation for the next leg. Dick Stoddart had received weather word from headquarters in New York: rain as far as the Polish border with thunderstorms in Poland itself. Rain over Lithuania. Favorable conditions over Moscow.

Ed Lund cornered HRH at the banquet. He told him he was concerned about the impact they felt on takeoff in New York. He said he wanted to give the ship a check while Standard Oil attendants filled up the tanks. HRH said, *wait, I'll go with you.* Ed Lund found a wrinkle on the skin on each side of the fuselage in the tail section. He opened up the tail cone and discovered the tail section of the fuselage had buckled badly where the shock absorption structure was mounted. French mechanics inspected the damage and said, *C'est fini, C'est fini.* No good solution appeared.

It would take a week to retool a new part. They could fly to Amsterdam where KLM worked on Lockheed aircraft. HRH appealed to Ambassador Bullitt who summoned his own American mechanic, an ex-American Air Corp sergeant named Cook. Cook arrived. He and Ed Lund rifled the aviation stockrooms for rivets, bolts, and angle iron. Ed Lund returned to the plane and found a French mechanic trying to tear down the cowlings and look at the engine.

Ed Lund was on edge. He was ready to slit the Frenchman's throat. HRH calmed him down. He induced the Mayor of Paris to bring in more soldiers to control the crowd and seal off the plane. Lockheed was notorious for fragile tail assemblies. Tommy Thurlow, Harry Connors, and Dick Stoddart tried racking out in beds supplied by the French Navy.

They couldn't sleep and returned to the hangar. HRH studied his black book and monitored progress of the repairs. Ed Lund and Sergeant Cook worked with assiduous Yankee ingenuity. They fabricated, bolted, riveted, and welded. They reinforced the fittings 20 times stronger than necessary. French dignitaries wanted HRH to return to the banquet in his honor.

He said he'd stay with the plane. The crew from Standard Oil topped out the tanks, 1600 gallons of 100 octane, plus 175 into the reserve tank to be used for takeoffs only. The crew didn't anticipate finding 100 octane fuel again until returning to the United States.

The plane was ready at 1:00 a.m., Paris time, Tuesday, July 12. The sky was pitch black; rain was falling. The hangar doors opened. Frenchmen swarmed. Soldiers carrying bayoneted rifles kept them at bay. LeBourget wasn't much better than the Orange County beet field in which HRH had crashed his H-1 Racer. It had no directional markers.

HRH asked the Airport Superintendent to guide the Lockheed with a jeep and position it for takeoff. They moved from the glare of flood lights into the black of an unlighted and unpaved runway.

Two huge towers illuminated with red lights loomed at the end of the runway. French instructions: take off between the red lights. HRH taxied behind the jeep and turned into the wind. The runway was a long undulating patch of sod. It was like taxiing on a bad soccer field. The Lockheed cranked up to 100 mph.

At that speed, the wheels were bouncing off the undulant sod and beating up the Lockheed's underside. The ship finally broke loose and lifted. Ed Lund reached for the controls to raise the landing gear. He felt another impact thud. Ed Lund choked down panic.

He thought: *It couldn't be the tail—it had to be the landing gear.* He reasoned: one wheel had hit the ground, causing a strut of the shock absorbers to strike bottom. The crew was edgy. HRH pointed to the accelerometer. He told the crew. *It's registering 2 G's. At 100 mph, no weight would press upon the wheels to cause damage.* He sensed their anxiety: *The landing gear can withstand acceleration. Your imagination is stretching. Just relax.*

HRH climbed straight for altitude and banked left heading for Moscow. Ed Lund relieved HRH after the plane leveled and was cruising. Ed Lund performed a quick calculation. He hadn't slept much the night before departure. Neither he nor Howard Hughes had slept more than an hour since they left New York 24 hours earlier. He shrugged. HRH returned to the controls. They climbed to 8,000 feet. They encountered zero visibility and ice.

The Lockheed was unequipped with de-icers. They flew by instruments. HRH was forced to gain altitude by employing more power than was fuel economic. The engines responded—the carburetors were unaffected by the ice. The silver plane broke through the storm at 16,000 feet. The crew sucked in oxygen at the higher altitude. They had been delayed eight hours with the repairs in Paris. They were anxious to make up for lost time. German instructions involved a circuitous course around Third Reich air space. HRH had other ideas. He decided to fly a straight line to Moscow. The straight line he had in mind crossed the heart of the Fatherland.

My dad was inside Germany in the summer of 1938. My dad majored in German at Cal and was teaching at Sonoma High School. His boyhood friend, Ozzie Hilton, ran a travel agency in Vallejo and had booked a bicycle tour across the Germany. He expensed my dad to lead to the tour.

My dad stashed my mother, then pregnant with my sister, with my Finnish grandmother in Berkeley. War clouds were bunching all over the Europe. Germany was mobilized. Hitler had already usurped part of Czechoslovakia. He conned British Prime Minister, *Peace in Our Time* Neville Chamberlain, into believing Nazi designs would stop with control of the Sudetenland. Hitler lied big. He was 14 months from sending up the balloon by invading Poland.

My father's brief in event of hostile outbreak were stark, and tri-partite: abort the tour, haul ass for a train station; ferry the tourists across the nearest border. My father saw Nazi mobilization up close, and it made a life-long impression. He saw the goosesteps and heard the heils. He watched a Nazi rally standing near enough to Joseph Goebbels to have fired a bullet into Goebbels' brain. My dad fantasized about taking out Goebbels. My dad might have been pedaling through the Ruhr Valley while *The New York World's Fair 1939* flew across verboten air space.

HRH pointed the plane toward Moscow through not around the German border. HRH had defied authority since birth. Adolph Hitler was a Charlie Chaplin Little Tramp look-alike: *The hell with them,* he said, *We have oxygen, we're at 16,000 feet, the weather is bad, and it's dark. We're in touch with the world by radio—they wouldn't dare try to shoot us down.*

The Germans were frantic hoping secret military installations along the straight-line route toward Moscow stayed covert. Dick Stoddart took over the radio and filibustered German *verboten* commands. He pleaded rainy and icy conditions. He relayed altitude and air speed. Paris piped in with a report of landing gear and undercarriage damage incurred in takeoff from LeBourget. Howard Hughes was displeased by Paris' inaccurate report broadcast to the world.

Dick Stoddart exploited the confusion to dissemble the Germans. He said, *I would like to say that Howard Hughes and his crew send their best regards. Everything is going great.* For a half-hour, Berlin relayed messages to Paris and to ships at sea which were picking them up and relaying them to America. The message transmitted to New York was exaggerated. Newspapers sent staff in motion to prepare HRH obituaries. Return messages tensed the crew: maybe something *was* wrong.

Ed Lund dropped the landing gear to test it. Howard Hughes leaned out of the left side window while Ed Lund lowered and retracted the gear. *It looks perfectly normal for a Lockheed retraction,* he said. Quelle Surprise*:* The French had panicked. In a

Bouncing Outside

Lockheed retraction, one wheel sometimes would remain in the landing position for a few moments before it retracts, giving the impression is failing.

On takeoff from LeBourget, the gear apparently had hit some undulant sod and kicked up a divot shower of dust and grass. French observers immediately went *C'est fini*. As the plane neared the border, the Germans flipped their mood. It sunk in finally: *The New York World's Fair 1939* was flying in sunshine above dense clouds that would make overflight spying on military buildup impossible.

Flying went smooth over Germany. Ed Lund thought of the war footing and its impact on aviation. While HRH was working on the Lockheed-14 in California, the British were negotiating with Lockheed to re-engineer 200 of the same model for what would become the Hudson Bomber.

Carl Squire, Lockheed VP in charge of sales, was in England trying desperately to land the contract. The Brits stalled—they were waiting to see how Howard Hughes' plane performed. Ed Lund had heard from Carl Squire in the days before liftoff on July 10. Carl Squire was pacing in a London hotel over the outcome of HRH's flight across the Atlantic. When the crew landed in Paris, the Brits placed the order for the 200 planes, a fantastic number for the times.

Moscow radio cut into the radio broadcast monitored by Dick Stoddart: *Hello, America. It is 4:10 a.m. here. Howard Hughes and his crew have circled the field and are coming in for a landing.* From his co-pilot's seat, Ed Lund looked ahead while Howard Hughes circled and landed pillow soft on the widest concrete runway he had ever seen.

Russian pilots had recently trail blazed the Polar route from Moscow to the US and were greeted festively by the Americans for their achievement.

Moscow wanted to reciprocate. They threw a banquet as lavish as the French at LeBourget.

The crew was hoping to lift off again as soon as possible. They had planned to fly from Paris to Moscow in seven hours, 20 minutes, but foul weather slowed it to seven hours, 50 minutes. Soviet air technicians cooperated. Soviet well-wishers didn't.

By prearrangement, Standard Oil rolled up a 2,000-gallon tank car. Soviet militia men, ragtag compared to the French soldiers, ringed the tarmac. Soviet press swarmed the plane and crew. Soviet citizens mobbed the ring established by the militia.

Ed Lund suggested to HRH: *You go with the big shots to the admin building, and the rabble will follow. I'll go ahead, gas up, and have plane ready in 30 minutes.* The crowd flocked behind HRH and the Russian entourage as expected.

Inside the building a banquet was on—food came in overloaded trays; vodka flowed like champagne had in Paris. HRH was implored to eat, drink and deliver speeches. The 30 minutes lapsed without him returning. The ship was refueled. Ed Lund looked at his watch. He walked around the tail section. He noticed the landing gear.

Apparently struck on takeoff from Paris *and* landing in Moscow, the wheel had dropped more than normal. A newsman near Ed Lund noticed the same thing and reported to radio control that the landing gear was damaged and what French had said was correct: the plane was in serious trouble. The news went inside the admin building, and HRH bolted out.

He and Ed Lund checked and rechecked. They shook out the landing gear, and every feature of the Lockheed's operating system and concluded nothing could be wrong, or the landing gear would not have retracted into position.

Bouncing Outside

The next stop was scheduled as Novosibirsk. The Russians advised against it. They said the landing strip was all mud. They recommended Omsk, even though Omsk was only a short hop from Moscow. That would mean overloading with gas at Omsk. Ed Lund didn't like the adjustment. They had made no arrangement with Standard Oil at Omsk and couldn't now. They were pushing two hours in Moscow. Russian officials handed over confidential maps to alternative landing strips in the event of emergency.

The crew lifted off at noon. HRH held the ship on the ground longer than necessary to gain speed before pulling up. He headed her toward an industrial complex beyond the end of the runway. The complex was dead ahead with smokestacks and guy wires rising 200 feet in the air. HRH cleared the stacks and wires by ten feet. Ed Lund took over controls, and Howard Hughes slept for the first time since leaving New York 42 hours earlier. Ed Lund flew three hours over a panorama of fertile fields and farming villages.

Clouds came billowing in below and obscured attempts to chart a course. HRH only catnapped. He woke and consulted the Russian maps. The maps were useless. They were detailed in 4/millionths scale, too small to yield accurate data on elevations or insight into terrain. They failed to include barometric pressures, so the crew could not calibrate the altimeter.

Overcast sunk in and stayed. They descended into the cloud bank to 9,000 feet elevation, and rain hammered the plane. Dick Stoddart was having trouble making radio computations by relay. When he finally made contact with New York, he reported they had crossed the Volga River at Kazama. They were headed toward the Ural Mountains, unable to chart elevation. HRH was back in control by now.

Steve Cassady

He descended slowly down to 3,000 feet to gain visibility. The crew tensed. Ed Lund alternated between watching the instrument panel and looking ahead for prospect of the Urals. He saw a mountain crest through the clouds. All information set the cloud ceiling at 1,000 feet. Ed Lund thought every second below 3,000 felt like an hour. In foul weather, celestial navigation is impossible. Through descent, rain came pelting down. Darkness engulfed just as they sighted ground on the west side of the Urals. They relied upon compass radio bearings which indicated Omsk dead ahead. They landed in zero visibility.

They landed on strip of mud without directional signals illuminated only by automobile headlights in zero visibility in a torrential squall. Howard Hughes' powerful nose-light innovation brought them from approach to touchdown and probably prevented them from crashing. Omsk was a remote station along the Trans-Siberian Railroad. 100 peasants, a few mechanics, and a female radio operator were on hand to greet them. The crew had withstood the worst weather of the trip. They lighted and sunk ankle deep into landing strip mud. The Siberians were confused. The plane said *New York World's Fair 1939*. The Siberians thought it still was 1938.

Refueling was as primitive as the surroundings. The gas sat in unlabeled 50-gallon drums. The peasants were not ESL fluent. The crew prevailed upon some peasants with sign language to help roll the barrels toward the plane. Ed Lund had to check each barrel, to make sure it contained gas. Octane level was anybody's guess. Ed Lund was drenched. His feet slid in the mud with every step. He had brought along some bottles of ethylene. He opened each of the 50-gallon drums and spiked in some octane and lead.

They funneled in the gas with a hand pump through a mesh screen which wouldn't permit water to pass through. The Siberians brought over an interpreter who passed along notice of another banquet in a little hut at the airport. She said, *we eat, we go to town, we sleep, everyone waiting.* Tommy Thurlow, Harry Connors and Dick Stoddart dealt Howard Hughes out of the mix.

They agreed to go with the interpreter to eat in exchange for meteorological information. Ed Lund stayed behind to supervise refueling, HRH to consult his ubiquitous black book. They were fully refueled by dawn. The right engine had developed a faulty solenoid and had to be started by an emergency shock cord with the help of some strong mechanics and a few hearty peasants. Ed Lund had them pick up two lengths of rope attached to the other end of the shock cord and stretch the cord as taut as they were able.

The tight cord whipped the blade, and the engine fired right up. The left engine started without a hitch. Rain was falling in sheets. The engines droned. Ed Lund turned on the million candle power nose lights. The next stop was Yakutsk, U.S.S.R. The flight had consumed 47 hours since lift-off in New York.

Conditions in LeBourget and Omsk conditioned the crew to anticipate disaster. Yakutsk was a long leg. The plane was overloaded with fuel. Takeoff would require taxiing speeds of 100 mph. The windshield washed with rain. The planed droned to a high rev pitch and skittered along the muddy runway.

A slight rise in the ground shot the plane into the air, and HRH eased back on the controls to avoid setting back on the ground. The overloaded plane hovered close to the field's surface. HRH turned it too close to the ground. It stalled and began falling off to the right wing. HRH cracked the throttles wide open.

Steve Cassady

He felt a surge of power and moved the controls wheels a complete turn to the left.

The surge activated the ailerons. The right wing rose, but the left wing started dipping. HRH turned the wheel slightly to the right, and the ailerons slowly picked the left wing out of danger. The plane began to gain some altitude. HRH red-lined the engine revs. The plane nosed up through the clouds and leveled into blue skies and sunshine.

It was Wednesday, July 13, 1938, at 5:00 a.m., New York time, 57 hours after departure. The crew circled for landing at Yakutsk, the last stop in Russia. The crew was happy to land on an adequate runway in sunshine and daylight—unhappy to see 50-gallon drums stacked on the runway instead of a tanker truck.

On the ground, minus the pelting rain, they replicated the laborious refueling of Omsk, spiking octane into gas barrels with ethyl and lead, warding off the same attempts at hospitality of the other stops, answering the same questions about a plane named 1939 in the year 1938.

They started the right engine with the shock cord again, and it fired up again on the first attempt. They had been on the ground three hours. HRH opened the throttles upon liftoff and began looking at maps. They would have to clear the 7,000-foot Verkhoyansk Mountains that rose between Yakutsk and the coastline of the Bering Sea.

Weather reports reassured: continued clear skies. Ed Lund took the controls while HRH went to the rear for sleep. Ed Lund looked up and saw the Verkhoyansk range. He pulled back the stick, and the mountains seem to rise. He pulled back until the plane reached 16,000 feet and cleared the peaks. Ed Lund put it on autopilot. 1938 aviation technology: the navigators control the direction of the flight; autopilot controls the altitude. Ed Lund adjusted the autopilot frequently as the plane encountered new mountains of which they had no record. Below, the land was desolate between the mountains, the barren heart of the Siberia.

The plane was making good time, catching up with the hours lost in Paris, Moscow, Omsk, and Yakutsk. Dick Stoddart re-established direct communication with World's Fair headquarters. The Lockheed headed northeasterly toward the tip of Siberia and the 60-mile width of the Bering Straits and Cape Prince of Wales on the extreme northwestern tip of Alaska.

The sun sank lower in the sky as they swung from northwest to north. It touched the horizon and below. The sun was below the horizon, but it still was light outside, and the crew could see mountains 40 or 50 miles away. HRH announced, *It's midnight.*

They flew across the land of the midnight sun in perspective shared by very few. They flew beyond the Siberian mountains. They flew over low swamps and tundra, interlaced with streams and spotted with ice. They were 2,500 miles from touchdown in New York. They had no check points until they hit the tip of the Bering Straits. They flew at 12,000 feet plotting a course to Nome but exploited excellent flight conditions and sped north to Fairbanks.

From that altitude, the Bering Sea appeared as an expanse packed with endless blocks of ice. They were flying at 203 miles per hour, 69 hours from takeoff at New York. The flight crew expected bad weather over the mountains into Fairbanks but encountered none. They landed at 8:15 p.m. EDT on Wednesday, July 13, 1938. Ed Lund saw a tanker truck with Pan Am ground personnel standing by for refueling.

Alaska was not yet a state. It had been purchased by the US in 1867. It was declared a territory in 1912 and wouldn't become the 49th state until 1959, but landing in Fairbanks felt like home. Wiley Post's widow was among the crowd greeting the plane. As the Pan Am men refueled the ship, HRH commandeered a car and drove the runway. He estimated it as 2800 feet long. Short. It ended abruptly in a stand of tall trees. HRH had the crew remove 1500 pounds of over-water emergency equipment. Minus 1500 pounds, the plane's balance was altered. It screeched down the runway, throttle wide-open. HRH lifted off and cleared the tree branches by what felt like inches. Upon impulse, he opened the inspection door beneath the fuselage and released a long trail of ping pong balls.

12 hours and two minutes out of Fairbanks, 85 hours after departure, they landed without incident or delay in Minneapolis. HRH cut the motors and waited while expert technicians filled the tanks with 100 octane fuel, the first 100 octane since LeBourget in Paris. They were gliding down a smooth concrete runway for takeoff 33 minutes later.

33 minutes after that, they ran into the worst thunderstorm Ed Lund had ever seen. The plane hit the simultaneous junction of a warm and cold front. It dropped like an elevator with a severed cable, plummeting 1,000 feet. The plane felt like it was being ripped apart. HRH and Ed Lund expected the windshield to crack open under a pounding fusillade of rain. They buttressed against the storm. They rose bent-kneed from their seats and placed their palms flat against the wind shield.

Up ahead they saw thunderheads extending to altitudes of 20,000 feet. They had no choice—no islands in the sky. They plunged ahead through the eye of the storm. Rain turned to hail. Hailstones pummeled them, large and hard as golf balls. Hailstones tattooed the fuselage. Hailstones dented the leading edge of the wings. HRH ordered the crew into the rear of the ship

Bouncing Outside

to watch the tail stabilizer. Ed Lund's and Sergeant Cook's Yankee ingenuity in Paris probably was keeping them airborne and alive. Lockheed was notorious for fragile tail assemblies. Three Lockheed-14 models in service for Northwestern Airlines already had lost their tail sections and crashed.

Tommy Thurlow asked HRH, *Do you think we should cut the speed and ease up our load. I don't believe our ship can stand up under this strain very many moments longer?* Howard Hughes was seldom inclined to retreat. He replied, *Don't worry, we've got it now—we're almost through the worst of it.*

Ed Lund felt no optimism; he didn't think HRH's plucky resolve was heartfelt. The storm didn't behave; it got worse. HRH throttled back, as Tommy Thurlow had suggested. He cut it as much as he could and still remain aloft. HRH and Ed Lund kept their palms pressed flat against the windshield.

It looked hopeless when a widening rift of blue appeared in the clouds. HRH headed for the rift at full speed. They cleared the cloudbanks. The air smoothed. The plane stabilized. The crew released from mortal terror. Dick Stoddart said, *You have no idea what is going on in New York.*

HRH didn't flinch while within a hailstone of doom. He freaked big time at the account Dick Stoddart was unfolding. He listened while passing the Statue of Liberty. He saw for himself while circling Floyd Bennett Field for a landing. It was variations on a single theme: human masses waiting cut loose, Howard Hughes cynosure of all frenzy.

HRH panicked at the sight—bumper-to-bumper strings of cars along every direction that contained a road. HRH relayed concern for the plane to flight headquarters. Flight headquarters reassured him of an orderly reception. Headquarters had commissioned

Steve Cassady

1,000 patrolmen on foot to control and restrain the masses. They had arranged a flying squad of motorcycle police to ring the plane once it landed and came to a stop. HRH scorched the wheels and sped in. Police and fire sirens wailed, bells rang, automobile horns honked. People in crowds estimated at 20,000 crushed against police barriers and chain link fencing straining to catch a glimpse of the silver monoplane. They stood, screamed, jumped, and waved newspapers, hats, and flags. Inside the airport fence, hundreds of VIP rushed the plane.

    They outran the motorcycle police just as a section of fence gave way and 15,000 celebrants broke onto the airfield. HRH taxied toward the Administration Building. He was petrified he would crush people under his wheels or hack them bloody with propellers. The crew stayed inside the plane until the police re-established crowd control.

    Millions of people all over the world were listening to their radios. Dick Stoddart's NBC people had hooked up complex broadcast capability directly to radio headquarters inside the Roosevelt Field Admin building. The first words they heard did not emanate from Howard Hughes. They heard: *Get out of here.* Then: *It's taking too much time.* Then, *Ah! Shut up.*

    Grover Whelan came on: *Did you have any trouble, Mr. Hughes?* HRH couldn't begin to answer. He lied: *No, none at all.* Mayor Fiorella LaGuardia piped in: *Seven million New Yorkers offer their congratulations for the greatest record established in the history of aviation. Welcome home!*

    HRH: *I am ever so honored thank you very much.* The crew unfolded their cramped bodies. They shook hands. They slapped shoulders. They were exhausted. They had just made history. It was 2:37 p.m. Eastern

Daylight Time, July 14, 1938. It seemed like forever, but they had been away 91 hours and 17 minutes.

Wiley Post and Harold Gatty had made somewhat the same journey five years earlier. HRH and his crew covered 14,824 miles, averaging 208 mph, and cut Post's and Gatty's record by more than half.

They had flown 71 hours and 14 minutes and spent 20 hours, three minutes on the ground. Dick Stoddart was the first to step from the plane. Dick Stoddart smiled and answered perfunctory questions. The rest filed down. HRH stepped out last.

Cheers rang out. Flush bulbs popped like Gatling gunfire. Ed Lund inspected the exterior. The fuselage looked like it had been beaten with a ball peen hammer. HRH was peppered with questions. He said, *All I can say is that this crowd is frightening me more than anything else that happened in the last three days.*

The crew was shoved into cars. Police motorcycles escorted them to mid-town to the Hampshire House on Central Park South. The next day, on July 15, 1,800 tons of ticker tape fell like snow from skyscrapers along Wall Street to honor an aviation milestone.

Politicians and dignitaries trumpeted tedious congratulatory oration. HRH presented a long speech professing ideal for the advance of aviation. This might have been the purest moment of his life.

He was selfless in the moment. He extolled technology for making his flight possible. He extolled man-hours of dedication by designers, engineers, and mechanics. He talked about his flight bringing the world closer. He talked about Italy holding the record for seaplanes; Germany, the speed record for land planes; England, the record for altitude; Russia, the record for distance.

HRH bequeathed the record just set to his own country. *If this flight may have demonstrated to Europe the fact that American Engineers and American workmen can build just as fine and just as efficient an airplane and its equipment as any other country in the world—then I certainly will feel it all has been worthwhile.* The ceremonies and celebrations last throughout the day. HRH bore up only to a point.

Once on the street, by prearrangement, he met William Randolph Hearst, Jr. They headed out to East River at 23rd Street, to the old New York Yacht Club Basin. Hearst Jr.'s 30 hp Aeronca was perched on floats in the basin. Hearst Jr. flew HRH in the Aeronca to Sands Point on Long Island Sound, where the Hearst family had a getaway mansion. Katherine Hepburn was waiting for him.

The movie, *The Aviator,* was released to theaters in 2004. Ed Lund would have hated it. It ran 170 minutes and belied its own irony: less than one minute of the 170-minute running time was devoted to the singular achievement of Howard Hughes' aviation career—the actual round-the-world flight of the silver monoplane, *New York World's Fair 1939.*

Not a single cockpit frame made the film. Such was the lurid appeal of Howard Hughes' bizarre iconography. 169 minutes pandering to his myth. A movie called *The Aviator* focusing predominantly on scandalous inference: plane crashes, Hollywood intrigue, Hollywood starlets, corporate intrigue, senate investigations, drug use, and phobic dementia.

Howard Hughes had opened the future for international commercial aviation. He flew the plane. He worked the stick. He stared down the elements. He was heroic and made history. He was an aviation age Lewis and Clark opening the Northwest Passage for westward expansion.

The moment was pure American aeronautic achievement, and it rated less than one minute in a 2004

Bouncing Outside

bio-pic of HRH titled *The Aviator*. On December 14, 1973, Howard Hughes was inducted into the Aviation Hall of Fame. HRH contacted Ed Lund and asked him to accept on his behalf.

Howard Hughes was nearing the end. He had lived in a secluded bubble more or less since 1958. He wired his appreciation and send Ed Lund as stand-in. Ed Lund was honored. He was conversant with all the lore—the tabloid spectacle that had become Howard Hughes' public image—and resented how widely it missed the mark of the man he knew.

Ed Lund was naïve. He invested more in human nature than human nature could ever return. Ed Lund hoped the Aviation Hall of Fame award would revive awareness of Howard Hughes' immense contribution to the Air and Space age.

In the days that followed HRH's induction Ed Lund read only critical accounts of *Mr. Elusive*: *Hughes Missing Again…Hughes Absent…Hall Show Gets off the Ground Despite a Truant Hughes…Hughes Won't attend Hall of Fame Induction.*

Ed Lund was incensed. He flew next to Howard Hughes when Howard Hughes transcended the rest. Ed could provide eyewitness testimony: HRH was an aviator for the ages. He had the story first-hand, not the whole story, but in his mind, the best story.

I knew Ed Lund for a short while in the late 1970s. I worked his material. I researched the rest. I read Bartlett and Steele. I saw *The Aviator* in 2005. I reworked Ed Lund's account, told his tale, and flashed a judgment: He was right. His story trumps the rest.

It is history big time live. It still excites.

Steve Cassady

9: Out of the Past—California Remains

...So, everything will live where the river goes.
                                                    --Ezekiel 4:9

Ground fog settles into the Central Valley by mid-December and stays unwanted more or less until February. It is ugly, low-ceiling fog turning January in Merced into a butt-ugly month. January in Merced is morose. The fog holds good moods hostage. Holiday glows have all but banked by New Year's Day.

Holiday bills come due in January. Half-heard on the news: a mathematician calculated with algorithms that a January day, the 24th actually, is the most depressing day of the year. I believe it. Payday seems distant. Nature lies dormant. Fields are fallow.

Lawns stunt and stay brown. Deciduous trees seem permanently leafless. Solar light cannot penetrate the hovering gray. Ground fog obscures sunrise and sunset both. Dawn breaks after seven. Darkness falls before five Dripping cold air permeates to the pores. The dew point sits in the low 40s. The great Central Valley in January might as well be Wales.

The weather perks only when it rains. Sunlight breaks the cloudbanks post-storm but only for a tease. January rains warm and wets the ground. Warmer, wetter ground releases humidity into cold air and forms more fog at the dew point. The thing cycles bleak for 31 long-ass days. Winter weather in Merced reminds me of holiday fruitcakes.

Holiday fruitcakes originated in the Middle Ages. Medievals baked holiday fruitcake from stuff they could preserve when winters iced them over. They spiked the dark gloppy results with brandy or rum. Fruitcake tastes like shit and probably tasted like shit to the medievals. Nobody with better options eats fruitcake. Medievals had no options. They did the best they could with what they had. Fruitcake is mid-winter penalty for not building in cheerier options.

I was sitting in TOGOs tucking into soup and a sandwich one day right after the first of the year. The skies outside were obdurate gray. I watched a teen-age kid schlep his tray to the next table. The kid styled out skate rat—light gray knit hat over long, dirty blond hair, sweat pants, black T-shirt, over a long-sleeve dingy white thermal undershirt. Both earlobes were studded with cubit zirconium. His sweatpants sagged below his ass, showing striped boxer shorts.

The kid exuded zit-pocked anger. His black T-Shirt was silk-screened with: *The Only Job I need is a Blow Job.* I double-took the T-shirt. I bifurcated the sentiment into *No Redeeming Values,* and *The End is Near.* I castigate post-millennium youth with impunity. I risk stereotyping and becoming a stereotype: middle-aged curmudgeon who forgot what it's like, bitter old guy deaf to teenage expression and angst.

I plead guilty but indifferent—I'm not seeking introspective reform on the subject of Generation X. I found the kid as depressing as the January weather. A thought sparked in. I had free time to kill before school started after MLK Jr. Holiday. I had just put new tires and brake pads on my Mustang. The depressing kid kicked me out of gray stasis. I conjured a road trip: Southern California to buy a coffee mug. Find solace, solitude and sunlight. Connect some dots.

I started drinking coffee at age 27 while working graveyard at a parking garage in San Francisco, 840 Sutter. I turned coffee snob my second or third year at Merced College, two decades before Starbucks baristas

Steve Cassady

were pimping foamy mocha frappes to Niles and Frasier yuppies. I'm old school. I drink coffee black, authentic. Jerry Salley, the evangelist turned hippie, had an office next to mine. He educated me on coffee blends. He pointed to a place in San Francisco, Freed, Teller, and Freed. Freed, Teller, and Freed was located on the corner of Polk Street and Frank Norris Alley, but it could have been set in London.

 Freed, Teller, and Freed smelled like what it was—a specialty shop with glass fronted dark wood display bins of coffee beans, and tea leaves. Freed's' roasted imported beans on the premises wafting intoxicant interior aromas. Freed's' beans marked the ideal point of the spectrum between brand name coffee in two-pound vacuum tins available at any grocery store, and the Starbucks profusion yet to invade from Seattle.

 Starbucks offends. Anything proliferating franchise links in a corporate chain like Starbucks is not a good thing. Anything spiked that strong with caffeine then cut that far back with high-fructose foam spells unexamined oxymoronic excess. Jerry Salley formulated a blend I haven't varied since: one-half Italian; one quarter Mocha Java; one quarter Celebes.

 I know where Italy is. I didn't know until taking a 2005 Cub Scout field trip with my ten-year-old to a dry-docked WW II submarine at pier 45 in San Francisco that Java and Celebes are located in Indonesia. I saw them on the patrol map in the ward room of the USS Pampanito. The USS Pampanito was the movie set for Kelsey Grammer's *Down Periscope.*

 Kelsey Grammer plays a smart-ass malcontent consigned to skipper an anachronistic diesel sub in the nuclear age. Freed, Teller, and Freed was located a block-and-a-half down Polk Street from Swan Oyster Depot. Swan Oyster Depot opened in 1912, and like Al The Wop's, hasn't had a new idea since opening day. It

Bouncing Outside

is narrow shop with a marble bar and 18 rickety stools. Swan is as pressed for elbow room as the interior of the Pampanito. Swan serves the best Crab Louis's on earth. Swan's Crab Louis's are assembled with lettuce, mountainous fresh crab and Louis dressing.

Swan is run by a family of Sicilian brothers, sons, nephews, and cousins named Sancimino. The Sancimino clan clings to exacting recipe standards. Swan sells 200 to 300 pounds of fresh crab a day. The Sanciminos scorn any crab Louis made with ingredients past lettuce, fresh crab, and Louis dressing, especially beets. Swan is not a secret. A line forms daily for a vacancy on one of the 18 rickety stools at the marble bar. Timing is everything. I would schedule visits to Freed's around an early lunch at Swan.

A great day defined: leave Merced in time to miss incoming SF traffic at the bridgehead and arrive to park in Frank Norris Alley prior to 11:20. Frank Norris Alley always yields a parking spot, atypical of San Francisco. Anytime later than 11:20, the lines to the marble bar at Swan start spilling out the door up Polk Street. Prior to 11:20, the day is set.

Run a tab at Swan—oysters on the half-shell, Crab Louis, bread, Chardonnay by the glass. Browse the used book store across the street. Buy blended beans at Freed's. Stop at the French Boudin French bread bakery out on Ninth Avenue and load up on sourdough rounds. Make it back across the bridge before afternoon commuter traffic bunches to clog the 580 through Castro Valley, Pleasanton, and Livermore. Cross Altamont Pass into the valley, along back roads—mostly Highway 33, and home by late afternoon.

The Loma Prieta earthquake in 1989 changed things. Freed's buckled. Freed's needed earthquake retrofits that wouldn't prove cost-effective. Freed's shuttered its retail store on the corner of Polk and Frank

Steve Cassady

Norris Alley. They opened a mail order operation in South San Francisco. Now I eat at Swan and buy sourdough rounds without buying coffee beans at Freed's on Frank Norris Alley. I don't have to. Freed's UPS's the beans to my door from a standing order.

Freed's enables a morning ritual that has captured me since I saw the *Ipcress File* in 1965. Michael Caine as iconoclastic British spy Harry Palmer begins his day grinding beans and French pressing his morning coffee. Director Sidney J. Furie zooms in on the scene and stays with it: Harry Palmer starts his day civilized. It made an incipient impression in 1965.

I since have adapted my own version. I rise before first light while my family sleeps. I walk our obstreperous beagle, Baskerville, so he can crap on the canal bank not on my lawn. I pull in three papers from the driveway, *the SF Chronicle, Modesto Bee the Merced Sun-Star*. I grind Freed's beans and drip a pot of coffee. I turn the stereo to FM-classical out of Sacramento, 91.7. I start with the Chronicle cross-word and work through the sports page, SF news, world and national news and on to the local rags. I drink coffee, listen to music, read papers.

I prep with ritual for an unfolding day. A coffee cup, a mug actually, plays in. China cups with saucers are incongruous. Fred Astaire drinks coffee from a china cup and saucer fighting a hangover in *Holiday Inn*. China cups and saucers are suitable for skinny guys in slacks who wear ascots and dance. Styrofoam is unthinkable. Common cups and mugs, chain-logo mugs, *World's Greatest*...mugs, souvenir mugs, mugs with precious hallmark sentiments, cartoon frames, pictures of pets, or holiday decoration are beneath ritual standard. The right mug needs distinction, heft, and grip and proper volume.

Bouncing Outside

My dad used to drink his morning coffee out of thick, off-white diner mugs, the kind they serve at Ole's in Alameda, or in Marny's in the Film Noir classic *Out of the Past,* starring Robert Mitchum as the doomed protagonist Jeff Baily and Jane Greer as the mantrap brunette, Kathie Moffat. My dad's mugs had heft. That part works, but not the grip. I could fit only my index and middle fingers through my dad's diner mugs.

In the proper grip, the thumb rests on top of the mug handle, the pinky finger on the bottom, and the three in the middle fit through the handle. The mug has to hold enough coffee for a full cup drunk down before the last sips have cooled, so two full cups carry through reading the papers. I know a source: a historic dive near Union Station in LA called *Philippe the Original.*

Philippe is old LA situated across Alameda Street from Union Station, across North Main from Olvera Street, a mile from Dodger Stadium, within view of the LA City Hall, and on the fringes of Chinatown. Philippe stays open 16 hours a day, six a.m. to 10 p.m., 363 days a year. Philippe closes on Thanksgiving and Christmas days. Philippe opened in 1908 and calls itself the home of the French Dip sandwiches.

Like Swan Oyster Depot and Al the Wops, Philippe doesn't innovate. It had long wooden tables with sawdust on the floor in 1908, and it has long wooden tables with sawdust on the floor in the new millennium. Philippe has ambience like Hurstwood's turn-of-the-century saloon in Theodore Dreiser's *Sister Carrie.* It caters to a turn-of-the-20th-century palate.

It serves dipped and carved roasted meat sandwiches—ham, lamb, beef, pork—on French rolls. It serves salads, sides, and deserts. It serves hardboiled eggs pickled in beet juice. It prepares and serves 300 pounds of pickled pigs' feet every week. It has a news and candy stand near the door. It sells distinctive logo

Steve Cassady

mugs with *Philippe* slant-scripted on the side, and *The Original* printed in a tail under the script. The mugs come in blue or red logos. The choice is easy. I can't do red. Fresno teams are red. Merced's are blue. Bloods and Crips. I had a blue Phillipe mug once but I broke it. I needed another one.

All the plan I had: break off a day-and-a-half January getaway: cross back roads into Southern California, reacquire a coffee mug with heft, grip, and volume. Not much of a plan, but I've found meaning in less. I left before at first light on Friday, January 6. The date checked in as a good omen. January 6 would have been the 100th birthday of Ed Lund. I headed south.

Weeks earlier I was listening to sports talk, KNBR-680 out of San Francisco. One of the morning guys, Brian Murphy, talked about attending the USC-UCLA football game the next day. He was leaving that day and driving. He spun off a frivolous talk-show topic. He said the three routes from the Bay Area to LA—Highway 1; Highway 101; Highway 99/I-5—define the personality types of the travelers.

Brian Murphy missed a route. I count four with four personality types. Mine was the fourth—freeway avoider—primarily via Highway 33. James M. Cain's, *The Postman always Rings Twice*, opens with the line: *They threw me off the hay truck at noon.* James M. Cain wrote pithy noir novels, *Postman, Double Indemnity, and Mildred Pierce*. His protagonist in *Postman* is named Frank Chambers. John Garfield plays him in the original 1946 movie; Jack Nicholson in the 1981 remake.

In the flick, Frank Chambers is bumming along pre-freeway California two-lane roads lined with T-top telephone poles strung with high tension wires, hitchhiking through towns that time forgot. Frank Chambers meets femme fatale Cora, played by Lana

330

Bouncing Outside

Turner, at a roadside diner owned by her sloppy Greek husband, Nick. Highway 33 feels like the road Frank Chambers bounced along when they threw him off the hay truck at noon.

Highway 33 cuts a roughly parallel course to SR-99 and I-5. It runs a slightly diagonal north-south from Tracy to Ojai, through every tumbleweed town of 10,000 population or less—some much less—strung along the west side of the San Joaquin Valley: Tracy, Westley, Patterson, Crows Landing, Newman, Gustine, Dos Palos, Firebaugh, Mendota, Coalinga, Avenal, McKittrick, Darby Acres, Taft, and Maricopa. I picked up 33 at Dos Palos, cutting over from 152, 20 minutes from my house. Night gave way to a low-light dawn and thick fog gray just outside Dos Palos.

Highway 33 isn't pure two-lane: it merges with I-5 for 12 freeway miles before ramping off and resuming two-lane west en route to Coalinga. The fog hung over farm labor towns Firebaugh and Mendota. The sun burned through at Three Rocks, less a town than a labor camp in the west side dust.

33 serpentines through low hills the other side of I-5 and flattens into oil fields congested with working derricks. Sun shone on the oil rigs and the green hills in the western horizon, but the fog returned on the other side of town and hovered for the 108 miles to Taft.

Fog camouflaged the desolate scenery from Coalinga to Taft: fallow ground, shriveled dry shrubs, flat expanse filled with oil rigs near Darby Acres and into Taft. Fog obscured all visual presence of the town of Avenal on the east side of 33 and its main industry, the state prison on the west side.

California prisons are built on cheap land cross-referred to a population without political juice to prevent an influx of inmate proximity. Avenal fits on all counts. The prison was constructed on jackrabbit

Steve Cassady

flatland next to an impoverished town economically dependent on a tax base from farm labor wages, the lowest in the system.

The fog burned off to stay past Taft up the hill to Maricopa and southwest into Cuyama Valley. I sped 80 miles from Cuyama Valley to Ojai through a lonely stretch of nut trees, grape vineyards, occasional farm houses, and mountain passes. 33 rises and winds through the Los Padres National Forest. It elevates to 6,000 feet before dropping into Ojai. Ojai has dominant Mediterranean architecture and has the look and feel of Tuscany. It sits high above Ventura and Santa Barbara, 15 miles from the Pacific Ocean. Howard Hughes attended prep school in Ojai, at the Thacher Academy.

Ojai is a lush garden town, population 10,000, sitting above the coastal winds and fog with year-round perfect growing conditions. It hit 76 degrees that January 6. Ojai is all vegetation: hibiscus, hydrangea, and bougainvillea bushes; citrus, palm, oak, and Manzanita trees. Highway 33 ends in Ojai. I dipped down highway 150 onto highway 101 South and ran into thick Friday freeway traffic and heavy overcast. The fog was allowable. Coastal fog follows marine conditions and has the good grace to stay high. It doesn't enclose and invade like ground fog in the valley. I detoured into Oxnard and Highway 1.

I drove past the Naval Air Station at point Mugu and down the Pacific Coast highway. I stayed right and kept within the flow of the traffic for the 50 miles along the Ocean to Santa Monica. The CHP assimilates local traffic laws through all along Route 1 on the 27 miles through Malibu to Santa Monica. Highway cops prowl for speeders. I have a Passport Solo on the dash of the Mustang. It keened with K-band signals all the way to Pacific Palisades. The Pacific shore on the right had turned gray and white-cap rough from mid-winter overcast. Traffic was thick. Surfers in wetsuits looked like upright seals roaming the beaches. I was hungry. I thought Pink's in Hollywood.

Pink's is an LA landmark. It features chili dogs and has since the Depression when a guy named Paul Pink sold hot dogs from a push cart for 10 cents. Paul Pink worked the corner of La Brea and Melrose. In 1939, Pink stationed his push cart in the weeds. In those days, La Brea and Melrose was out in the sticks. Paul Pink built his current stand in 1946. Pinks might be the most famous hot dog stand in America. Pink's has its own web site. It has walls full of celebrity photos from Steve Martin to Doctor Phil to Henry Winkler.

I'd never eaten at Pink's. Pink's is open from 9:30 a.m. to 2:00 a.m., 3:00 a.m. on weekends. Pink's clientele is diverse, ranging from winos to tourists to movie stars. Patrons stand in line to eat chili dogs at Pink's. Celebrities limo up to the corner of Melrose and LaBrea and order Pink's chili dogs. Howard Hughes ate chili dogs from Pink's when he still was sane.

I cut off PCH on Sunset at 2:30. La Brea is 20 miles inland from PCH. Sunset was impacted all the way. In Brentwood, a jogger stopped to power walk up a block long grade. The jogger reached the top of the grade before I did. Sunset bisects the 405 on an overpass in Westwood. I looked down. The 405 was dense with traffic stalled in both directions. I stayed with Sunset past UCLA and Bel Air. I broke at Doheny in Beverly Hills and scaled downhill to Santa Monica Boulevard. Santa Monica was better but not much. I turned right onto La Brea at 3:50. Typical LA Friday afternoon: 20 miles traveled in an hour 20 minutes.

25 people waited in line in front of me at Pink's. 25 people stood in line when I was leaving the dining patio. Lines are a constant at Pink's. Pink's was

disappointing. Pink's has landmark features and mediocre chili dogs. I am a connoisseur. I had a better chili dog at Cupid Dog in Chatsworth a month earlier. I eat better ones at Darla's in Atwater ten minutes from my house. The meat and buns at Pink's were okay, but the onions didn't crunch. The chili was scooped high, but tasted mealy. The couple behind me in line had never eaten at Pink's. The husband was blue-collar. He was butt-crack, belt-below-the-boiler large. He ordered four chili dogs for himself with two diet cokes, a chili dog and a diet coke for his wife. They were digging in when I left. Pink's chili ingests with alarming potential to talk back. I was glad I wasn't riding close-quartered with the guy and his wife devouring five chili dogs between them.

 I drove down La Brea to Wilshire and turned left toward downtown. Past two p.m., freeway traffic anywhere in LA is impossible, especially on Fridays. In 1984, I dropped into LA on a Friday. I was in town that year to attend Skipper McNally's funeral. Skipper McNally died a skid row death. He collapsed on the street in downtown LA without ID.

 He was toe-tagged a John Doe and stayed in the county morgue for three months before a Raiders front office guy, Mike Ornstein, noticed he hadn't been around and made inquiries. Mike Ornstein later was the agent for Reggie Bush who was accused of brokering improper payments to Reggie Bush while Reggie Bush still was participating with USC.

 The Raiders made arrangements at a Catholic Church in El Segundo. Skipper had no family—or any that claimed him. The Raiders were it. They made sure the service was well-attended. The pews filled with front office people, some players, church ladies standing in as mourners. Al Davis attended. Tommy

Bouncing Outside

Grimes delivered the eulogy and broke into tears as he talked. The service ended around two p.m.

I had figured to bum around LA for at least a day before heading north. I flashed on Friday traffic and made an impulse decision. I could clear traffic before 2:30 and leave all congestion behind or fall mired in it for the duration of the day. I got the hell out. I hit the Lincoln Highway to PCH in Santa Monica, sped up Highway 1 exited on 150 at Ventura, up the hill to Highway 33 in Ojai and home. I haven't been back to LA since, except on quick in and out business.

Overcrowding turns the place dreadful. I was changing gears this trip. I was immersing in LA Friday traffic. I was picking at things. I avoided the freeways. I drove down Wilshire into Hancock Park past 100 Fremont Place where Patty Barham hosted Ed Lund and me in the first of the Howard Hughes inquiries. Happy 100th birthday, Ed.

100 Fremont Place still lies behind a stone pillared entry with parking arm and rent-a-cop guardhouse security. Surrounding buildings range from newer low-rise business centers architected to fit the surroundings and landmark art-deco structures still in use like the Wilshire-Ebell Theater. The marquee at the stately First United Methodist Church a few blocks down speaks to new diversity in old LA. Pilipino services are held at 8:30 on Sunday, English at 9:30, Spanish at 10:30, and Korean at some time listed in a string of Korean language characters.

LA intrigues me, always has. I picked at an insight—*I love LA except for the traffic*—and branded it oxymoronic. That's like saying *I love the beach except for the sand.* Amended: I love old LA standing in low relief from new LA. New LA is smog-choked traffic snarls. New LA is meretricious: glass and chromium

Steve Cassady

high-rise buildings, silicon tits, tanning booth skin, almond Botox eyes, and collagen lips.

Old LA remains visible and redeems: swaying palms lining the boulevards, historic art deco buildings, warm rushes of soft heat in January, tropical pastels, hacienda architecture, adobe court apartment buildings, foliage made lush by hydration claim-jumped from the Owens Valley in the early part of the 20th century.

New LA is everything about California ruined beyond repair. It is overcrowded, overpopulated, overbuilt, polluted, ecologically despoiled, but old LA comes across as mythic film noir sound stage settings. Film noir was bean jumping through my skull while I drove around LA. Pure film noir is 1940s and 1950s black and white, an edgy undertow to LA's smooth surface glamour. Film noir runs dark themes through doomed protagonists and lurid femme fatales.

It employs stark camera angles, high contrast lighting, and chiaroscuro effects. Film noir—from the French *noir* for *black*—plots out inescapable fate through the media of guilt, greed, retribution, recompense, and moral reckoning.

Audrey Totter was a B-movie film noir moll. Audrey Totter plays the siren lion tamer that lures Frank Chambers into an affair in the 1946 *Postman Always Rings Twice.* Audrey Totter plays Robert Ryan's suffering wife in the RKO boxing noir movie, *The Set-Up.* Howard Hughes ran RKO in 1949 when *The Set-up* was produced. Audrey Totter is the female lead in Robert Montgomery's *I am the Camera* version of Raymond's Chandler's *Lady in the Lake.*

For a period of months in 1965, I saw Audrey Totter on her front porch five days a week. In college at UCLA I drove a school bus for private school rich rids attending The Brentwood Military Academy and Bel-Air School. My boss was a bald-headed heart-attack-waiting-to-happen guy named Price Dickey who couldn't understand how I could return to the barn ahead of schedule after every route. He was an okay guy. He was skeptical that *light traffic* was true every morning and afternoon. He always looked at his watch nervously and shook his head. He may have suspected me of pushing his buses a little hard.

On my route daily, I stopped at a house in the VA complex off Veteran and Sepulveda to pick up a fourth-grade girl named Mea Fred. Mea Fred had knobby knees and wore glasses and a Bel-Air school uniform—navy/white plaid skirt, collared white blouse and navy sweater. Her father was a VA doctor. Her mother was Audrey Totter. Audrey Totter might have been waving goodbye to Mea Fred every morning, but I fantasized otherwise: a film noir siren, one hand clasping her robe across her knees, the other beckoning toward me.

In 1976 John Wiebusch at NFL Properties hired me for a two-week trial run to check if I would fit an editorial opening at Properties. Properties occupied the 24th floor of the Douglas Oil Building at the corner of Wilshire and Westwood. My first day, Wiebusch guided me through the office.

He walked me into the art room and introduced me to an assistant to the art director, a young lady of about 21. She wore tortoise shell glasses and had a yellow #2 pencil sticking out of her long auburn hair. John Wiebusch said her name was Mea. I eyed her desktop nameplate. Last name, Fred. I clicked it fast. I said, *Yeah, I know, Audrey Totter's daughter.* I'd apparently made a huge impression as her fourth-grade bus driver. She had no recall without protracted prompts.

Weird how things connect.

I drove down to Union Station and parked. I walked over to Philippe to buy my coffee mug and stayed to read the LA Times over a slice of cherry pie

Steve Cassady

and milk. I had time to kill. I worked in produce fields with Mexican Braceros as a teenager in Salinas. The Braceros didn't shake native habits; they worked in huaraches. Huaraches are awful: hard-leather lattice strapped tops with tire treads as soles. Breaking in Huaraches raises heel and toe blisters.

Huaraches are so bad I had to have a pair. I've worn them ever since. Authentic huaraches are hard to find. Border towns hold no charm. I won't drive to Tijuana for any reason including a $20 pair of sandals. I know a dry goods store in the Mission District of San Francisco that carries huaraches, but its stock is unreliable. Olvera Street is best. The tire tread on last summer's pair separated from the insole in the fall. I was here. I bought huaraches at a stand on Olvera Street. I checked my watch. Six p.m.—I hadn't killed enough time. Decisions. I went back to the waiting room in Union Station and parsed the variables.

The freeways would be packed sardine-tin tight until eight p.m. Figure a hotel room in downtown LA as a give-up move. I didn't want to return the way I came or stay stuck in traffic on the Golden State and 405 just to climb the Grapevine and negotiate I-5 or 99 through tule fog. I had allowed for a 36-hour getaway.

I had to administer a basketball game in Merced at seven p.m. Saturday. I had 24 hours left. I flashed a thought: Maybe I'd spent so much avoiding congested traffic I had lost visceral touch with gridlock. Maybe I needed deeper immersion to revalue the freedom of lonely back roads. Secondary thought: I wanted roads I'd never driven. Tertiary recognition: I was impatient to move. I caved at tertiary.

I retrieved the car and accessed the 101 Hollywood Freeway. I clover-leafed in four directions from the 101: south on the 110 Harbor, southwest on the 10 Santa Ana, northeast on the 5 Golden State and east on

I-10, the San Bernardino. It is impossible to fathom the mass of automobile traffic in LA without ramping onto multiple freeways during rush hour on Fridays. Four-lane waves of oncoming halogen headlights, four-lane waves of red lights in front blinking from futile applications of brakes. Traffic sprawl on Friday nights is prodigious. It doesn't move; it oozes.

Drivers change lanes for no reason and stall things further. Drivers honk horns without purpose for the illusion of command. I stayed contained. I was stuck in traffic by choice. I wouldn't do this twice daily—ever. I may never do it again. I had no need to fret. I was feeding the contrast to habitual back road options, anticipating somewhere remote tomorrow. I resigned myself to slow. I found an FM classical station, 105.1 and listened to a Mozart hour. I drifted into thought and weighed itinerary choices.

I had left the parking garage at Union Station at 6:15. By 7:15, without shifting past second gear, I approached the city limits of Rosemead. Union Station to Rosemead: 11 miles. Commuting on LA freeways twice daily would flip me insane. Traffic finally abated at 8:15. I revved into normal speeds moved past El Monte, Claremont, Walnut, and Pomona.

I exited onto 15N toward Barstow and Las Vegas just before San Bernardino. Somewhere near San Gabriel, I had settled on a destination. I had never been to the Owens Valley. The Owens Valley is film noir thematic, at least neo-noir. Jack Nicholson's Technicolor 1974 *Chinatown* captures a fictional slant of the Owens Valley land grab with collateral corruption. The title stands metaphoric for all that is unfathomable and dark about human events.

John Huston plays the evil antagonist in *Chinatown,* old Noah Cross. Noah Cross once owned LADWP before it becomes part of public

Steve Cassady

administration. He anticipates hydration via aqueduct from the Eastern Sierra. He conspires to acquire cheap tracts of arid land in the San Fernando Valley. He is filthy rich already. With water for irrigation and development, land values skyrocket, and Noah Cross becomes richer than Farouk. Noah Cross is down-to-the-bone a creep. He fathers his own granddaughter by his own daughter. Incest is a common theme in American Literature. William Faulkner uses it in his Yoknawtapha novels as metaphoric for natural corruption involving land. More or less, Faulkner says despoiling nature by greed is tantamount to feeding on one's own. Faulkner's definition applies to *Chinatown*.

In an epiphanic moment, the Jack Nicholson character, private eye Jake Gittes, braces Noah Cross. Jake Gittes cannot grip why someone so rich would sell more of his soul for additional wealth. He asks, *What can you buy that you can't already afford.* John Huston caught the moment. John Huston as Noah Cross smiles with the leering mask of Mephistopheles, replying, *Why the future, Mr. Gittes, the future.*

The film ends on Alameda Street not far from Philippe with Noah Cross walking away comforting his incestuous daughter/granddaughter. Noah Cross' other daughter, his granddaughter's mother, has just been shot through the eye socket by police. Jake Gittes was protecting the mother while she was trying to escape her father's control. Jake Gittes rages at incomprehensible injustice. His partner explains it: *It's Chinatown, Jake.*

I had never driven 395 past the intersection of Highway 58 at Kramer's Junction at the southern tip of the Sierra. Kramer's Junction is 120 miles below Lone Pine, maybe 100 miles below the southern tip of the Owens Valley. I was flying along I-15 with new purpose when traffic stopped to a trickle across all four lanes. Traffic crept along for 60 minutes before diverting from the middle lane to the right and left around an apparent obstacle. I passed the obstacle picking up welcome speed, using third, fourth and fifth gears for the first time in an hour. The obstacle, a rusted out neo-Joad yellow Nissan pickup with a bulky load tarped to its bed, sat stalled in the center lane, hazard lights blinking, no driver in sight.

The stalled Nissan had choked four-lanes of traffic to first-gear speeds for 15 Interstate miles. Ten minutes later, I exited onto two-lane 395 toward Adelante/Bishop. I'd been on the road since 6:30 in the morning. I found a motel in Adelante. I avoid fleabags if I have a choice, my concession to comfort evolved from earlier indiscrimination.

Adelante's best is someplace I would have patronized in the 1980s traveling cross-country with Michael Zagaris—a 60 dollar a night Day's Inn that looked like Days Inn had repoed it from Motel Six. Room 115 was redolent with bad motel room smells—disinfectant and air freshener mixed with sour transient mold. I was too tired to care. I was asleep by ten and on the road again by 5:30. A low moon to the west ameliorated the pre-dawn darkness. I caught dusky glimpses of desert sagebrush, the bare outline of the Eastern Sierra in the background.

The Sierra Nevada spins the compass needle with its readings. It runs 400 miles north-north-west to south-south-east in the central part of Eastern California. It stretches from Fredonyer Pass in the north near Lake Tahoe to Tehachapi Pass in the south. The Sierra is bounded on the west by the Central Valley, on the east by the Great Basin Desert.

Highway 58 runs east-west and crosses Tehachapi pass into the Central Valley. Highway 58 used to hook with Route 66, the road the Joads took from Oklahoma

Steve Cassady

to Bakersfield during the Dust Bowl, before Route 66 was decommissioned and subsumed by freeways. I crossed 58 at Kramer's Junction at daylight into new territory on 395. The sky was crystal blue, free of pollution. The Eastern Sierra differs from the other side. The principle of the Orographic Lift applies: Pacific weather air masses expand and cool as they rise to the Sierra peaks. They cannot hold the moisture they build. They dump the whole humid load before they cross the peaks. Rain and snow from the marine conditions keep the western mountainside fertile and green. The eastern side receives only precipitation on the peaks and runoff from melted snow.

Its flanks are dry and brown below the snow line. Rivers flowing from the Sierra Crest on the west side of the range eventually reach either the San Joaquin or Sacramento Rivers, meet at the Delta and drain into the Pacific Ocean. Melted snow packs from the east side of the range form as rivers and flow into the Great Basin. They stay contained with no ocean destination. Highway 395 staggers with eastern Sierra/Great Basin topographic drama.

Towns don't intrude. They are small, picturesque, and compact. Surrounding desert terrain to the east is abundant with sagebrush and runs vast toward the White Mountains. The Sierra to the west looms majestic. The range increases in height gradually from north to south. It crests near Lake Tahoe at 9,000, at 13,000 feet near Yosemite.

It peaks in the south with Mt. Whitney then diminishes quickly in elevation down to Tehachapi pass. Mt. Whitney at 14,494 feet is the highest point of the continental United States. 80 miles east, Death Valley is the lowest point at 280 feet below sea level. Highway 395 runs midpoint between the continental high and low elevations. Mt. Whitney, often visible from Lone Pine, was lost in the clouds the day after Ed Lund's 100th birthday.

I imagined the view through clouds from a side street in Lone Pine. The street looked like the setting for Humphrey Bogart's *High Sierra,* in which hard-case felon Roy *Mad Dog* Earle leaves Marie (Ida Lupino) and her dog *Pard* in a 1941 Plymouth coupe while scaling heights to his film noir showdown with the posse of riflemen stalking his trail.

Lone Pine is the southernmost of four towns along Highway 395 in the Owens Valley. The others are Independence, Big Pine, Bishop. Independence is near Manzanar where the US Government interned Japanese-American citizens after Pearl Harbor according to Executive Order 9066. The Owens Valley sits at 4,000 feet elevation and extends 75 miles from Haiwee Reservoir near the shanty town of Olancha to Sherwin pass at 7,500 feet 24 miles above Bishop.

The Owens Valley is an LA story rife with subplot corruption. LA would still be as arid as Inyo County without water drained from the Owens Valley. One-third of LA's domestic water is piped in from the Owens Valley. In the early 20th century the city of Los Angeles carpet-bagged Owens Valley water rights to 300,000 acres though questionable land tract acquisition schemes. The LA Department of Water and Power under Superintendent William Mulholland planned and constructed a 223-mile aqueduct which diverted water from Owens River.

Investors who knew it was coming bought LA land on spec and became richer. The purchases led to angry revolt and aqueduct sabotage by Inyo and Mono County farmers. The LADWP aqueduct diverted inflows to Owens Lake. Owens Lake dried up and left alkali flats in the wake of its recession. Alkali dust storms followed with annoying frequency. In 1970, LADWP completed

Steve Cassady

a second aqueduct from Owens Valley with more eco-disastrous results. Ground water was pumped into the aqueduct. Owens Valley springs and seeps dried up and disappeared. Ground water-dependent vegetation shriveled and died like neglected house plants.

Litigation followed. Inyo County pushed it. The Sierra Club pushed it. Owens Valley citizens group pushed it. The groups pressured LAWP to sign a memo of understanding agreeing that the lower Owens River would be re-watered by June, 2003. LADWP missed the deadline. New suits followed. The State of California was named. LADWP promised to re-water the lower Owens Valley by September of 2005. Deadline missed again. Pumping water to LA continues at a higher rate than the rate at which water recharges the aquifer. Long term prognosis: not good—without ecological intervention, chronic desertification.

I wanted to reach Bridgeport in Mono County, 90 miles beyond Bishop. *Out of the Past* begins and ends in Bridgeport. *Out of the Past* is archetypal film noir. The movie opens idyllic with frames of Bridgeport's small-town charm. Jeff Bailey owns a filling station and is planning to marry the town's blond virgin named Ann. Jeff Bailey is out fishing with blond Ann in the East Walker River. Jeff Bailey's real name is Jeff Markham. A man in a dark topcoat and black hat drives into Bridgeport out of Jeff Markham's shady past. Jeff Markham is dragged back to a snarling sequence of murder, cover-up, and extortion.

He is innocent of all crimes except involvement with the wrong woman, dark mantrap Kathie Moffat, and employment by her jilted lover, criminal Whit Sterling, played by Kirk Douglas. Jeff Markham tells blond Ann the story, and the film flashes back through intrigue in New York, San Francisco, LA, Reno, and

Lake Tahoe. Jeff Markham returns to the past to clean it up and ends up shot dead by dark Kathie.

As with the best of film noir this one has a nasty little moral: manage choices so the present turns into a past from which escape is possible. The movie ends in Bridgeport with Jeff Bailey dead while blond Ann walks away with her boring local suitor, the fish-and-game warden who drives a government-issue Plymouth coupe and has loved her since the fourth grade. Bridgeport was an RKO film noir movie set in 1947. I was 90 miles away, but conditions threatened.

I'd read the weather page of the LA times over breakfast in Ridgecrest. South to north on 395: Bishop, 51/24 and dry. Mammoth Mountains, 27/15 and snow. Highway signs warned of chain restrictions 38 miles above Bishop. Highway signs listed the closure of mountain passes into the Central Valley, the passes over 4, 120, 88, and 89. Bearing on, I'd have to keep moving north and return home through Reno and down I-80 over Donner Summit.

Bishop's roadside campground and golf course were blanketed in snow. 24 miles later, I hit Sherwin Summit at 7400 feet elevation. Storm was imminent. I never backtrack. Emerson had a relevant notion, widely misquoted. Emerson is often citing as saying, *Consistency is the hobgoblin of little minds.* What he really wrote: *A foolish consistency is the hobgoblin of little minds.* I paid attention and challenged the temptation toward foolish consistency.

I was driving into threatening clouds on a sharply elevating road with wide Z-rated tires in a fast car with no rear end weight. I envisioned fishtail skids and snowbank collisions. I had no chains. Outside temperature was dropping. Dark clouds were pressing down. I scanned the surrounding terrain: white blanket of snow. I wanted to reach Bridgeport. I never backtrack. Donner Party visions jumped in: foolish consistency consequences.

I rethought. I own a DVD of *Out of the Past*. I could see Bridgeport stage-set in my living room. I had driven through Lone Pine, Independence, Big Pine, and Bishop—all ambient similar. Bridgeport was higher in elevation in a different county, Mono, but it couldn't be significantly different from the towns in the Owens Valley. I could *extrapolate* Bridgeport.

I hair-pinned at Tom's Place and sped down to more forgiving elevations. I drove through the Owens Valley north to south and caught a different take en route from snow to desert sand. I marveled at the irony.

LA is overrun to the point of being unlivable. LA is symbolic of California's ruin from overgrowth. LA developed to the point of unregulated disaster because it snatched water rights and hydration from the Owens Valley. The Owens Valley is ecologically disfigured but has preserved God's own balance between civilization and nature—partially because it lacks water sufficient to grow. One way to view it: LA stole its own destruction with Owen's Valley water, but saved the Owens valley from similar doom, ecological spoilage notwithstanding. Promethean stuff. Film noir fitting. Law of unintended consequences applied. Evil never wins. Nature never loses.

I back-tracked 125 miles on 395 before I saw the first chance to cross toward home. I saw the signs for Highway 14 to Palmdale. I cut off and drove 15 miles to the intersection with 178. I've never traveled 178, but I knew it ends in Bakersfield and crosses the southern Sierra at about its lowest elevation. The roads were dry, the sky was blue. The air was clear. Road signs marked 178 into virtual halves—42 miles to Lake Isabella, 87 miles to Bakersfield, meaning 45 miles from Lake Isabella to Highway 99. The leg to Isabella

Bouncing Outside

winds up and around abundant groves of high-elevation Joshua Trees. I passed few cars and saw only smatterings of life.

The serpentine mountain road mesmerized into high-level contrast with LA the day before. The solitude of upper 178 mocked LA freeway congestion. I tabbed it as a place where God kicks back to laugh at commuter snarl. I passed the hamlet of Onyx. I dropped down into view of Isabella, a Kern River reservoir, and detoured 13 miles north to the lakeshore town of Kernville. The road looped around to another lakeshore town named Wofford.

In Wofford, I saw the road sign intersection for Highway 155 toward Alta Sierra and Glennville. I knew 155 feeds into 99 at Delano above Bakersfield. I took it. Wofford is maybe 4000 feet elevation. Highway 155 climbs to 7,500 in fifteen miles on a two-lane blacktop donkey trail. 155 was precipitous and slick at 6000 feet. Dark clouds bunched in. Donner Party visions of the next 1500 feet of elevation jumped back in. I backtracked again, to Wofford and followed 155 the other way to the town of Lake Isabella, where it connected to 178. Good choice.

178 parallels the Kern River coming out of Lake Isabella all the way into Bakersfield. The Kern is wild, fast, and remote. It is a winding two-lane road all alive with southern Sierra panorama. White water shooting through granite rocks in the Kern River Canyon for 45 breathtaking miles.

My family won't accompany me on my getaway bursts. They are averse to long-time confinement in a car. They dislike whipping around remote roads until motion sickness sets in. They aren't thrilled by boycotting fast foods and eating in diners, even in landmark joints like Pink's or Philippe. They miss a lot. By the time I hit SR 99, I was tranquilized by the

Steve Cassady

trip. LA confirmed a charge. The state of California is, at congested points, a wreck beyond repair. LA is emblematic of civilization unleashed without control.

But so much of California still remains. Highway 33 past Taft and the Cuyama Valley; 395 through the Owens Valley; 178 winding past the Joshua trees; 178 following the wild Kern River—all roads through lands that time forget, all accessible within a few hours from my house. The trip invigorated.

Even 99 was inoffensive. Rain had poured through the valley and washed away the January fog. Traffic was fast and had dwindled. At Delano I looked east toward Glennville and Alta Sierra. Dark edged cumulinimbus clouds gathered to obscure the snow-capped southern Sierra peaks. Most days, smog off Highway 99 obscures the mountains to the east. After a rain, without the clouds, the Sierra peaks would be visible, snow caps etched against the blue horizon.

Socked-in peaks validated an earlier choice. Snow was falling on 155 near where I backwatered to 178. I would have been trapped. I stopped in downtown Tulare at Nielson's family diner for a New York steak and baked potato. I flew home on autopilot. I was in the Merced College gym by six o'clock for a 7 p.m. game. I had been gone 36 hours, in the car for all but 10 of them, and loved it. I found what I had sought: mid-winter reaffirmation: patch of blue breaking through dispiriting gray and this knowledge: California in spite of itself still is getaway friendly, all majestic and sparse on a good bounce to the outside.

In spite of its ruins, California remains—enough of it to provide transcendent relief from the overcrowded insanity that has become its temporal truth.

Epilogue: Elkhorn Slough

...I am part of all that I have met...
       --Alfred, Lord Tennyson,
              from Ulysses

The coastal mountain chain of central California links four major ranges: Diablo, Gabilan, Santa Cruz, and Santa Lucia. The Gabilan and Santa Lucia parallel each other roughly 20 miles apart for about 100 miles. They extend from the ocean shores between Santa Cruz and Pacific Grove to a place called Jolon on Highway 101 just below King City.

On the northwest end of the valley, the two ranges decline into sand dunes and ice plants beaching the Pacific around Monterey Bay. On the southeast, they overlook arable soil around backwater farm communities, Chualar, Gonzales, Soledad, Greenfield, King City. In between lies the fertile, windswept Salinas Valley. Cold marine air blows with monotonous frequency through the Salinas Valley. It blows in as afternoon and overnight fog. It burns off, if it does at all, by mid-morning the next day. Daily fog and wind: Salinas. I was born and raised in Salinas. I left without regret owing to a climate I found aversive.

John Steinbeck was born in Salinas in 1902. John Steinbeck earned the bulk of his literary fame writing about his home turf. He sensed the soul of tillable nature. He vibrated to the rhythms of the land. He resonated with the seasons. He was imbued with the salt air and its surroundings. He fed off the weather. I read Steinbeck voraciously. I jazzed on his prose but I never appreciated his settings. I couldn't actualize Steinbeck's

Steve Cassady

truth through the dank gray fog or funereal winds of my upbringing. The place was cold when good places were warm, during spring and summer.

I didn't appreciate: the Salinas Valley is as naturally productive as any place on earth. Its unique meteorology ordains it. Cold ocean air and morning fog mix with nutrient soil, ample water and favorable drainage. They produce lettuce, broccoli, strawberries, cauliflower, celery, spinach, artichokes, and wine grapes. Ugly conditions permit prolific production. Farmers rotate crops to replenish soils. They plant and harvest year-round. The Salinas Valley produces 80 percent of the nation's lettuce, 50 percent of its cauliflower and mushrooms, 25 percent of its celery, 60 percent of its broccoli, and 90 percent of its artichokes.

I worked in the fields every summer from age 15 through 19. I hated it. Grunt work in produce kills any romance over the miracles of sowing and reaping. I hoed beans, cut celery, shagged empty lettuce cartons to packers, wind-rowed filled lettuce cartons ahead of the stitching truck, hauled irrigation pipes.

Eddie Cochrane sang *Summertime Blues*. I felt the blues. A contemporary song from when I was 16: *The Lazy, Crazy, Days of Summer*. It drilled me from the transistor radio during the long-ass work days. I failed to relate. I worked 60 hours a week in summers at wages ranging from 87 ½ cents an hour when I began with the Braceros in the lettuce fields at age 15 to $1.50 working for my brother-in-law from ages 17 to 19.

I worked during the growing season, end-of-school in the spring to post-Labor Day. I worked six days, 10 hours/day. I fell asleep in movie theaters on Saturday night dates. I dreaded the speed of passing time on Sundays, my only day off. I despised every minute of field work but persisted for two Dutch stubborn reasons: pride (most everyone that started with me quit) and money. Alternative to #2: asking parents for teenage screw-around money when I knew neither parent (nor older brother and sister) would have done the same at the same age. I worked and followed suit.

I bought my own gas, clothes, fast food, and weekend entertainment. I opened a bank account and hoarded the rest. From age 16, I drove a dumb-ass 1941 Plymouth coupe handed down from my mother's Finnish stepfather. I was saving for a slicker whip. At age 18, I bought a lime green second-hand 1957 MGA ragtop. It had removable Isinglass side curtains. It had neither heat nor air. It was a shitty car that handled smooth. It was built for weekend jaunts along winding lanes using lab robes in the chilly British Isles.

It broke down during long hauls on hot California Freeways. Didn't matter. I dropped the top in April. I left it off until October. The car seduced. It cornered like an ocelot. It malfunctioned chronically. I went broke with repair bills. I drove the crap out of it. It was an old-world ride—engineered from concepts never retooled for post WW II technology, produced with rising post-war United Kingdom labor costs. I loved the MGA; it rocked. Tricky wheels for an early phase of an overlong post-adolescent spree.

I left Salinas at age 20 for dryer, wind-free conditions and didn't return but for brief family visits. I was peripatetic through three decades. I lived in LA three times, San Francisco twice (a cold-weather exemption happily conferred), and Dutch Flat before settling in Merced in the San Joaquin Valley, with an asterisk attached to the word *settling*.

Headquartering is more accurate. Before I was married and had children, I worked 175 days of year teaching college. The other 190: I was on the road more than I was home. I face retirement age without feeling the need to retire. I still like my job. All things

Steve Cassady

anticipated in retirement—freedom, travel, pursuit of hobbies—those are things I've already done. I became domesticated over time. I sunk roots without knowing it. I have grown curious about deeper roots.

The boat sponsored post-millennium searches and returned me to waterway beginnings. I had dabbled into Elkhorn Slough and Monterey Bay but never penetrated. It was time. I picked a late December day when my wife and sons had driven to Arizona to visit my daughter. They took with them an over-laded cargo hold of stuff for my daughter's first apartment.

They took a grandmother-in-law, a mother-in-law, and a young nephew. I bailed. My wife's extended-cab Yukon was packed like the Joad's 32 Ford pickup when the Joad's left Sallisaw. In-laws and family stuffed into close quarters for an 11-hour drive across the desert: the arthritis in my neck cinched up just imagining. I foresaw *Das Boot* suffocation. My wife said, *You aren't going, then?* I laughed. She understood. I was five days free with a choice. Burrow into an empty nest—or bounce to the outside. I bounced.

December on the central coast: blue sky respite from bleak valley gray. December: the best weather month of the year in the Salinas Valley. Crisp, cold mornings; warm afternoons; calm winds; bright azure sky, fog restrained obediently off-shore. My sister had died young. Contact with her children becomes increasingly sporadic. It settles in as an inarticulate, unmet need. I felt a spur to reconnect.

I phoned my only nephew who had taken over the family farm when my brother-in-law retired. The farm is partly fallow in December. My nephew had free time. My nephew is teenage physical in his 40s. He skateboards, surfs, mountain bikes, hang glides. He was all over a kayaking trip. I picked him up at eight in the morning. My nephew has inspiring history. He lost his mother when he was 21. At 22 he was diagnosed with bone cancer just below one knee.

Initial prognosis: 15/85 chance of survival. His dad had sufficient money for the best medical care. That helped save his life. So did the skill of the best MDs his father's money could buy. Mostly it was him. They went the Mayo Clinic. Diagnosis confirmed: the same strain of carcinoma as the Kennedy kid that lost his leg at the knee. Mayo said, amputate. My nephew said, *second opinion.* He went to Stanford. Stanford said, *operate, and we save the leg, though without full use.* Nick said, Go. He was on the table 18 ½ hours attended by 16 surgeons.

He came out of anesthesia in mortal pain, his leg in a plaster cast to his hip. The doctors were optimistic about cure and survival. They always are. They said they had excised the tumor and arrested the spread. They weren't optimistic on mobility and use. They projected one leg shorter than the other, a prosthetic shoe, and lifelong use of a cane. Nick chafed during recovery. He hated the cast. He hated the idea of physical inhibition. He pushed his rehab.

He was indefatigable. He said finally, *I know my body better than they do.* He dismissed their PT regimen. He sawed off the cast six months before the doctors authorized and went at it. He was relentless. He surfed. He rode his bike. He flew to Europe to visit his sister in Holland. He took his bike with him. He pedaled 500 miles across Europe. The doctors' pessimism didn't account for Nick's will. Nick's legs are now the same size. He danced at his wedding seven years after initial diagnosis.

We took the back roads from the farm on Old Stage Road to Elkhorn Slough. I'd been to Elkhorn Slough and scoped its wild life, mostly harbor seals, otters and more waterfowl than Alfred Hitchcock

Steve Cassady

imported into the set of *The Birds*. I had scoped it too shallow in previous runs. I hadn't realized the eco-complexity. I saw it now. Elkhorn Slough is seven miles of wetlands inland from the jetty at Moss Landing harbor spread over 7,000 acres of salt marsh, originally the mouth of the Pajaro and Salinas Rivers. Indians, Chinese, immigrant farmers in their turns diked, ditched, channeled, and drained the wetlands for the purposes of for harvesting salt and growing produce. Over time they overproduced.

 Overproduction fucked up things as it always will. Pesticide-polluted runoff threatened the estuary ecology. Ecological conscience was alarmed and intruded. Vigilant environmental effort since has reclaimed the slough. Birdwatchers and naturalists have ID'd 400 species of fish, 200 species of birds from brown pelicans to avocets and plovers. The place thrives again with coastal life.

 Kayaking in Elkhorn is tide-dependent. I don't read tide tables and don't want to learn. I called ahead. The tide was falling out at three feet until 12:45 pm. I translated: paddle outbound from the boat ramp at Kirby Park to the harbor and back, not the reverse. We hit the water about nine am and rode a sucking ebb tide four miles to Moss Landing in 54 minutes. Fast. We couldn't return with the flood until the tide slacked and turned at 12:45. I called my brother. He works in Watsonville, five miles away. We connected.

 It was my brother's birthday, also the day he was retiring from a company he built from the ground during a recession then sold and was re-hired as CEO. My brother's company invents, constructs, and markets electronic control systems for industrial washing machines. My brother's professional life is the grown-up version of the same shit he did when we were kids: disappear into the garage and make things.

Bouncing Outside

My brother was precocious. He's older by 18 months. When he was 17, he drove an automatic transmission 1956 Chevy. The transmission went out. My brother took the Chevy to a transmission shop. The tranny guys tore into it for an estimate. They estimated high. They figured my brother for a teenage sap. They said they could replace the defective parts, but new parts wouldn't mesh with old—the whole thing would have to be rebuilt. My brother said, *box it up*.

He had the car towed home. He bought standard transmission and clutch conversion kits. He disappeared into the garage for a few weeks. He emerged with a four-speed stick that shifted from the floorboard hump.

While he was at it, my brother reconfigured the windshield washer. He replaced the rubber tubing from the reservoir with copper extensions and re-routed the copper through the firewall to the upper lip of the glove compartment. He attached swivels and an elbow. He rigged it so the passenger could reach unto the glove compartment, find the copper tubing under the lip of the compartment, lower the elbow, pull it six inches into the cab and swivel it down.

The swiveled elbow was a spigot. The windshield washer on a '56 Chevy was activated by a button on the wiper knob. My brother pushed the button. Reservoir contents flowed through the copper tubing and elbow spigot. My brother tended to fill the reservoir with vodka. He tended to place a cup of orange juice under the spigot and spike a screwdriver. My brother never had open containers in the car.

When we were 14 and 12, my brother subscribed to *Popular Mechanics* magazine. One month, PM featured an article on construction of a ten-foot plywood, fiberglass composite hydroplane. My brother sent away for the plans. He bought materials with paper route money. He disappeared into the garage. He jig-sawed the plywood into parts. He joined the parts with ring nails. He fiber glassed the joints and exterior surface. He sanded it all smooth. He painted it red and white. He emerged with a flawless craft. He used some more paper route money and purchased a second-hand Evinrude outboard motor.

I contributed small. I used paper route money and bought water skies, a $26 outlay. We skied every time we could scam someone with a driver's license to chauffeur us toward a waterway. One time my sister—five years older than I—was in breakup phase with her future husband, Nick's dad. A guy named Don Shirk pursued her. Shirk tried hard. My sister was mostly indifferent. She was using Shirk, working my future brother-in-law. Don Shirk drove a root beer colored 1952 Pontiac. One Saturday, he wanted to take my sister to Coyote Lake near Gilroy.

Henry and I camped on. Don Shirk thought he could impress my sister by taking us and the boat. Susan hated the idea and thought even less of Shirk for letting us con him. We skied while they sat on the beach. They took a nature hike. We ran out of gas for the outboard. They were still out of sight.

We hustled on shore with a five-gallon gas can fitted with rubber hose and a suction pump. We stuck one end of the hose into Don Shirk's gas tank, the other into our gas can. We palm-pumped a couple gallons. We skied until Don Shirk and my sister returned. We were assholes. We've always gotten along, my brother and I. I have no conception of sibling rivalry. I have never known it.

Nick, Henry, and I went to lunch at Phil's Fish Market in Market in Moss Landing, the only adult males left in the family. My nephew is cryptic. He speaks softly and rarely elaborates. He said something about the water. Something like, *it's funny how the water lures us all.* He was right. His observation ran deep. Henry has sailed a *Santa Cruz 27* out of Santa Cruz harbor for 30 years. He has taken up sculling. He races his sailboat. He has raced in the harbor, through the Golden Gate, in Baja...Nick surfs and wind surfs, mostly within a tight radius of Monterey Bay, often in Moss Landing not two miles of where we are eating soft shell crabs at Phil's...I run kayaks through flat water in Northern California.

It all started not far away—at the mouth of the Salinas River, Twin Bridges, between Castroville and Fort Ord. The Salinas River feeds into the ocean at Twin Bridges. The mouth of the Salinas probably is the worst waterway any of us has ever used. Ambient scenery: artichoke fields and traffic snarls on Highway 1. The river is narrow. The water is mud brown and butt cold. Twin Bridges sits on the windward side of the sand dunes of the Pacific shore.

Marine air hovers. At 14 and 12, we didn't know anything about wet suits—or giving in to cold. The boat rode on top of the car. We cushioned it with inner tubes and roped it down through the open windows of my dad's two-door 1954 Ford V-8. My dad drove us to Twin Bridges on spring and summer Saturdays and waited while we skied out our gas. No way would we siphon fuel from my father's tank. He was too sharp; he'd catch us. We wouldn't do it anyway. With my dad, we drew lines of love and respect. We stayed on our side of the lines.

We were fearless on the water. We took turns driving the boat and skiing. We red-lined the Evinrude and strung along behind it. Our teeth chattered. We endured shrinkage. We froze our lips blue. We carved out high-spray rooster tails on sharp turns. We whipped the tow rope into thrilling arcs. My father was a water guy as well. During summers in college, he lifeguarded at beaches along the Russian River. He witnessed drownings of heedless youth taking bad risks.

He was always gesturing us to back throttle. We never did. I don't recall my father having much fun on boating trips.... We talked through lunch. Henry was happy with impending retirement. He scored. His company retained him to travel eight days a month to outpost branches he had developed as the company grew—to Brazil, China, Australia, and England.

Nick and I rode the marshland flood tide back through the harbor seals and waterfowls to the car at Kirby Park. I stowed the boat trailer at the ranch. I activated the rest of a 48-hour plan. I had called one of my wife's 4-H kids to feed the goats, geese and sheep. I had kenneled Baskerville, the obstreperous beagle.

I was two days unfettered, loose in the area of my rambunctious youth, blessed by one of the best weather days of the year: clear cold morning, bright blue sky, windless air, full color dawns and dusks. I checked into the Hyatt at *Hotwire*.com prices and fell asleep between high thread-count sheets anticipating the next day.

I was up before dawn and caught the CNN account of vengeful Shiites dropping the trap on Saddam Hussein. I exited the hotel in starlight and headed toward the water. I breathed in Monterey Bay eco-facts: underwater canyons as deep as 12,000 feet spawning wondrous arrays of marine life.

Monterey Bay is home to 26 species of marine mammals from seals and otters to bottle nose dolphins; 94 species of sea birds, 345 species of fish, four species of turtles, 31 types of invertebrates, 450 species of large marine algae. John Steinbeck's buddy, hard-core scientist Doc Ed Ricketts, lived in Cannery Row for good reason. From tide pools to undersea grottos, Monterey Bay is endless with Marine Biology. I stood by a palisade rail at the foot of Cannery Row taking in sunrise over the Santa Lucia.

As kids, we went to the beach as a family. We usually went to Lover's Point in Pacific Grove. I remember green salt-water shadowed dark with seaweed foaming onto shore; shorebirds scratching trident tracks in the sand pack; pelicans honking. I remember: shivering blue-lipped from overlong immersion in cold ocean surf; romping in the sand; gawking at tourists crowded in glass-bottom boats tooling around the cove.

I remember drooling to the smells of the burger shack above the beach. The place looked good in memory. It beckoned it real time. A month earlier I kayaked Monterey Bay. I put in at a dune across Del Monte Boulevard from the Naval Post-Graduate School. The water was calm for Monterey Bay. I paddled easily past the wharf, Cannery Row, and past the Aquarium. I had visions of bending right near an outcrop of rocks filled with barking seals and paddling around the rocks into the memory of the protected cove of Lover's Point beach. I recognized real-time truth at the right-hand bend: the rocky outcrop borders the open sea. Most days, even when the inlet is calm, the open sea is violent at the edges.

It pounds the rocks with treacherous currents and tides. Conditions chop and back swell. They endanger paddling. I imagined being washed against the rocks or swept to sea by crosscurrents ripping strong with the ebbing or flooding tide. I turned back. Today, at sunup, it would have worked. I drove up Foam Street to Pacific Grove and saw the cove at Lover's Point and its surrounding waters rippling crepe paper flat to a gray horizon still rimmed pink with sunrise hues.

Steve Cassady

I hung around the Bay and walked the fishing wharf until the town woke up. I backtracked to 17-mile drive and remembered: the Crosby Clambake, the Pro-Am golf tournament. It was homespun then. Bing Crosby and his celebrity clan wearing flat hats, smoking cigars—fighting elements for 72 holes and having unpretentious rich guy fun.

It's all corporate now. It's called the AT & T. We went annually as teenagers and never paid. We parked off the road, jumped down a dune, walked down the sand pack toward Pebble Beach and scrambled up a dune between golf holes. We blended with the gallery scoping Pros and Amateurs—Jack Lemmon, Clint Eastwood, and Walter Matthau; Jack Nicklaus, Tom Watson, and Arnold Palmer. We walked random paths from pin to tee mixing with the rich and famous.

I followed 17-mile drive until it went this way and that and wound around behind Monterey Peninsula College. I pulled into a parking lot. I can't pass another JC without driving in and checking their athletic facilities. MPC was revamping with bond money—new athletic facilities construction for all sports.

I was envious. Merced College passed a bond recently. Merced College exempted any expenditure on athletics. I ventured to the baseball field. I stood by home plate. I flashed back to1963, my sophomore season at Hartnell. We were playing Monterey at MPC. I remember: I struck out the first at bat. The strikeout followed a string of four K's from the previous game. I was streaking. Jess Regli was the coach.

Jess was prototypical old school: bandy-legged, broad-shouldered and gray haired, a poor man's Casey Stengel, at least in appearance. He was a four-sport letterman at San Jose State. Jess Regli tended to let things slide. He scheduled the season, rolled out the balls for practice, hit fungoes, coached third base, and wrote the lineups. We did the rest. I started my freshman season in left field. I was faster than the sophomore centerfielder. The sophomore centerfielder thought we should switch. We changed positions without consulting Jess. Jess didn't interfere.

We were pretty good though not especially civilized. Guys fired up smokes on the bench during games. Jess didn't interfere with that either. My dad braced him once on the smoking thing. He said, *Cass, I don't like it either, but if I tried to stop them, they'd all quit on me.* Two times each year, Jess scheduled double-header trips to Soledad prison, one to the farm, one to the main block. We played the inmate teams. I had a monster game one of those years on the farm, went five for seven in the double header. I remember the pitcher, a left-handed light-skinned black guy with freckles. He threw the first screwball I ever faced.

Our second year, we had a tall (6-7), skinny first-baseman named Jim Harris. Harris was one of the smokers. We were playing inside the walls. Guards had escorted us through the barred gates. We were sitting down near the field lacing up our cleats. A group of inmates shuffled by wearing watch caps and baggy denims. Harris recognized one of them. Harris and the convict had a brief reunion. They had been friends from a previous experience.

I was up for my second at bat against MPC. Jess Regli called time. He strolled toward the plate. I walked toward him. He put both hands on my shoulders and looked into my eyes. He said, *Hit the ball.* He turned and walked back to the third-base box. I thought, *that's it? You called time out for that advice?*

The pitcher, Duke Quinones snapped off a high inside curve that wobbled off its rotation and hung. I picked up the spin. I turned on it with my front shoulder down and hands inside. I rolled my wrists hard

Steve Cassady

on contact. I hit it over the left field wall. Two runners were on. Next at bat, two more runners on base. Same result. I batted twice more. I hit singles with a runner at second in both ABs. I made two dead-run full extension diving catches with runners on base, one angling in toward shortstop, one in deep right center robbing some poor MPC Lobo of a triple.

I was never as good before or since, but that day was all mine: two home runs, two diving catches, two singles, eight RBIs in a game we won 11-10. I saw it again after 43 years. I still felt the jazz.

I jumped back on highway 68 and drove into Salinas. I went downtown toward the Steinbeck Museum at the foot of Main Street. The area was shabby in my youth, perfect for middle-class teenagers roaming small town urban blight in search of significance. We frequented the area. We played pool in smoke-filled halls and bought pocket knives and cheap wrist watches from seedy hock shops.

We got flat-top haircuts from Rick Obesa at the Crystal Barber Shop. We chose Rick Obesa on merit. He advertised the best flat tops in town. He permitted 15 year olds to paw through piles of pornographic magazines while waiting turns in the chair. The Crystal barber shop is gone. It was situated next to the Crystal Theater, which ran Mexican and Pilipino features.

It was on the other side of the Crystal from the Rodeo Café, where my best friend Bob Robertson's brother Barry ate at 2 am after playing piano with his jazz trio at a Market Street dive. One night Barry Robertson sat at the counter at the Rodeo Cafe and ordered a steak sandwich. The cook plated the sandwich and set it on the counter at the serving window. The waitress dealt it to Barry Robertson. Barry Robertson put the sandwich to his mouth. He bit down with every molar into pure gristle.

Bouncing Outside

Barry Robertson was combustible. He once was flagged for speeding on a straightaway in Bolsa Knolls north of town: 100 in a 25. The highway cop shook with rage while he wrote the citation. Barry Robertson stood 6-4. He rose to full height. He straddled the stool. He grabbed the sandwich with long piano-playing fingers. He crushed it into a glutinous wad. He wound up and fired. He splattered the wad into the wall behind the counter, bellowed, *This is shit!* and left. The Crystal Theater swallowed Rick's Barber Shop and morphed into an upscale 14-screen multiplex called the Maya Cinema. The Rodeo Café has morphed into a trendy eatery called Sang's.

Bob Robertson had a strange upbringing. His mother was a lush. His father bootstrapped himself from dust bowl roots. Gene Robertson started as a field hand and was active in farm labor issues. He was kicked out of town during the produce strikes of the 1930's that John Steinbeck wrote about in *In Dubious Battle*. He evolved into management and became a produce executive for Harden Farms, one of the largest growers in the Salinas Valley.

Gene was stable but seldom around. Bob's house had zero parental supervision. I was 13 the first time I went to Bob's house. From his exposure to the produce fields he had gained an extensive vocabulary of gutter Spanish. Bob's house was cool. Gene had built it himself: two stories with a western ranch theme. Bob's house was the first I encountered with extension telephones. That initial visit we hit a lull while Bob was sitting near one of extensions. He reached over and uncradled the receiver. He dialed.

He cut loose a string Mexican profanity and hung up. I asked, *who'd you call?* He said, *The Black Cat Café*. *The Black Cat* was a storefront whorehouse in Chinatown. Bob Robertson was impressive for 13.

Steve Cassady

Eventually his parents had to sell the house. Maureen, his mother, had tanked the family finances with profligate drinking and spending.

Gene moved them into a series of apartments until the inevitable divorce. Bob worked summers in the sheds. He had to rise early. He was attempting sleep one summer evening, while living in an apartment on Iverson Street across from Palma High School. The house behind his apartment bedroom window belonged to a family named Scattini. The Scattinis had a nice house. Their backyard patio separated from Bob's apartment complex by a six-foot cedar fence.

Their patio was illuminated by a floodlight on the eave above a sliding glass door. Bob's bedroom window had no curtains. The bedroom window was elevated slightly above the Scattini fence. The Scattini floodlight shone through Bob's window trashing his attempts to sleep. Bob Robertson had the same DNA as his brother Barry. He snapped.

He grabbed a pellet gun from the closet. He opened window, aimed, and fired. Glass shattered, but patio light still flooded his bedroom. Bob had missed the floodlight but hit the slider. Broken glass spread over the Scattini's patio doorstep. Bob swore and said, *Whoops.* He hid the pellet gun in a closet shelf and climbed under the covers. He stayed in bed until the cops rang the doorbell. He answered in his underwear, rubbing his eyes. He lied credibly. He had been asleep, he said. He had seen and heard nothing.

Bob stayed with us a good part of the time. My parents loved him. They weren't as fond of us as friends. They thought we enabled each other's lesser qualities. My mother was delighted when after JC I went to UCLA, and Bob chose Berkeley. Bob was erratic and tended toward blasphemy. He tended to blame the Almighty for his own imperfections. Once he threw dirt clods toward the sky and dog-cussed God for giving him teenage acne.

Once we were swilling beer while watching *Spartacus* at the drive-in movie on Market Street. Bob teared up during an intense scene dramatizing the grace of God. That was a clue. Bob Robertson converted to Christianity at Cal, though it took a while for religion to file down the rough edges. The summer after our junior year in college, Bob's dad procured him a job at the produce market in downtown LA. Bob was driving a beat up early 60s VW Beetle. He was ready to leave Berkeley for the summer when his battery died.

He was broke, of course. He reverted. He roamed his neighborhood streets past midnight until he found an unlocked bug. He popped the boot and jacked the battery. He left the next morning for LA. While descending the Grapevine toward the San Fernando Valley, his windshield shattered. He interpreted it as a sign—a message from God that lifting a battery constituted sin. He knew he still had work ahead in the area of salvation.

He had enough money for gas and food in LA until his first paycheck two weeks hence. He couldn't afford a new windshield. He stopped at a sporting goods store. He dipped into his food and gas money and bought a cheap pair of swimmer's goggles. He reamed out his shattered windshield with a tire iron. I was living with my cousin Pete in a fleabag duplex on Overland in west LA, just south of the Mormon Temple. Bob was bunking with us for the summer.

Bob showed up at our apartment wearing his goggles with no windshield on his bug. He looked ridiculous. My cousin Pete still remembers: Bob didn't change his sheets all summer. Near Labor Day, when he was packing for his return to Berkeley, Bob folded the sheets, now gray and 90 days used and returned them carefully to the linen closet.

One weekend that same summer, Bob said The Campus Crusade for Christ was holding some big event—I don't remember what they called it, Jamboree, Conference, Camp meeting, Convention, Chautauqua Tent Revival—at Lake Arrowhead in the San Gabriel mountains above San Bernardino. Bob said we should go. I said I was broke. He said he was too.

I asked about a registration fee. Bob said he wasn't planning to register. I had a relative in Lake Arrowhead—a female cousin from my father's generation on my father's mother's side. She and her husband were retired. I said, *Let's go.*

We took the MG. It was terminal by then. The cooling system was gunked up. The engine dripped oil through a crack in the block. We rationalized the MG could make it. We figured we could drive round-trip to Lake Arrowhead on one tank of gas and five quarts of extra oil. We pooled our cash. We splurged on gas and oil. We looked at what was left after exiting the gas station: one dime. We reasoned a single dime would accomplish nothing. The dime was Bob's. He threw it out the open top before we hit the freeway.

We found the CCC grounds and scoped security. It had no security. Apparently, every other attendee had pre-paid for registration, food and lodging. CCC hadn't accounted for the prospect of free-loaders. Perfect. We took fast inventory of the set-up. We discovered an expanse of cabins. We discovered some of the cabins were obscure, located on the edge of the grounds near the woods. We discovered the cabins nearest the conference rooms and dining hall were the most fully occupied. We discovered the outer cabins were mostly vacant. We discovered not all windows on the unused cabins were locked.

Bouncing Outside

We let ourselves into one of the cabins on the edge of the pines. It was quite satisfactory. We had a place to flop. Meals were served cafeteria style in shifts. Again, security was non-existent. Conventioneers merely showed up and grabbed plates from a stack and filed through the chow line. We grabbed plates from a stack and filed through. The food proved edible, the price agreeable. We spend a weekend in the woods.

Bob went to his CCC meetings. I worked the wilderness and lazed around like Huckleberry Finn on Jackson Island. We left late on Sunday morning and tracked down my cousin Lou and her husband Walter. They had a house amid the pines on a slope overlooking the water. Lou fed us a big Sunday dinner.

Walter repaired TV sets as a retirement hobby. His workroom was stacked with cast-aside but now-functional TV sets. Lou said a college student needs a TV set. I agreed. Walter gave me a 13-inch B/W GE portable for my bedroom. We left at sunset. We made it home without spending a dime. Bob Robertson evolved from blasphemous teen to man of God. He has been a Christian Missionary in Amman, Jordan since graduating from college. Barry Robertson retired early as a high school English teacher.

I strolled two blocks more. I saw the El Rey Theater. It's beautiful. It has been restored to full art deco splendor. When we were in junior high, high school, and junior college, the El Rey was managed by a man named Si Gertz. Si Gertz was a big man with balding black comb-over hair. He had what looked like a dueling scar traced from his left earlobe to his lower mandible. Si Gertz came across hateful. The dueling scar fomented Foreign Legion rumors.

Si Gertz was as territorial as a pit bull. He was ubiquitous inside his darkened theater. He patrolled with a flashlight and a snarl. Si Gertz shined his light on teenagers making out. He flashed it at kids who stretched their legs over the seats in front of them. He hushed kids who dared to converse. He guarded the exit doors with a scowl. Si Gertz was vigilant. He snarled at adolescent offenders. He never smiled. Si Gertz was a local legend tagged as an ogre that hated kids.

Si Gertz's goat was easy to get. Every kid with spunk tried him. One time in high school, we were dragging Main in my 41 Plymouth. We passed the El Rey. I saw a kid shagging from the theater alcove. The kid bolted across traffic through screeching brakes and honking horns. I looked closer. It was my brother Henry. Henry looked around. I looked around. I saw what he saw: Si Gertz darting through the same brake squeals and car horns.

Si Gertz was high-stepping through moving traffic in hot pursuit. Henry picked it up. Henry bolted down the sidewalk. Si Gertz, in black suit, and tie, wearing brogans, was right behind him but losing ground with every stride. It was a mismatch. The teenage grandson of Uuno Railo dogged on a straightaway by wing-tipping Si Gertz. It was over before Henry passed Montgomery Ward on the corner of the next block.

No telling how many kids snuck into the El Rey while Si Gertz was chasing my brother. My brother's offense: He was walking by the theater with his buddies. He diverted to the El Rey's lobby doors, opened them and yelled in something loud and disrespectful, probably *Si Gertz*. Gertz was near the door, and it was on. Salinas was a small town without much for teenagers to do. We all bought into Gertz's legend and hectored him for amusement.

In adult retrospect, the legend was probably false. Probably, Si Gertz just resented post-pubescent assholes giving him constant shit. His only probable sin: he was easily provoked. He probably had friends who cared and family that loved him. He was probably very nice to adult patrons.

I finished my Old Town tour at the Steinbeck museum. I like the Steinbeck museum, with its running dialogue from *The Grapes of Wrath* and its restoration and display of *Rocinante*, the green camper truck Steinbeck took around America with his poodle in *Travels with Charley*. John Steinbeck is iconic in Salinas, ironically so. Steinbeck wrote *In Dubious Battle* about the 1930s produce strikes in Salinas and *Grapes of Wrath* about grower abuse of the Dust Bowl Okies. Steinbeck wrote the truth as he saw it.

He characterized the fate of the disenfranchised. Contemporary public opinion thought he slandered his home town industry. Public opinion branded him a communist. Steinbeck rebutted. Paraphrased, Steinbeck said the communists aren't even communists. He cited Stalin. He said communist Stalin led one of the most murderous and reactionary regimes in world history. Public opinion wasn't moved by the distinction. Steinbeck eventually migrated to New York where he could write about his home town in spiritual freedom. When he was awarded the Nobel Prize for Literature in 1962, public opinion softened.

Salinas named the town library after him. Salinas restored his ancestral home and converted it to a B & B. Upon announcement of Steinbeck's Nobel award, the English faculty of Hartnell College sent a congratulatory telegram. Steinbeck wired back a generous sentiment of appreciation. After my father died, my brother and I leafed through my parents' safety deposit box. We found Steinbeck's wire. My father obviously had palmed it. We couldn't divine the rightful owner.

We were pretty sure my father had noble motives—he was meticulously honest by his own definition. We believe he didn't trust the hairball politics within the English Department faculty for proper disposition of the wire. By then, Salinas had paid its full tribute to the once reviled Steinbeck with creation of the National Steinbeck Center at the end of Main Street. Salinas either had forgiven the prodigal son, gravy-trained his lasting fame, or both. We had the document appraised. We donated it to the Museum, and wrote off its value on our estate income tax. I like to think my father would have approved.

    I hitched the boat at the ranch and drove back roads, Old Stage to Natividad, through Crazy Horse Canyon, to 101 just below 156, the turnoff toward San Juan Bautista and Hollister. I turned toward Los Banos at the junction of 152. I crossed the Diablo at 1300 feet over Pacheco Pass and dropped into the valley past San Luis Reservoir and home on two-lane Highway 59 through El Nido. I was rejuvenated. I blinked ahead to prospects that still transcend. I reckon I'm in my sixties with the final years coming on. But cutting back is not an option. I won't go gentle. I will always find jazz on Northern California waterways and roads.

    I plan on bouncing to the outside until they sift my ashes into the urn.

www.ingramcontent.com/pod-product-compliance
Lightning Source LLC
Chambersburg PA
CBHW032038090426
42744CB00004B/50